FamilyFun
Cookbook

FamilyFun Cookbook

By Deanna F. Cook
and the Experts at FamilyFun Magazine

EDITIONS

New York

This book is dedicated to
the readers of Disney's *FamilyFun* magazine

Most of the recipes and photographs in this book
were previously published in *FamilyFun* magazine.

FamilyFun magazine is a division of the Walt Disney Publishing Group.
To order a subscription, call 800-289-4849.

FamilyFun Magazine
BOOK EDITORS: Alexandra Kennedy, Deanna F. Cook, and Katherine Eastman
PRODUCTION EDITOR: Paula Noonan
RECIPE TESTERS: Cynthia Caldwell, Vivi Mannuzza
PRODUCTION DIRECTOR: Jennifer Mayer
PRODUCTION ASSISTANT: Martha Jenkins

Impress, Inc.
DESIGNERS: Hans Teensma and James McDonald
PHOTO AND ART ASSOCIATE: Tobye Cook
ASSISTANT DESIGNER: Leslie Tane

FOOD STYLIST: Cynthia Caldwell
PHOTOGRAPHY: Lightworks Photographic

The staffs of *FamilyFun* and **Impress, Inc.**
conceived and produced *Disney's Family Cookbook* at
244 Main Street, Northampton, MA 01060

In collaboration with
Hyperion, 114 Fifth Avenue, New York, NY, 10011

Pre-press Production by Aurora Graphics, Portsmouth, NH
Printed in Hong Kong by Wing King Tong Co. Ltd.

Library of Congress Cataloging-in-Publication Data

ISBN 0-7868-5355-7
First Edition
1 3 5 7 9 10 8 6 4 2

Acknowledgments

Special thanks to the following *FamilyFun* magazine writers for their wonderful recipes and activities: Barbara Albright, Laurie Joan Aron, Diane Baker, Betty Belanus, Ruth and Steve Bennett, Lynne Bertrand, Laurie Winn Carlson, Carol Case, Nancy Castaldo, Cynthia Caldwell, Clare Collins, Tania Cowling, Sandy Drummond, Teresa R. Edminston, Jeannette Ferrary, Phyllis Fiarotta, Cathryn Harding, Beth Hillson, Coral Jordan, Mollie Katzen, Amy Killinger, Heidi King, Valerie Kohn, Drew Kristofik, Vivi Mannuzza, Shoshana Marchand, Sam Mead, Maggie Megaw, Joyce Rita Malley, Susan Milord, Jean Mitchel, Catherine Newman, Rebecca Lazaer Okrent, Valerie Orleans, Darlene Polachic, Susan G. Purdy, Tracey Randinelli, Betsy Rhein, Barbara Rowley, Mary Beth Sammons, Elizabeth Schwartz, Jeanne Skvarla, Shannon Summers, Emily B. Todd, Susan Todd, and Dede Wilson.

And to the following *FamilyFun* readers who shared the priceless ideas and recipes that have been a success with their families: Margi Ackerman, Bonnie Alexander, Lois Andrews, Sawyer Paull-Baird, Patti Barnes, Kathleen Bostrom, Ted Belsches, Janet Buckley, Jennifer Byers, Beth Comer, Julie Dunlap, Shanden and Lauren Field, Sue Jones, Jean Law, Karen Telleen-Lawton, Sherri Maunsell, Ann McDonald, Rachael Muro, Cindy Miles, Jacob Mulhern, Jenny Mulligan, Lori Nienau, Nancy Ojeda, Lorrie Paull, Andrea Rohms, Sarah Rosemarino, Ian and Abigail Rowswell, Miriam Sagan, Jacob Sandmire, Alexa Scally, Louann Sherbach, Teri Shilling, Cindi Tripken, Glenda Ulrich, Tricia Vega, Nancy Weber, Brenda Wollenberg, and Mallory Wright.

With gratitude to all the staff of *FamilyFun's* art and editorial departments, who directed much of the original work — especially to the following staff members for writing recipes and activities and generating ideas: Rani Arbo, Deanna F. Cook, Katherine Eastman, Clare Ellis, Pamela Glaven, Ann Hallock, Alexandra Kennedy, Ed Kohn, Cindy Littlefield, Paula Noonan, Susan Roberts, Lisa Stiepock, Maryellen Sullivan, Priscilla Totten, and Mike Trotman, and to David Kendrick and Ginger Barr Heafey for their art direction.

Special thanks to all the photographers, stylists, and models for their excellent work, which first appeared in *FamilyFun* magazine.

This book would not have been possible without the help of the staff at Impress, Inc.: Hans Teensma, James McDonald, Tobye Cook, and Leslie Tane; and the staff at Hyperion: Bob Miller, Wendy Lefkon, Monique Peterson, and David Lott.

ABOUT THE EXPERTS AT *FAMILYFUN*:

Deanna F. Cook is the Food Editor of *FamilyFun* magazine and the author of *The Kids' Multicultural Cookbook.* She and her husband live and cook in Northampton, Massachussetts.

Mollie Katzen is the author and illustrator of *Moosewood Cookbook, The Enchanted Broccoli Forest,* and *Still Life With Menu* and coauthor of the children's cookbook *Pretend Soup.* She is the writer of the "Teaching Kids to Cook" recipes in this book, which she develops with the help of her two children, Eve and Sam.

Rebecca Lazear Okrent, a regular contributor to *FamilyFun* magazine and the editor of *LivingHome Online,* writes about food and travel from her home in New York City, which she shares with her husband, Daniel, son, John, and daughter, Lydia.

Barbara Albright, former Editor-in-Chief of *Chocolatier,* is the author of *Simply Scones, Mostly Muffins, Quick Chocolate Fixes,* and the coauthor of *Cooking with Regis & Kathy Lee.* Her daughter, Samantha, and son, Stone, are her official taste-testers.

Contents

Build a Vegetable Bug: *page 170*

Scrambled Eggs with Tomato and Basil: *Page 21*

At Home Deli: *Page 46*

Fluttery Creations: *Page 83*

6

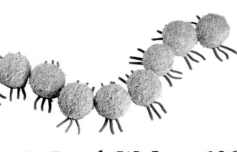

CHAPTER 1
Getting Ready

A S THE FOOD EDITOR of Disney's *FamilyFun* magazine, I like to root around in our file cabinets and pull out letters from our readers whenever I need a boost. Hearing a parent thank us for the recipes in the magazine is satisfying, but looking at a child's expression in the accompanying photo — holding up a Father's Day cake or a homemade apple pie — makes my day. A child's excitement as he offers up a slightly lopsided creation is proof that cooking is about family, about making something good to eat in the kitchen, and sharing it with someone you love. Forget the flowers — say it with spaghetti and cupcakes.

Since we started *FamilyFun* in 1991, families have come to rely on us for our cooking tips and recipes. They've clipped and saved and spilled flour all over them — the mark of good recipes. We decided it was about time to gather our most popular recipes in one place for the busy parents who want to put good meals on the table and enjoy them with their kids. In this cookbook, you will find recipes for real food, meals parents actually make and kids actually eat. And they're fun, from the preparation to the table.

Over the years, our contributors and readers have shared their tricks for satisfying every eater at the table. I am relieved to report that none of them involve preparing a different meal for each family member — a strategy some exasperated parents resort to. A couple of the tricks appeal particularly to kids. For starters, the names of the recipes are clever — Carrot Stick Salad, Veggies in a Blanket,

Shopping Wisely: Page 12

Turtle Bean Burritos. This may be a small point to an adult, but to many a picky child a catchy name makes a meal more appetizing. An innovative presentation is also key to making food more tempting. We won't pretend that every mom and dad has time to carve radishes into flowers, but some simple tricks — cutting sandwiches with cookie cutters, arranging sliced fruit into faces, or serving fun pasta shapes — win over the kindergarten set.

If you have finicky eaters in your household (and who doesn't?) you can still present nutritionally balanced meals. For the child (or adult) who turns up his nose to a tomato slice tucked in a grilled-cheese sandwich, for example, we say offer him a host of healthful add-ins — avocado, salsa, onion, broccoli. After all, things taste better when you have a choice.

Try to expand your repertoire in other ways as well. When I was a kid,

the most exotic thing my family ate was Swedish meatballs. Now we can't imagine a week without stir-fry. (My six-year-old nephew told me that pesto is the best thing you can eat on tortellini. Granted, he is the nephew of a food writer, but I don't think he's the only kid in his school who brings pesto for lunch.) The trend is that families in the nineties are eating out more and tasting new flavors all over town: Mexican, Chinese, Japanese, Thai, Italian, Greek, Caribbean. As our palates become more sophisticated — more receptive to a broad range of ingredients and cooking methods — we are expanding our choices. Grocery stores have responded, too, with shelves stocked with fresh herbs, specialty vegetables, and seafoods unheard of a generation ago. This recipe collection takes advantage of our global education with easy-to-follow recipes that introduce exotic foods in not too exotic ways.

Although most families' lives are

too overscheduled for three-course dinners every night, the special occasions call for extra effort. For those days, we have included some of my favorite holiday recipes. I always marvel at the fact that when my family reminisces, the conversation often comes back to food — especially the traditional dishes. For my younger sister it might be the memory of the green cupcakes my mom made for her St. Patrick's Day birthday; for my older sister it is the baklava my grandfather made at Christmas. Holiday recipes make parents (and grandparents) heroes in the eyes of their kids, and they create traditions our children insist we maintain year after year.

The kitchen is the family room — the core of the home, where everyone gravitates, not just for eating, but for learning and growing as a family. We hope these recipes will bring your family as many happy memories in the kitchen as they have brought the readers of *FamilyFun*. Now get ready to share some deliciously good times.

Eat dinner together. For many busy families, the evening meal is often the only time of day the crew gets to spend together. It is a good time to share ideas, catch up on news, and enjoy each other's company, and it may be the only time your kids get your undivided attention. Make sure the television is off and that all phone calls will be returned after dinner is over. At the dinner table, the best family entertainment can happen spontaneously through storytelling, laughter, and the appreciation of a good meal shared.

Plan menus ahead and save time. An hour spent planning meals on a Sunday will save you time all week long. Brainstorm new recipe ideas, try a more ambitious Sunday meal (with enough leftovers for lunch), or cook a sauce for a spaghetti dinner, freezing half for

Table Topics

When Karen Telleen-Lawton of Boulder, Colorado, wanted to make dinner a more fulfilling time for her family, she inaugurated Table Topics, a list of subjects in a basket on which they could speak extemporaneously. There are only two rules: You can choose to talk about whatever you wish rather than the topic drawn; and the speaker is allowed uninterrupted time, until he or she requests comments. Karen found that whether the assignment was to discuss something fun they had done in the last few days or to talk about something embarrassing that happened, her kids reveled in the undivided attention. Best of all, their practice of regular communication taught them a lot about each other.

Getting Ready

later. If you need ideas, peruse the chapters with your kids and involve them in the selection process; kids who participate in menu planning are more likely to eat the meals. Make a menu plan out of construction paper or create one on your word processor, then post it on the refrigerator. Be sure that each meal is complete — with a protein, grain, vegetable, and dessert. When you have a menu, you can compile a grocery list and avoid the tedious daily trips to the market. **Shop wisely.** Although your kids might say "there's nothing to eat" unless you buy bags of junk food, it's important to have the following basics on hand for snacks, lunches, and last-minute dinners:

☛ Vegetables: Scan the produce aisle for the freshest vegetables — usually those that are in season. Some staples you want to keep in your crisper or pantry are lettuce, onions, garlic, mushrooms, broccoli, cauliflower, peppers, tomatoes, squash, carrots, potatoes, peas, and corn on the cob. During off-seasons, pick up frozen peas, corn, and green beans, which taste better and are more nutritious than produce shipped thousands of miles.

☛ Fruits: Besides standbys such as oranges and apples, take advantage of berries, grapes, melons, and tropical fruits. Always have a lemon on hand for fresh lemon juice.

☛ Grains: Fiber is an important part of any diet, so pick up whole grain cereals and breads and replenish your supply of whole wheat and all-purpose flour, popcorn, rice, couscous, cornmeal, and rolled oats.

☛ Dairy: This primary source of calcium is most healthful when it is low- or no-fat. Try skim milk and low-fat yogurt and eat low-fat cheese, if your kids are game. Butter and margarine are too high-fat to be worthwhile sources of calcium.

Eggs, another dairy case staple, are healthful in moderation.

☞ Pasta: You can stock your shelves with everything from dry bow ties to wagon wheels. In the freezer, keep on hand fresh tortellini and ravioli.

☞ Meats and poultry: For fast dinners, pick up fish, chicken, ground beef and turkey, sausages, or tofu. Many grocers now carry free-range meats, which are more expensive, but leaner and chemical-free.

☞ Baking essentials: For impromptu baking projects, stock up on baking powder, baking soda, yeast, honey, granulated, brown, and confectioners' sugar, salt, vanilla extract, dried fruits and nuts, flavored and unflavored gelatin, food coloring, sprinkles, baking chocolate, cocoa powder, and chocolate chips.

☞ Sauces and condiments: Be sure to have in your refrigerator salsa, mustard, mayonnaise, catsup, chutney, relish, and soy sauce, as well as barbecue and spaghetti sauce.

☞ Oils and vinegars: Invest in virgin olive oil, as well as vegetable oil, and in red wine, white, and balsamic vinegars.

☞ Canned foods: Although canned goods once had a bad name, they are excellent time-savers. Try canned beans, such as chickpeas and kidney beans, canned tomatoes, and canned fruits in their juice.

☞ Stocks: Bouillon cubes and chicken broth are great for instant soups.

☞ Herbs and spices: Grow or pick up fresh herbs to snip over food and use as a garnish. Have the following dried herbs and spices on hand: cinnamon, basil, bay leaves, thyme, parsley, oregano, rosemary, dill, curry powder, chili powder, cumin, and any other favorites.

☞ Nuts and nut butters: Peanut butter, sesame

Grocery Savings

Buy in bulk: Pick up extra-large packages of frequently used items like cereal and juices.

Take advantage of special sales: Stock up on nonperishable items, such as canned goods and paper products.

Check the newspaper: Food sections will keep you up-to-date on the best produce buys.

Shop at double-coupon stores: Some stores will give you twice the face value of your coupons — a substantial savings.

Buy produce at local food stands: It eliminates the cost of a middleman — and lets you support local business.

Grow your own: For less expensive, better-tasting produce, plant some vegetables and herbs.

When *FamilyFun* reader Lori Nienau's son and daughter began to show an interest in food preparation, she organized a kids cooking class, held in her Kirkland, Washington, home. Lori collected recipes and asked both kids to invite a friend to attend their course. Their one-and-a-half-hour sessions took place one day a week after school and ran for four weeks. Lori began introducing the young chefs to the four food groups, cooking terminology, and the importance of a clean kitchen. After the kids learned to make an item, they placed the recipe in a three-ring binder and took home samples of their creations to share.

seeds, sunflower seeds, and walnuts add protein to sandwiches and salads.

Be prepared. The better equipped you are, the more likely you can efficiently whip up dinners, desserts, and other involved dishes. Consider the following checklist:

☛ Pots and pans, including a non-stick frying pan and small, medium, and large saucepans with fitted lids, a large soup pot, and a roasting pan.

☛ Utensils, such as a wooden spoon, whisk, garlic press, slotted spoons, spatula, ladle, rubber spatula, pastry brush, and pot holders.

☛ Small, medium, and large mixing bowls, as well as dry and liquid measuring cups.

☛ Baking tools — a rolling pin, pastry wheel, cookie cutters (regular, mini, and giant cutters, as well as aspic cutters, which are available at specialty shops and well worth the investment), pastry bag and decorator's tips, and Popsicle sticks.

☛ Baking pans, including two cookie sheets, a 13- by 9- by 2-inch pan, two 8- or 9-inch round cake pans, 9-inch pie pans, an 8½-inch and a 5-inch loaf pan, muffin tins (mini, regular, and giant) and paper liners, and a wire cooling rack.

☛ Appliances — an electric mixer, food processor or blender, and a microwave oven.

Raise healthy eaters. The key to good nutrition is not counting every calorie or avoiding all fatty foods: It's eating small portions of a variety of foods. In other words, it's okay to serve your child a cupcake as long as you also serve a healthy sandwich, carrot sticks, and a glass of skim milk. Be sure to set a good example by eating healthy foods yourself. Many of the recipes in this book are for special occasions — so eat those in moderation. And don't deprive your kids of their favorite foods; just be sure to dole them out carefully. Good tastes are linked with happy childhoods.

Introduce one new food every week. Taste is a learned behavior. It's tempting to serve hamburgers and pizza seven nights of the week, but it's more important to educate your children's palates so they can learn to love a wide range of foods. Introduce a new fruit or vegetable on a regular basis, and if your children don't like it, reintroduce it a few months later. Kids' tastes change over time. Try sneaking a new food into a dish they love or offer it as an optional topping. For inspiration, see the At Home Deli, page 46, the At Home Soup Bar, page 92, and the At Home Hamburger Joint, page 134.

Eat out one night a week. Eating out can be a fun way to spend time together. *FamilyFun* reader Shelly Cronin, who is from the magazine's hometown of Northampton, Massachusetts, reserves Friday nights for eating out with her family and Saturday nights for eating out with her husband. She says this tradition is a wonderful way to enjoy her kids' company and to maintain a close relationship with her husband. If you can, make a point of taking each of your children out to breakfast or lunch once a month and let him or her be the center of attention.

Teach your kids to cook, set the table, and clean up. Learning to cook is an important life skill and a great hobby to get your kids hooked on. In each chapter, our "Teaching Kids to Cook" recipes by Mollie Katzen will help you introduce young chefs to the right way to cook. Mollie encourages kids to be creative in the kitchen — to smell fresh herbs and decide whether to add them to the soup, for example — and to enjoy the process of making something to eat. Let your kids thumb through those sections and pick out the ones they want to try. For a complete cooking course, test one a week, then enlist the kids' help with the cleanup afterward.

Designer Table Setting

In *FamilyFun* reader Nancy Weber's household, table setting is transformed from a chore into an art form. The person setting the table gets to set it any way he or she sees fit — as long as four people can dine with the result. Sometimes they have plates under the chairs and all the knives and forks in a pile in the middle of the table; other times they have origami napkin swans; sometimes everyone has a different shape and color glass, and the napkins are tied around the rungs of the chairs. And one night Dad made a model of the starship *Enterprise* using forks, knives, and plates.

Step 1. Arrange a napkin on the diagonal and pull one layer down.

Step 2. Flip the napkin over and fold in the two sides.

Step 3. Turn it over again and fill with silverware.

CHAPTER 2

Breakfast: Rise and Shine

O A CHILD, Sunday breakfast is the best meal of the week. You get to sleep late, read the Sunday comics, and eat in your pajamas. The fare is as sweet as dessert: Maple syrup poured over a stack of pancakes, warm blueberry muffins, or cinnamon rolls straight from the oven. Weekday breakfasts, however, bear little of that romantic charm. The morning becomes a rush hour, and some kids (and parents) would rather just not bother fixing breakfast or eating, despite the knowledge that the first meal of the day is the most important. So, how can you turn breakfast into a favorite meal every day without getting up before dawn to start baking?

On weekdays, make it fast and eat slow. Fill your freezer with whole grain cereals, breads, and other nutritious baked goods. Keep a supply of fresh fruits (cut into bite-size pieces), low-fat milk, and juices in the refrigerator. Store cereal on a shelf your children can reach, so they can help themselves. For a real time-saver, set the table for breakfast each night as soon as the dinner dishes are cleared.

Bake breakfast treats on the weekends. Muffins, scones, and homemade pancake mixes all can be made ahead to save time. Let your child browse through this chapter and pick a recipe to try each week; if invited to help make it, he might also be more inclined to eat it.

Serve small portions. You don't want to load your child up on heavy breakfast foods before school, or it will slow him down. Serve a variety of lighter foods, including protein, starches, fiber, and fat:

No-Frills Loaf: *Page 118*

Puffed Pancake: *Page 25*

Breakfast on the Run

If your kids need to dash off with a lunch box in one hand and breakfast in the other, here are some manageable quickies:

Warm yesterday's pancakes or waffles in the toaster and serve with jam.

Make a peanut butter and banana sandwich on toast.

Fill a pita with a scrambled egg and a slice of ham.

Mix ricotta cheese with cinnamon and sugar and serve with sliced apples inside a whole wheat pita.

Mix granola into a container of yogurt.

Blend a banana with a little milk or OJ and pour into a thermos.

Apple-Walnut Pancakes: *Page 23*

fruit and milk on a high-fiber cereal, for example, or a batch of scrambled eggs with whole wheat toast.

If your child can't eat first thing in the morning, brown-bag her breakfast. If your child honestly can't bear the idea of breakfast — and the only way to keep her at the breakfast table is forcibly — pack her a school breakfast that includes a juice box, a muffin or high-quality cereal bar, and an easy-to-eat piece of fruit, such as a banana or an apple.

Define breakfast loosely. Nowhere is it written that breakfast must consist of eggs, pancakes, and sausage. If your child prefers cold pizza or tuna fish sandwiches for breakfast, just consider yourself lucky that he doesn't start the day with a cola.

Enjoy weekend breakfasts. If eating dinner together every night is unrealistic, plan on eating breakfast together on a weekend morning. Turn off the TV, make a big breakfast or brunch, and catch up on the busy week.

Sunday Morning Omelets

Kids like to choose their own fillings for this classic egg dish. Encourage them to invent combinations from whatever leftover vegetables, spreads, cheeses, and meats you have on hand. How about a jelly and cream cheese omelet?

½   tablespoon butter or margarine
2   eggs
1   tablespoon water
    Salt and pepper to taste
Filling options:
1   tablespoon grated cheese, such as
        Cheddar or Mozzarella
1   tablespoon cottage cheese,
        Boursin, or flavored cream
        cheese (see page 35)
2   tablespoons diced, cooked chicken
1   tablespoon crispy bacon pieces
2   teaspoons jam or jelly
2   sliced mushrooms
2   cherry tomato halves
1   tablespoon diced green or red
        pepper
1   tablespoon diced onion

In a large, nonstick frying pan, melt the butter or margarine over medium-high heat. Beat the eggs with a fork in a small bowl and stir in the water, salt, and pepper. Pour the egg mixture over the butter, swirling the egg until you have coated the pan with a thin layer of uncooked egg. Sprinkle the desired fillings over the omelet and cook for 1 to 3 more minutes, or until desired doneness. To serve, hold the pan at a 45-degree angle and, with a spatula, gently fold the omelet in half. Makes 1 generous omelet.

Breakfast Burrito

The morning after a Mexican meal, I use up my leftover tortillas, grated cheese, chopped onion, and salsa in this delicious roll-up sandwich.

1   tablespoon butter
6   eggs, beaten
4   to 6 8-inch flour tortillas
Filling options:
½   cup grated Monterey Jack cheese
1   plum tomato, chopped
1   small onion, diced
¼   green or red pepper, chopped
½   avocado, diced
    Salsa
    Sliced olives

Over medium-high heat, melt the butter in a large, nonstick frying pan and scramble and cook the eggs to your liking. Meanwhile, warm the tortillas for a few minutes on the rack of a 250° oven, then fill with the egg and your choice of ingredients. Fold into a burrito (see page 159 for directions). Serves 4.

Breakfast Burrito

EGG HEADS

For a silly activity that makes terrific use of eggshells, you can make Egg Heads with wild grass-dos. For each, you'll need a raw egg, a needle, grass seed, and potting soil. First, use the needle to make a hole about the size of a quarter in one end of an egg, then drain the contents and rinse out the shell. Gently draw or paint faces on the shell and set in an egg carton to dry. Spoon soil into the shell, then plant the grass seeds according to package instructions. Moisten, cover with plastic wrap, and place in a sunny window until the seeds sprout — about one week. When the Egg Heads have a thick head of hair, remove the covering and style with scissors. Water your Egg Heads regularly.

Breakfast: Rise and Shine

Well-Timed Eggs

Soft-Boiled Eggs: In a saucepan, cover eggs with water and bring to a boil. Reduce the heat to a simmer and cook for 2 to 3 minutes more. Remove each soft-boiled egg and let sit until it is cool enough to handle.

Hard-Boiled Eggs: Cook eggs as you would for soft-boiled, but simmer for 15 minutes. Plunge into cold water to halt the cooking and make peeling easier.

Note: Add 2 minutes to cooking times if the eggs are straight from the refrigerator.

Royal Ham 'n' Eggs

This dish is a favorite at my mother's inn in Woodstock, Vermont. The vegetables listed can be substituted with ½ cup of sliced mushrooms, chopped broccoli, shredded zucchini, or cubed boiled potatoes; instead of ham or sausage, you can add strips of prosciutto or bacon pieces.

1½	cups French bread cubes
½	pound cooked ham or sausage, cubed
1	8-ounce package frozen chopped spinach, thawed and drained
12	cherry tomatoes, sliced in half
8	ounces Cheddar cheese, grated
8	eggs
1	teaspoon dried mustard
¼	teaspoon pepper
1	cup milk

Preheat the oven to 350°. Butter a 13- by 9- by 2-inch baking dish and line with the bread cubes. Cover with layers of ham or sausage, chopped spinach, cherry tomatoes, and grated cheese. In a separate bowl, whisk the eggs, dried mustard, pepper, and milk. Pour the mixture over the casserole. Bake for 30 minutes, then broil for 2 minutes, or until the cheese turns golden brown. Makes 8 to 10 servings.

Royal Ham 'n' Eggs

Breakfast Pizza

Better known as a frittata, this egg dish can be topped with everything your kids like on pizza. Prepare it the night before and serve at room temperature.

4	eggs, beaten
¼	to ½ cup grated mild Cheddar or Monterey Jack cheese
¼	cup diced ham, pepperoni, mushrooms, or other pizza topping
1	tablespoon butter or margarine

Preheat your broiler. In a medium-size bowl, mix the eggs, cheese, and pizza toppings. Melt the butter in an 8-inch frying pan with a metal handle over medium heat. Pour in the egg mixture and cook until the bottom is golden, about 7 minutes. Remove the pan from the stove and place it under the broiler for about 3 minutes, or until the top has puffed up and lightly browned. Cool slightly and cut into wedges. Makes 1 frittata.

The Best Way to Nuke Bacon

☞ **Microwave slices of bacon between 2 paper towels so you can throw the mess away. For crispy bacon, heat 4 slices on high for 4 minutes.**

Scrambled Eggs with Cream Cheese and Chives

Learning to scramble eggs is a great cooking lesson for kids. Fresh chives and cream cheese create a creamy embellishment.

- 1 tablespoon butter or margarine
- 2 eggs
- 1 to 2 tablespoons cream cheese, cut into ½-inch cubes
- 4 fresh chives, snipped into pieces

Melt the butter in a small saucepan over medium heat. Beat the eggs, pour into the pan, and stir for 1 minute. Add the cream cheese and chives and cook to desired doneness. Serves 1.

Cottage Cheese and Dill:

Add 1 heaping tablespoon cottage cheese and 2 teaspoons chopped fresh dill (or 1 teaspoon dried dill) to 2 nearly cooked scrambled eggs.

Cheddar Cheese and Bacon:

While stirring, sprinkle 1 to 2 pieces of cooked, crumbled bacon and 2 teaspoons grated Cheddar cheese into scrambled eggs. Let the cheese melt before serving.

Tomato and Basil:

Toss half a small, diced tomato and 1 to 2 teaspoons chopped fresh basil into your scrambled eggs before serving.

Salsa, Cilantro, and Sour Cream:

Mix 1 to 2 tablespoons salsa, 1 teaspoon chopped fresh cilantro, and 2 teaspoons sour cream into scrambled eggs while cooking.

GREEN EGGS & HAM, I AM, I AM

To celebrate Dr. Seuss's birthday, kick off March 2nd by reading *Green Eggs & Ham* and whipping up a batch of green scrambled eggs. Just add a few drops of green food coloring to your family recipe.

Variations on Scrambled Eggs (clockwise from bottom left):
- ☛ Tomato and Basil
- ☛ Cheddar Cheese and Bacon
- ☛ Cream Cheese and Chives
- ☛ Salsa, Cilantro, and Sour Cream
- ☛ Cottage Cheese and Dill

Breakfast: Rise and Shine

Eggs in a Nest

Eggs in a Nest

This clever perennial, which has been called Eggs in a Nest, Eggs in a Saddle, One Eyes, and Egyptian Eggs, has helped to launch a thousand wary kids into the delicious world of eggs. Use whole grain bread to up its nutritional value.

1	slice of bread
1	teaspoon butter or margarine
1	egg
	Salt and pepper to taste

Use a 3-inch cookie cutter (hearts, stars, and circles are all possibilities) to cut a shape out of the bread. Melt the butter in a griddle or frying pan. Place the bread in the pan and break an egg into the hole. Lay the cutout shape in the pan wherever it will fit and toast until golden brown. Sprinkle the egg with salt and pepper.

When the egg is cooked on the bottom and before the bread becomes too brown, flip the egg nest to toast the other side and finish cooking the egg, about 1 minute. Serve with the toasted shape. Serves 1.

Oven-Baked Home Fries

As any diner cook could tell you, home fries are a delicious accompaniment to an egg breakfast. When you add extras, such as cheese and bacon pieces, they practically become meals unto themselves. Note, though, that the high fat content makes home fries a better breakfast treat than a staple.

4	medium-large, unpeeled potatoes, in ½-inch cubes
3	tablespoons butter or margarine
1	medium onion, diced
1	to 2 crushed garlic cloves (optional)

Place a large, cast-iron skillet in the oven and preheat to 350°. Place the potatoes in a saucepan, cover with water, and boil for 10 minutes. Drain the water and cool. Remove the cast-iron pan from the oven, swirl in the butter, and add the potatoes and onions. Stir to coat and return to the oven for 30 to 40 minutes, occasionally flipping to brown on all sides. Add the garlic during the last 5 minutes. Serves 4 to 8, depending on if they are a main or side dish.

Deluxe Home Fries:

Melt cheese over the home fries and sprinkle crumbled bacon on top.

A Mountain Man Breakfast:

Add 1 scrambled egg to Deluxe Home Fries.

Pancakes & Waffles

The Perfect Pancake Mix

FamilyFun contributor Becky Okrent developed this vitamin-packed mix to encourage her family to make pancakes in short order.

- 3 cups all-purpose flour
- 3 teaspoons baking soda
- 4½ teaspoons baking powder
- 1½ teaspoons salt
- 1 tablespoon sugar (optional)
- 2 cups whole wheat or oat flour, or a combination
- 1 cup seven whole grain cereal (available at health food stores)
- 1 cup cornmeal
- 4 tablespoons wheat germ (optional)

In a large mixing bowl, sift the all-purpose flour with the baking soda, baking powder, salt, and optional sugar. Drop in the remaining flour, cereal, cornmeal, and wheat germ and stir until thoroughly blended. Store in an airtight container and, if using wheat germ, refrigerate. Makes 7½ cups, enough for 15 batches of 5 pancakes.

Perfect Pancakes:

You can store leftover batter in the refrigerator for two days and reheat leftover pancakes in a toaster.

- 1 tablespoon butter
- 1 egg
- ½ cup nonfat yogurt, buttermilk, sour cream, or milk
- ½ cup Perfect Pancake Mix

Set a griddle or skillet over medium heat and melt the butter. Lightly beat the egg with the yogurt, buttermilk, sour cream, or milk. Add the pancake mix and stir just until smooth.

Ladle the batter onto the skillet. Turn the pancakes when you see air bubbles on the surface (about 1 minute). Serve with maple syrup, jam, yogurt, or confectioners' sugar. Makes about 5 medium pancakes.

Perfect Blueberry Pancakes:

Stir ½ cup fresh or frozen blueberries into the batter before cooking.

Pancake Specials

Apple-Walnut Pancakes: Toss chopped walnuts, sliced apples, and ½ teaspoon cinnamon into your batter.

Cranberry-Orange Pancakes: Add ½ cup cranberries, 1 tablespoon orange juice, and 1 teaspoon orange zest to the batter.

Banana Pancakes: Top pancakes with sliced bananas before flipping.

Pumpkin Pancakes: Mix 2 tablespoons of mashed pumpkin and 1 teaspoon of allspice into the batter.

Personalized Pancakes: Shape the batter on the griddle into animals, cartoon characters, or your child's initials.

Perfect Blueberry Pancakes

the mixture from becoming lumpy. Beat in the eggs, one at a time.

Over medium-high heat, brush an 8- to 9-inch nonstick frying pan with a small amount of the melted butter, swirl in ⅓ cup of the batter, and cook for about 1 minute, or until the edges are dry and bubbles appear in the center. Carefully flip the pancake and cook the other side until golden brown. Serve immediately or keep a stack warm in a 250° oven. Continue until you've used up the batter and butter. Makes about 10 8-inch pancakes.

Raspberry Syrup

FamilyFun contributor Susan Purdy's no-cook pancake syrup takes only a few minutes to prepare. The kids can join in by straining out the raspberry seeds. This tangy syrup also goes well over fruit salad or melon slices.

    3 cups fresh raspberries,
       or a 12-ounce bag of frozen
       unsweetened raspberries
    1 cup light corn syrup
    2 teaspoons fresh lemon juice

Place fresh or frozen berries into a blender or food processor (in small batches if necessary) and process into a smooth puree. Set a strainer over a bowl, pour in the puree, and stir to remove seeds. Add the corn syrup and lemon juice and blend until smooth. Taste and adjust flavorings. Store in a jar and refrigerate. Makes about 2 cups.

Pancake Tips

☞ **For lowfat pancake cooking, try using a small amount of salt in place of butter on the griddle.**

☞ **Add a tablespoon of maple syrup to pancake batter for extra flavor.**

☞ **For very light pancakes, use club soda in place of the usual liquid in the batter.**

Swedish Pancakes

The best way to serve these pancakes, known as *plättar* in Sweden, is to set up a buffet with bowls of fillings, such as jam, crispy bacon, grated cheese, hot applesauce with cinnamon, strawberries, and whipped cream.

    1½ cups flour
     1 tablespoon sugar
     ½ teaspoon salt
     3 cups milk
     2 eggs
     3 to 4 tablespoons butter, melted

Sift the flour, sugar, and salt in a large mixing bowl. Add the milk, a little at a time, whisking well to keep

Gingerbread Pancakes

On a cold Sunday morning (or for a special winter supper), serve a stack of gingerbread pancakes with real maple syrup and mugs of hot mulled cider.

- 1 cup all-purpose flour
- 1 tablespoon sugar
- 1 teaspoon baking powder
- 1 teaspoon ground ginger
- ½ teaspoon salt
- ½ teaspoon baking soda
- ½ teaspoon cinnamon
  Dash of ground cloves
- 2 tablespoons molasses
- 1 tablespoon vegetable oil
- 1 cup buttermilk
- 1 egg, lightly beaten

In a large bowl, combine all the dry ingredients. In a small bowl, whisk the molasses, oil, buttermilk, and egg. Slowly pour the liquid mixture into the flour mixture and stir until uniform. Lightly grease a griddle or pan over medium-low heat and cook the pancakes for about 3 minutes on each side. Makes 6 medium pancakes.

Puffed Pancake

This soufflé wanna-be is a fun variation on the usual pancake. Be sure the kids are around to see the puff collapse.

- 3 tablespoons butter
- 3 eggs
- ⅔ cup milk
- ¾ cup flour
- ½ teaspoon vanilla extract
- 1 cup strawberries, sliced
  Confectioners' sugar

Preheat the oven to 450°. Melt the butter in a 9-inch pie pan in the oven (watch that it doesn't burn). Meanwhile, whisk the eggs and milk, then sift in the flour, whisking it until well combined. Mix in the vanilla extract.

Remove the pie pan from the oven and pour in the mixture. On a low shelf, bake for 20 minutes, or until puffed and golden brown. Remove from the oven and fill the center with the strawberries. For a finishing touch, powder with confectioners' sugar. One pancake serves 2 to 4 people.

Very Berry:

Pile a baked Puffed Pancake with blueberries, raspberries, blackberries, and whatever else you can find in season. Sprinkle with confectioners' sugar.

Peaches and Honey:

Coat sliced peaches with honey and mound onto a baked Puffed Pancake.

Apple Spice:

Warm applesauce and cinnamon in the microwave, then spoon onto a baked Puffed Pancake.

Gingerbread Pancakes

Breakfast: Rise and Shine

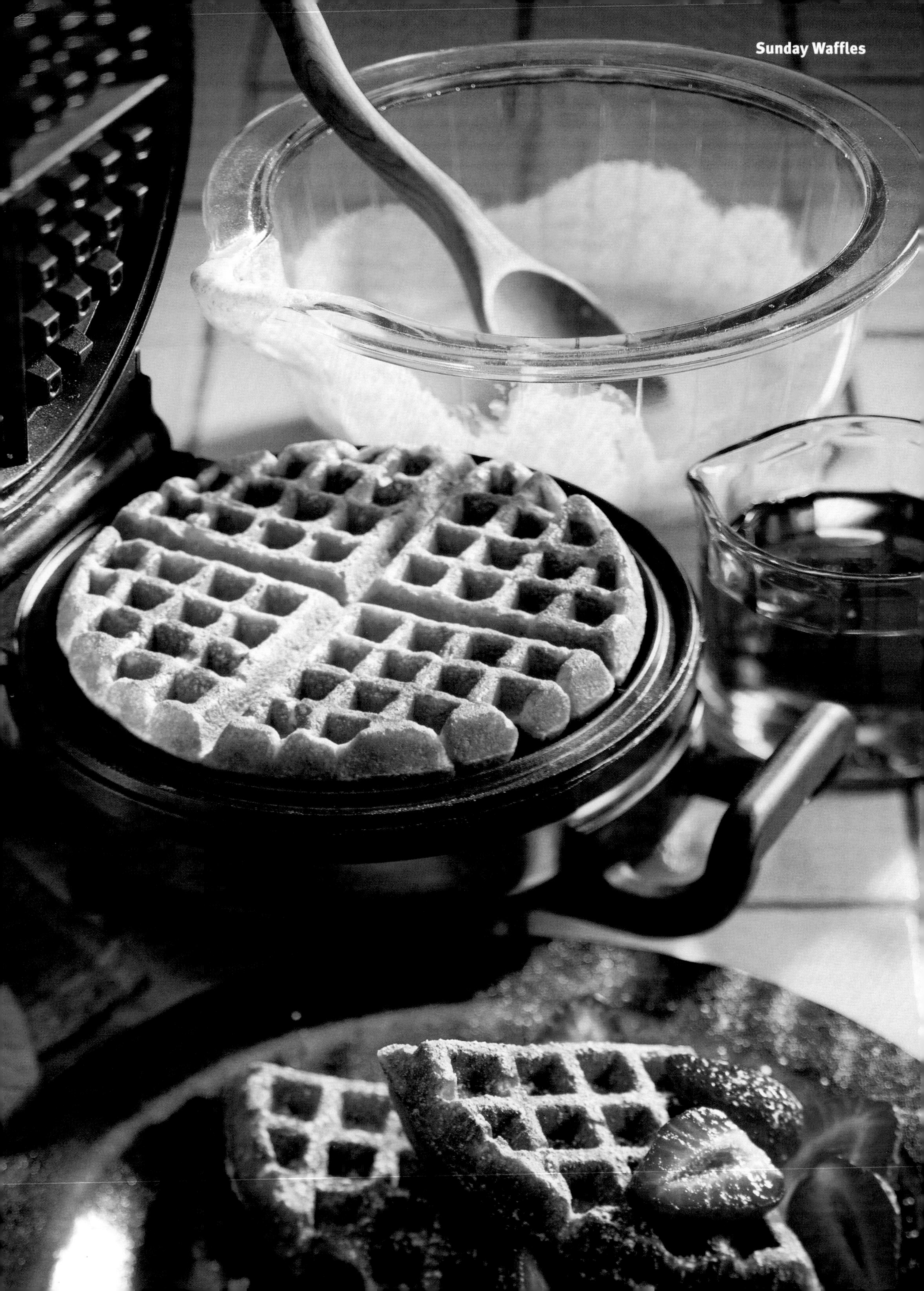

Great Toppings for Pancakes, Waffles, and French Toast

Children love the opportunity to get creative with toppings. Here are some ideas:

- ☛ Confectioners' sugar
- ☛ Cinnamon Sugar (see page 36)
- ☛ Strawberry jam
- ☛ Unsweetened yogurt
- ☛ Sliced fresh fruit or berries
- ☛ Honey
- ☛ Lemon Curd (see page 35)
- ☛ Cream cheese and jelly
- ☛ Flavored butters (see pages 35 and 52)
- ☛ Vanilla yogurt and granola
- ☛ Raspberry Syrup (see page 24)
- ☛ Applesauce and cinnamon

Waffles on the Run

The next time you pull out the waffle iron, remember to make an extra batch for mornings when your family needs to grab a quick bite. Cook the waffles, leaving them slightly lighter than usual, cool, then place in a sealable plastic bag and freeze. To reheat, pop one in the toaster, then garnish with your favorite toppings or one of the suggestions above.

Sunday Waffles

The leisurely pace of Sundays means extra time for *FamilyFun* contributor Becky Okrent and her family to make waffles, using her Perfect Pancake Mix.

- 2 eggs, separated
- 1 cup milk
- 3 tablespoons vegetable oil or melted butter
- 1 cup Perfect Pancake Mix (see page 23)

In a bowl, combine the egg yolks, milk, and oil or butter. Stir in the Perfect Pancake Mix. Beat the egg whites until stiff and gently fold into the batter. Cook on a greased waffle iron until lightly browned. Makes 4 to 6 waffles.

Banana Split Waffles:

Top a waffle with 1 tablespoon of plain or vanilla yogurt, sliced banana, and a sprinkle of granola.

Poppy Seed Waffles:

Add 1 tablespoon of poppy seeds to the batter before cooking.

Strawberry Cream Cheese Waffles:

Spread Strawberry Cream Cheese (see page 35) on a waffle and cut into pie-shaped wedges.

Pick an Orange Orange?

Because most oranges are dyed to improve their appearance, don't judge an orange by its color. Pick a sweet orange by examining the navel: the bigger the better. For 1 cup of juice, you will need 3 sweet medium juice oranges.

Breakfast Milk Shake

This make-ahead healthy shake is so thick, some kids insist on calling it banana ice cream.

- 2 bananas
- 5 to 10 whole strawberries (optional)
- ¼ cup blueberries (optional)
- ½ cup milk or orange juice

Slice the bananas into 1-inch chunks. Wash and stem the berries. Seal the fruits in a plastic bag and freeze for 3 hours or overnight. Place the frozen fruits in a blender or a food processor (if they are rock hard, let them slightly defrost). Add the milk or orange juice and puree or process until smooth and thick. Pour into a glass, bowl, or mug and serve with spoons or straws. Serves 2.

Cinnamon French Toast

FamilyFun *contributor Mollie Katzen says, "I can't think of a more perfect recipe for beginning cooks than French toast. I've made it with three-year-olds, twelve-year-olds, and many ages in between and, somehow, it's appealing to everyone."*

2 eggs and a whisk

½ cup milk

¼ teaspoon vanilla extract

a shake of ground cinnamon

1 Ask your child to break 2 eggs into a large bowl. Cracking eggs is simple and fun for even the smallest child if the bowl is big enough and the egg is whacked hard enough.

2 The next step is to add ½ cup of milk, a shake of cinnamon, and ¼ teaspoon of vanilla extract. Have your child beat it all up with a whisk.

Cooking Tip: Young kids can successfully measure milk if they pour it from a small pitcher, which is easier to wield than a big milk carton. (Don't worry if the milk spills a little or the measurements are not exact.)

3 The chef can carefully pour the batter into a shallow dish or pie pan. This makes it easier to dip the bread without bending or breaking it.

Cooking Tip: If there is a little batter left over after cooking up one batch, just add it to the next round.

4 Ask your child to dip the bread on both sides until it is soaked through. For best results, pat the bread with a fork to get it wet, then transfer it to a plate.

Cooking Tip: Dry or stale bread actually holds together better than fresh bread. If fresh bread is all you have, just soak it briefly, so it won't fall apart.

3 to 4 slices of bread — stale, if possible (challah, French, Italian, or sourdough is best)

butter

syrup

confectioners' sugar

sliced strawberries

5 Show your child how to turn the heat to medium-low or an electric skillet to 375°. Melt 1 tablespoon of butter in the pan. Then place the bread in the pan, being careful not to splatter the hot butter.

Cooking Tip: An electric skillet is ideal for cooking with kids. Set it up on a tabletop at their level, which is easier for them to reach than a stove.

6 Cook one side of the bread until it is brown. This will take a few minutes — your chef can use a spatula to peek. Then flip it over and cook on the other side until brown on the bottom. Use the spatula to lift it onto the plate.

Cooking Tip: Remind your child that the pan is hot and to avoid touching any part but the handle.

7 Put syrup, confectioners' sugar, and sliced strawberries on the table. Let the kids eat the French toast with toppings of their choice. Serves 2.

Cooking Tip: Instead of syrup and strawberries, encourage your kids to come up with other toppings. Suggest Cinnamon Sugar (see page 36), jam, yogurt, or sliced fresh fruits.

Muffins & Scones

Good Morning Muffins and Best Apple Butter

flours, baking powder, salt, and cinnamon. Blend the dry ingredients with the apple mixture until just combined. Spoon the batter into the muffin tins and bake for 25 minutes, or until golden brown. Makes 12 muffins.

Best Apple Butter

As I learned from my mother, who created this recipe, the best part of making apple butter is that your house fills with a sweet, cinnamon aroma. It isn't a lot of work, but it takes a long time to bake, so plan to make it when you are working around the house. Nothing is better when spread on muffins, scones, or toast.

9 to 10 apples, peeled, cored,
     and cut into 1-inch chunks
1 cup apple cider
2 teaspoons apple pie spice
     (available in the spice rack at
     your grocer's)

Place the apples in a large, nonreactive saucepan with the cider. Cover the pot and cook for about 30 minutes over low heat, or until the apples are soft. Cool, divide into two batches, and puree each in the bowl of a food processor or blender. Pour all of the pureed fruit into a 13- by 9- by 2-inch baking dish, sprinkle with the apple pie spice, and stir well.

Stirring every 20 minutes, bake in a preheated 300° oven for 2 to 3 hours, or until your apple butter is deep brown and thick. Cool and then scoop it into a clean jar with a sealable lid. It will keep for up to 2 months in your refrigerator. Makes 1½ cups.

Hot Mulled Apple Cider

Combine a gallon of cider with 4 cinnamon sticks, a few cloves, ¼ teaspoon of ground nutmeg, and several orange slices. Gently warm over medium heat. Strain and transfer to mugs. For extra flavor, add a cinnamon stick and orange slice to each serving.

Good Morning Muffins

Thanks to these nutritious muffins, my brother gets his kids to eat apples and carrots for breakfast.

3 eggs
½ cup sugar
½ cup vegetable oil
1 cup grated apples
1 cup grated carrots
1 cup whole wheat flour
1 cup all-purpose flour
1 tablespoon baking powder
¼ teaspoon salt
1 teaspoon cinnamon

Preheat the oven to 375°. Lightly grease a 12-cup muffin tin or line it with paper liners and set aside. Blend the eggs, sugar, and oil until well combined. Stir in the grated apples and carrots. In a separate bowl, sift the

P B & J Surprise Muffins

The inspiration of *FamilyFun* contributor Beth Hillson, these moist peanut butter muffins hide a secret jelly or jam filling. She lets her son pick the flavor and puts him in charge of spooning the surprise into the batter. Her advice: Make a batch on a Sunday so your child can enjoy them as breakfast treats all week long.

1¾	cups all-purpose flour
⅓	cup sugar
2½	teaspoons baking powder
½	teaspoon salt
½	cup creamy peanut butter
1	large egg
¾	cup milk
⅓	cup butter, melted
½	cup strawberry, raspberry, or grape jelly or jam

Preheat the oven to 375°. Line a 12-cup muffin tin with paper liners. In a large bowl, combine the flour, sugar, baking powder, and salt. In a separate bowl, mix the peanut butter with the egg; add the milk, a little at a time, then add the butter. Mix well. Pour the wet batter into the bowl with the dry ingredients and stir gently to combine (the batter will be stiff).

Put a heaping tablespoon of batter in the bottom of each muffin cup. Use a finger to make an indentation in the center and put a teaspoon of jelly in the hole. Cover with another heaping tablespoon of batter, or enough to fill each cup about two thirds full. Spread the top batter gently until no jelly is visible. Bake for 20 minutes, then turn the muffins onto a wire baking rack to cool. Be careful — the jelly centers can get hot. Makes 12 muffins.

PB & J Surprise Muffins

2½ cups blueberries, washed
    and stems removed

Preheat the oven to 375° and line a 12-cup muffin tin with paper liners. In a large bowl, cream the butter and sugar. Add the eggs, and stir in the milk and vanilla extract. In another bowl, sift the dry ingredients. Stir them into the butter and sugar mixture, then fold in the blueberries. Fill the muffin cups almost to the top and bake for 25 minutes, or until light brown. Makes 12 muffins.

Blueberry Buckle

This foolproof coffee cake is a specialty in Maine, America's blueberry capital.

Topping:
    ⅓ cup sugar
    ½ cup all-purpose flour
    1½ teaspoons cinnamon
    ¼ cup butter, softened

Batter:
    ¼ cup butter
    ¾ cup sugar
    2 eggs
    ½ cup milk
    2 cups all-purpose flour
    ½ teaspoon salt
    2 teaspoons baking powder
    2 cups blueberries, washed and
        stems removed

To make the topping, stir the dry ingredients and butter with a fork until the mixture crumbles. Set aside.

Preheat the oven to 350° and grease a 9-inch square pan. In a mixing bowl, cream the butter and sugar, add the eggs, and stir in the milk. Mix until smooth. Sift the flour, salt, and baking powder into a separate bowl. Gradually stir it into the batter. Fold in the blueberries, then spread the batter in the pan. Sprinkle the topping over the batter. Bake for 35 to 40 minutes, or until a toothpick inserted in the middle comes out dry. Serves 8.

Very Blueberry Whole Wheat Muffins and Blueberry Buckle

Go Blueberry Picking

For the sweetest blueberries, head to a local farm and pick your own. To find a blueberry farm in your area, call your county extension service or state department of agriculture. Be sure to pick extra for freezing — just toss them in a sealable plastic container. You'll welcome the berry taste in the middle of winter.

Very Blueberry Whole Wheat Muffins

If you are trying to introduce your kids to whole grain flours, a basket of these sweet blueberry muffins is convincing evidence that unprocessed flours taste the best.

    6 tablespoons butter, softened
    ¾ cup sugar
    2 eggs
    ½ cup milk
    1 teaspoon vanilla extract
    1 cup all-purpose flour
    1 cup whole wheat flour
    1 tablespoon baking powder
    ¼ teaspoon salt

Strawberry-Almond Muffins

Fresh strawberries and slivered almonds are excellent flavor companions, but if your kids rank among the many who are not nut fans, you can substitute Grape Nuts cereal for the almonds.

½   cup butter, softened
¾   cup sugar
2   eggs
½   cup milk
1½   teaspoons almond extract
1½   cups all-purpose flour
½   cup whole wheat flour
1   tablespoon baking powder
¼   teaspoon salt
2   cups strawberries, chopped
¾   cup slivered almonds

Preheat the oven to 375° and line a 12-cup muffin tin with paper liners (a good job for kids). In the bowl of an electric mixer or food processor, cream the butter and sugar. Add the eggs, one at a time, and blend until fluffy. Mix in the milk and the almond extract. In a separate bowl, sift the flours, baking powder, and salt. Add the flour mixture to the milk mixture and blend until just combined. Fold in the strawberries and almonds. Fill the muffin cups to the top and bake for 30 minutes, or until golden brown. Makes 12 muffins.

STRAWBERRY SLUSH

Strawberries stack up third, right behind papaya and cantaloupe, on a list of the most nutritious fruits compiled by the Center for Science in the Public Interest. That's because they are so high in vitamin C (ounce per ounce, they outrank even oranges).

6 ice cubes
16 strawberries
**½ cup frozen
    concentrated limeade**
½ cup water

Place the ice cubes in a blender or food processor and pulse until crushed. Add the strawberries, limeade, and water. Puree until smooth and thick. Pour into tall glasses with flexistraws. Serves 2.

FunFact
To dream of strawberries is a sign of good things to come.

Strawberry-Almond Muffins and Strawberry Slush

Fruit-Filled Scones

Fruit-Filled Scones

A traditional teatime treat, scones make a delicious breakfast, too. Serve them warm with butter, jam, or homemade Lemon Curd (opposite). On special occasions, you can also make a pot of decaffeinated tea to serve to your kids with lots of milk.

2	cups flour
¼	cup sugar
1	teaspoon cream of tartar
1	teaspoon baking soda
½	teaspoon salt
½	cup butter or margarine
⅔	to ¾ cup milk
¾	cup raisins, currants, or chopped dried apricots

Preheat the oven to 400°. Sift the dry ingredients and cut in the butter or margarine until the mixture is coarse, resembling cornmeal. Gradually add the milk to make a soft dough. Add the dried fruit and knead the dough three to four times. On a lightly floured surface, roll out the dough to a ½-inch thickness and cut out the scones with a 2-inch round cookie cutter. Place on an ungreased cookie sheet and bake 10 to 12 minutes, or until golden brown. Makes 10 scones.

Jamming with Jam

A sweet song from the classic children's book Bread and Jam for Frances *by Russell Hoban*

Jam on biscuits,
jam on toast,
Jam is the thing
I like most.
Jam is sticky,
jam is sweet,
Jam is tasty,
jam's a treat—
Raspberry,
strawberry,
gooseberry,
I'm very
FOND...
OF...
JAM!

English Muffins

Mound an English muffin with toppings and you've got a wholesome breakfast.

☛ **Make a breakfast sandwich by topping toasted English muffin halves with slices of ham, scrambled eggs, and cheese. Broil until the cheese melts, then sandwich together the halves.**

☛ **Spread a toasted English muffin with peanut butter and Best Apple Butter (see page 30).**

☛ **Toast to crispy brown and top with Honey Butter (see page 119).**

☛ **Layer fresh Granny Smith apple slices and Swiss cheese on a toasted muffin.**

☛ **Spread peanut butter on a toasted muffin and arrange banana slices and raisins into a funny face.**

☛ **On a toasted muffin, layer pear slices over Real Cashew Butter (see page 52).**

☛ **Poach an egg, sprinkle it with salt and pepper and a jolt of hot sauce, and pile it on a muffin.**

☛ **Daub a slice of sweet ham with mild mustard, top with a lettuce leaf, and layer between toasted muffin halves.**

☛ **Melt Gruyère cheese on a muffin and sprinkle with chopped bacon.**

Lemon Curd

This light and sweet English curd makes a great topping for many American breakfast foods. *FamilyFun* contributor Vivi Mannuzza swears this is the best recipe we've ever run in the magazine.

2   large eggs
2   large egg yolks
¾   cup sugar
⅔   cup fresh lemon juice
2   teaspoons grated lemon zest
⅓   cup unsalted butter, cut into pieces
⅛   teaspoon salt

In a saucepan, whisk the eggs and yolks. Add the sugar, lemon juice, and zest. Add the butter pieces and salt. Cook on low heat, stirring constantly for 8 minutes, or until the curd thickens enough to coat the back of a spoon. Don't let it boil. Pour into a glass dish, cover, and refrigerate for at least 4 hours. Makes 1½ cups.

Strawberry Butter

Sweet on toast or bagels, this spread has won over many breakfast-haters.

½   cup unsalted butter, softened
½   cup strawberries, fresh or frozen
3   tablespoons confectioners' sugar

Combine all the ingredients in a food processor and blend until smooth. Makes ⅔ cup.

Strawberry Jam Butter:

Blend ½ cup unsalted butter, softened, and ¼ cup strawberry jam until smooth.

Apricot Butter:

Blend ½ cup unsalted butter, softened, with ¼ cup apricot preserves.

Blueberry Butter:

Blend ½ cup unsalted butter, softened, with ¼ cup blueberry jam.

CHURN YOUR OWN BUTTER

Kids can try their hands at the Early American chore of butter-making by constructing a coffee-can churn. Place a potato masher or wooden kitchen mallet in a clean 1-pound can and cut a hole in the plastic lid to fit the handle. Fill the churn with 2 cups room-temperature whipping cream, then snap on the lid with the handle sticking through. Take turns beating the handle up and down with a steady rhythm. In about 25 minutes, curds of butter will float to the top (if they don't, beat with a hand-held electric mixer until the curds form). Scoop the curds out, saving the leftover buttermilk for pancakes. Rinse the butter in a sieve under cool water, then refrigerate. In 1 hour, add salt to taste and shape into balls or sticks. For creative shapes, use cookie cutters or butter molds.

How To Flavor Cream Cheese

In a bowl, soften 4 ounces of cream cheese with a wooden spoon (add 1 tablespoon yogurt, ricotta cheese, or sour cream for a smoother spread). After flavoring cream cheese, spread it on bagels, toast, rice cakes, celery, or apple slices.

Veggie Cream Cheese: Add 1 tablespoon of diced carrots, snipped chives, or diced white or red onions.

Strawberry Cream Cheese: Add 6 to 8 fresh or defrosted strawberries.

Cinnamon and Raisin: Add ½ teaspoon cinnamon and 2 tablespoons raisins.

Sun-dried Tomato: Add 2 tablespoons chopped sun-dried tomato with ½ teaspoon olive oil and a dash of salt (omit yogurt or other dairy for softening the spread).

Double Olive: Add ½ cup sliced black olives and green olives stuffed with pimento.

Mandarin Orange: Add ½ teaspoon cinnamon and ½ cup mandarin orange sections, cut into small chunks.

Cinnamon Sugar

At Home Resort

FamilyFun **readers Brenda and Mark Wollenberg of Edmonton, Canada, told us one of their favorite weekend ideas: their family temporarily transformed their house into their own bed-and-breakfast called the Red Rose Inn, where they were the royally treated guests. Among the treats: The kids played breakfast waiters and chefs, serving their folks croissants and fruit, then everyone headed out for a day of sight-seeing in their own hometown.**

Cinnamon Sugar

Top your toast with butter and a sprinkle of any of the sugars below. Vanilla and cocoa powders are available in specialty food stores; they're a bit expensive, but a little goes a long way.

   ¼   cup sugar
   1   tablespoon cinnamon

  Mix the cinnamon and sugar and break up any lumps. Makes ¼ cup.

Nutmeg Sugar:

Substitute 2 teaspoons nutmeg for the cinnamon.

Vanilla Sugar:

Instead of cinnamon, use 1 teaspoon pure vanilla powder or a few drops of vanilla extract.

Chocolate Sugar:

Use ¼ cup high-quality cocoa powder, such as Cadbury, instead of cinnamon.

Your Cup of Tea

Black Tea: For true flavor, use a blend of loose cut black tea leaves. (Many of the bagged varieties contain remnant leaves and powder.) Rinse out and preheat a ceramic or porcelain teapot with hot water, then pour out the water. Add your tea leaves: 1 teaspoon per measured cup of water, plus 1 teaspoon for the pot.

  Meanwhile, fill a tea kettle with 1 cup of fresh water per person and bring it to a brief, rolling boil. Pour the water into the teapot and steep for not more than 5 minutes. Stir before pouring to disperse flavorful oils.

  Immediately serve in cups by running the tea through a strainer. If it's going to stand before serving, strain the tea into another warm pot to avoid "stewing" the leaves. You can add sugar or honey and a cloud of milk or cream to each cup.

Cambric Tea: Given to youngsters in England as a soothing tea variation, this blend uses 2 to 3 tablespoons of prepared tea mixed with ¾ cup hot water and ¼ cup milk. Stir with a teaspoon of honey or sugar.

Shepherd's Tea: For a warming, caffeine-free cup of comfort, mix equal parts of hot water and warm milk or cream with a little sugar or honey.

Gadzooks Granola

Gadzooks Granola

When her daughter Lydia insists that granola looks like bird food, contributor Becky Okrent points out that sunflower seeds, the key ingredient, give birds energy to stay warm through the winter. Let your child help you assemble this treat, and she can learn all about measurements.

- 3 cups rolled oats or an equal mixture of oats, wheat, rye, or barley flakes
- ⅓ cup unprocessed coarse bran
- ⅓ cup sesame seeds
- ⅓ cup raw hulled sunflower seeds
- ½ cup honey or maple syrup, or a mixture of the two
- 1 cup coarsely chopped nuts (peanuts, cashews, or pecans)
- ¼ teaspoon allspice
- ¼ teaspoon cinnamon
- 2 cups mixed dried fruit (dried berries, cherries, raisins, or chopped dried apricots)
- ½ cup toasted wheat germ

Preheat the oven to 350°. Spread the oats, bran, and seeds on a jelly roll pan and bake for 15 minutes, or until golden brown. Meanwhile, put the honey, nuts, and spices in a large bowl. Stir in the hot grain mixture when it's ready. Return the mixture to the pan, spreading it out evenly. Toast in the oven, stirring occasionally, until it's evenly browned, about 10 minutes. (Granola burns easily, so watch it carefully.) Toss the mixture with the dried fruit and wheat germ. Cool completely before storing the granola in airtight containers. Makes 9 cups.

Make a Breakfast Sundae

Fill a parfait glass with fresh fruit (peaches, berries, or apples), add plain or flavored yogurt, sprinkle with granola, and top with a cherry.

Peanut Butter Granola Bars

Caption: Peanut Butter Granola Bars

Peanut Butter Granola Bars

FamilyFun contributor Cynthia Caldwell packs a couple of these energy boosters for her family before they head out the door. They make an excellent midmorning pick-me-up.

- ¾ cup creamy peanut butter
- ½ cup plus 2 tablespoons honey
- 2 cups granola
- 1 cup old-fashioned oatmeal
- 1 cup raisins or chopped dried apricots
- ½ cup sunflower seeds
- ½ cup chopped walnuts or peanuts
- 2 eggs, lightly beaten
- 2 cups crispy rice cereal

Preheat your oven to 325°. Grease a 13- by 9- by 2-inch baking pan. In a saucepan over low heat, melt the peanut butter and honey. Let cool. In a large bowl, mix the granola, oatmeal, raisins, sunflower seeds, and walnuts. Stir in the peanut butter and honey mixture to coat. Slowly mix in the eggs. Gently stir in the rice cereal and press the mixture into the prepared pan.

Bake for 20 to 30 minutes, or until lightly browned on the edges. Cool and cut into squares. The kids can help wrap them individually in foil or plastic wrap. Store in the refrigerator. Makes about 20 bars.

MATH IN THE KITCHEN

If your family eats a multi-colored brand of cereal, you can turn a few minutes in the morning into a quick lesson in graphing for your child. Pour out a handful of cereal and have your child estimate which color is the most prevalent (no counting allowed). Next, have your child arrange the cereal in rows according to color, thereby creating a picto-graph. The longest row in the graph wins. Try the exercise a few more times. The math expert can, of course, then eat the graph.

Chocolate Chip Granola Bars:

For an after-school snack version of this recipe, add 1 cup chocolate chips instead of the sunflower seeds and walnuts.

Cranberry Granola Bars:

Mix in ½ cup dried cranberries at the same time as the raisins. The red color gives the bars a cheerful look, and the subtle tartness complements the peanut butter.

A CEREAL CHEAT-SHEET

Kids love the cereal aisle for all its cartoon characters — and parents should, too, for all the nutrition available in a quick breakfast. These guidelines will help you pick the healthiest of the bunch.

☞ Look for cereals that list a grain first on the ingredient list.

☞ Check for at least a couple grams of fiber. Watch out for cereals high in sugar, fat, and sodium.

☞ To add even more nutrition to the morning meal, add skim milk and fruit to your cereal.

☞ Other ideas? Try mixing two brands of cereal or pour fruit juice over the cereal instead of milk.

Three Bears Porridge

Try serving comforting, old-fashioned oatmeal as a breakfast standard. To entice your little bear into eating all his porridge, try the variations.

2½ cups water
¼   teaspoon salt (optional)
1½ cups rolled oats (old-fashioned, not instant)

In a medium saucepan, bring water to a rolling boil, add salt if desired, and pour in the oatmeal, stirring to mix. Over medium heat, cook the oatmeal for about 5 minutes, stirring occasionally, until all the water is absorbed. Serve with various toppings. (For inspiration, see our ideas at right.) Makes about 6 cups.

Goldilocks Porridge:

Drizzle maple syrup over cooked oatmeal. Stir in 1 tablespoon of raisins and 1 teaspoon cinnamon. Top with a sliced apple or peach.

Mama Bear Porridge:

Mix in 1 tablespoon crème fraîche or whipped cream, 1 teaspoon grated orange zest, and ½ teaspoon honey.

Papa Bear Porridge:

Add 1 tablespoon chopped walnuts, ¼ teaspoon molasses, and a small pat of butter.

Baby Bear Porridge:

Mix in 1 tablespoon mashed banana, 1 tablespoon plain yogurt, and a drop of vanilla extract.

Help-Yourself Breakfast Bar

Create a do-it-yourself breakfast bar with a variety of toppings for hot and cold cereals. Try fresh berries, honey or maple syrup, applesauce, dried fruits or berries, or a sprinkling of wheat germ, sesame seeds, or whole grain cereal.

Goldilocks Porridge

CHAPTER 3

Lunch Specials

COMING UP with creative lunch ideas for kids five days a week, nine months out of the year, is no easy feat. You're not alone if your child sometimes eighty-sixes your latest healthy concoction in favor of a hot dog from the school cafeteria. What we perceive as a delicious, well-balanced lunch box full of goodies may seem boring, weird, or just plain gross to kids.

FamilyFun contributor Becky Okrent says it's important to be sensitive to your child's style when packing a lunch from home. "I have two kids who are exact opposites. My son refuses to take anything conspicuous, such as a chicken drumstick, and if I pack anything so garish as a slice of homemade bread, he will think I'm trying to humiliate him in front of his friends. My daughter wants all the frills. She finds crustless sandwiches cut

into heart shapes a testament of my love."

The challenge is to prepare lunches that are nourishing, palatable, and appealing to each child. So, exactly how do you do that, especially when you aren't at school at lunchtime to see how your efforts are paying off? These tips from Okrent and other *FamilyFun* contributors are key.

Make lunches at home. Although many school lunch programs have lightened up their menus, it's smart to make your lunches at home where you can save money and control the nutritional value. If that isn't realistic, call the school cafeteria and find out its nutritional guidelines. School lunch programs vary from school system to school system — some prepare all their foods from scratch, and others offer vended meals. Keep a copy

Purple Passion Shake and Spiral Sandwiches: *Page 58*

Chinese Sesame Noodles: *Page 60*

A Week of Lunches

Monday:
Spiral Sandwich (page 58), Wild Oatmeal Cookie (page 192), juice box

Tuesday:
PB and Jellyfish sandwich (page 43), bug juice, gummy worms

Wednesday:
Chinese Sesame Noodles (page 60), orange wedges, iced tea, fortune cookies

Thursday:
Chicken Nuggets (page 60), Sweet Potato Chips (page 72), Cubcakes (page 196)

Friday:
Soft Taco (page 47), tortilla chips and salsa, star fruit

of the weekly menu posted on your refrigerator and discuss the healthy choices with your children.

Start with the lunch box. In September, let your children pick out favorite lunch boxes or reusable bags that they feel express their individuality. Be sure lunch boxes include or can accommodate a thermos with an opening wide enough for a spoon (for soup, pasta, or yogurt). A mini ice pack is also a worthwhile accessory.

Plan well-balanced menus ahead of time. Before you go shopping, agree on the lunches for the week and post the list on the refrigerator. You might even allow one day for leftovers and another, as a treat, for a school lunch.

Involve the kids in preparing their lunches. If they have a little time invested, they will be more likely to eat

them. They can help with everything from shopping to cooking to packing.

Make lunches the night before. In most homes, it's too hectic on school mornings to make lunches, but it can be a fun collaborative project the night before. Over the weekends, you can also make lunch-box treats — muffins, cookies, or a pot of soup — to enjoy all week.

Serve small portions. Many parents make the mistake of sending too much food to school with their children. Try small amounts of a variety of foods.

Get creative with your presentation. One way to make lunches enticing is to come up with clever packaging ideas. Pack the fixings for a sandwich and let your child assemble it at school, or send sesame noodles in a Chinese take-out container with chopsticks.

Remember that lunchtime is social time. Don't send anything too conspicuous in your kids' lunch boxes, such as foods with strong odors, without running it by them first.

Send a little bit of home in the lunch bag. Pack a lunch-box surprise, such as a note, sticker, or lollipop. It's a simple gesture that will let your kids know your thoughts are with them even when you're not.

Sandwiches

Something Fishy

Even picky preschoolers won't throw back this clever lunch. Serve it with Goldfish crackers and gummy worms.

- 2   slices whole wheat or white bread
- 1   6-ounce can tuna in water, drained
- 2   tablespoons mayonnaise
     Lettuce
- 1   tomato, thinly sliced

Stack the bread slices and cut out the fish shape below, or use a fish-shaped cookie cutter. Make a tuna salad with the tuna and mayonnaise, then layer it with the lettuce and tomato. Serves 1.

PB and Jellyfish:

For variety, try a peanut butter and jelly sandwich on the precut, fish-shaped bread.

Mini Muffuletta

Salami fans always order up this smaller take on the New Orleans classic.

- 1   small hard roll
- 2   slices salami
- 2   slices ham
- 1   slice provolone
     Diced onion (optional)
     Sliced olives (optional)
     Sliced radishes (optional)
     Olive oil
     Vinegar

Cut the roll in half and place the salami, ham, and provolone on the bread. Add the onion, olives, and radishes, if desired. Drizzle the bread with olive oil and a splash of vinegar (too much will make it soggy). Serves 1.

Easy Lunch-box Stuffers

- ☞ **Carrots, celery sticks, or broccoli florets** with a small container of salad dressing for dipping. (To prevent the veggies from drying out, wrap them in a damp paper towel.)
- ☞ **Fresh fruit:** Try sliced apples rubbed with lemon juice, fresh or canned pineapple chunks, melon in season, fruit salad, or a fruit smoothie.
- ☞ **Pretzels, salted peanuts, or popcorn**
- ☞ **Celery sticks** filled with cream cheese or peanut butter and raisins
- ☞ **Fruit yogurt** packed in a thermos
- ☞ **Crackers** served plain or sandwiched with peanut butter, jelly, or cheese
- ☞ **Mozzarella sticks or string cheese**
- ☞ **Graham crackers,** plain or sandwiched with peanut butter
- ☞ **Dried fruit:** Raisins, apricots, apples, or pineapples
- ☞ **Tortilla chips** with a small jar of salsa
- ☞ **Pasta salad or soup** in a thermos
- ☞ **Pickles, olives, or hard-boiled eggs**
- ☞ **Stickers or a note from you**

Something Fishy

SuperSub

The Yumbrella

While your kids are out splashing in the rain, you can prepare them a healthy lunch that looks like an umbrella.

> 1   slice of bread
>   Mayonnaise, mustard, or butter
> 1   slice of cheese or salami
>   Red or green pepper
> 1   radish or carrot
>   Parsley or bean sprouts

Spread the bread with mayonnaise, mustard, or butter. Cut the cheese or salami slice into the shape of an umbrella (a round slice should give you two umbrella tops). For the umbrella handle, cut a ¼-inch slice straight through the red or green pepper and use the natural curve at the bottom for the handle (one slice will yield two handles). Add squirts of mustard on the umbrella for raindrops. Surround the umbrella with radish or carrot flowers and parsley or bean sprout grass. Place the bread on a plate and squirt more mustard raindrops around it. If it's especially wet outside, you can complete the meal with a cup of hot soup. Serves 1.

The Yumbrella

SuperSub

Faster than a hot dog, stronger than spicy mustard, SuperSub gives the basic hero extra-special powers by adding kids' favorite fixings — onions, peppers, black olives, or sweet pickles.

> 1   medium hero roll
> 4   to 6 slices of thinly cut cheese
>   and/or luncheon meats
> 4   thin tomato slices
> ½   cup shredded lettuce
> 2   teaspoons vegetable oil
> 2   teaspoons red wine vinegar
>   Salt and pepper to taste
>   Special fixings

Slice the hero roll in half lengthwise. Line the roll with the cheese and luncheon meat. Top with the tomato and lettuce. Sprinkle with the oil and vinegar and season with salt and pepper and any special additions. Close up the sandwich, then cut it in half and wrap it in plastic wrap. Makes 1 large sub.

Happy Lunches

Kathy Bostrom's kids enjoy getting children's meals at fast-food restaurants, but it isn't always economical. So now she makes her own. While Kathy fixes lunch, she lets the kids color a white paper lunch bag. For the ever-popular toy, she saves cereal box prizes and buys gumball trinkets. Her kids pretend to drive through the kitchen, picking up their lunches at the counter.

Sailboat Sandwiches

These novel sandwiches — filled with tuna salad and topped with Cheddar cheese sails — give kids a real feel for the seashore. Set these treats in a plateful of blue corn tortilla chips to complete the nautical theme.

    4   dinner rolls
    1   cup tuna salad
    4   slices Cheddar cheese
    8   toothpicks

Slice the tops off the dinner rolls and hollow them out. Fill the rolls with the tuna salad or any other filling your kids like. Slice the Cheddar cheese into rectangles about ⅛ inch thick and cut the rectangles on the diagonal to make triangles. Insert a toothpick into each triangle to make little sails and add them to the top of your "boats." Makes 4.

Veggies in a Blanket

The young *FamilyFun* readers Ian and Abigail Rowswell entered this burrito-like concoction in our Kids' Snack-off Contest, and their recipe got rave reviews. The siblings, ages nine and six, from Medina, New York, say the sandwich is kind of like a wrapped-up salad.

    2   6-inch flour tortillas
    2   tablespoons cream cheese
    1   medium carrot, grated
    2   lettuce leaves

Wrap each tortilla in a paper towel and microwave for 15 seconds (or warm in a cast-iron pan on low). Spread 1 tablespoon cream cheese over each tortilla, add carrot and lettuce, and roll. Makes 2.

SPROUT YOUR OWN

For a healthy crunch on your child's sandwich, try this indoor gardening project. Measure ½ cup of dried beans (alfalfa, radish, wheat berry, mung, lentil, or adzuki) into a 2-quart, widemouthed plastic jar. Cover with nylon mesh or cheesecloth and secure with a rubber band. Fill halfway with cool water and set the jar away from direct sunlight for 8 hours. Gently drain the water through the mesh cover and return the jar to its shady spot. Twice a day for the next three days, fill the jar with tepid water, drain the water, then set the jar back in the shade. By the fifth day, your crop should be ready to harvest. Your sprout growers need only to reach into the jar and gently pull out handfuls of the mature sprouts. Toss them with salad dressing or stuff them into a sandwich and enjoy. To store leftover sprouts, wrap them in a double thickness of paper towel and refrigerate in a plastic bag.

At Home Deli

Leftovers & Cold Cuts

Cold meat loaf
Taco meat
Chicken or turkey breast
Stuffing
Roast beef
Salami
Ham
Bologna
Bacon

Spreads

Cream cheese
Egg salad
Tuna, chicken, or shrimp salad
Crabmeat
Hummus
Refried beans
Peanut butter
Fruit spread or jam
Catsup
Mayonnaise

Mustard
Salad dressing
Butter
Horseradish
Salsa
Cranberry sauce
Relish
Chutney

Cheese

American
Boursin
Gouda
Cheddar
Feta
Muenster
Swiss
Provolone
Mozzarella
Monterey Jack

Vegetables

Lettuce
Coleslaw
Sliced cucumbers
Grated carrots

Bean sprouts
Sliced tomatoes
Fresh spinach leaves
Sliced mushrooms
Avocado
Three-bean salad
Onions
Roasted veggies
Green pepper
Fresh herbs

Breads

Tortillas
Whole wheat
White
Sourdough
Light or dark rye
Pumpernickel
Crackers
Quick breads
Hot dog bun
Bulky or onion roll
Pita
Bagel
English muffin
Croissant

Sandwich Shortcuts

Having everything ready makes the addition of greens and other fresh vegetables to sandwiches easier (and more likely).
☞ **Washed lettuce or spinach:** When you return from the market, drop the greens into a sink full of cold water, give them a few rinses, and tear them into pieces. Then let the kids have their way with the salad spinner. Wrap in a dish towel and store in the crisper drawer.
☞ **Grated carrots:** Peel, grate, and store in a water-filled container.
☞ **Tomatoes, peppers, onions:** Slice them thinly and refrigerate in sealable plastic bags.

Turkey Stroller:

Cut open a large piece of pita bread (or use a single tortilla), spread with mayonnaise and top with sliced turkey, tomato, and shredded lettuce. Roll up and eat like a hot dog.

The Mexican Roll-up:

Spread refried beans on a tortilla, top with grated cheese, lettuce, and salsa, and fold like a burrito. Warm and serve.

Hungry Man Special:

Layer thinly sliced roast beef with horseradish on pumpernickel bread.

Cucumber Tea Sandwiches:

Spread a layer of butter or cream cheese on a slice of white bread, top with paper-thin cucumbers and a second slice of bread, then cut off the crusts.

Ham and Cheese Special:

Spread mustard on two slices of bread, pack with ham and cheese, then bake or microwave just enough to melt the cheese (kids especially like these when cut into sandwich "fingers").

Down by the Sea:

In a food processor, blend cooked shrimp and cocktail sauce, then spread a tablespoon between two crackers.

The Big Chicken

Whenever you have chicken leftovers, you can whip up this zesty chicken salad.

> 1 cup cooked chicken, cubed
> 1 stalk celery, chopped
> ½ cup diced cucumber
> 2 tablespoons mayonnaise
> 1 tablespoon sour cream
> 1 tablespoon chopped fresh parsley
> 2 tablespoons chopped red onion (optional)

Mix all the ingredients together. Pile the salad on a deli roll or into a hot dog bun. This makes enough for 2 sandwiches.

The Big Chicken Curry:

Add 1 tablespoon curry powder to the ingredients above for an Indian-flavored salad.

Turkey Apple Salad

FamilyFun contributor Katherine Eastman makes this turkey, apple, and raisin combo with Granny Smith or Golden Delicious apples — she says either variety will give this salad the right zing.

> ½ pound boneless, skinless turkey breast, cooked and cubed
> ¼ cup plus 1 teaspoon mayonnaise
> 1 teaspoon vinegar
> ½ cup raisins
> 1 large apple, cored and diced
> ¼ cup chopped walnuts (optional)
> 1 tablespoon chopped fresh parsley
> Salt and pepper to taste

Combine the turkey, mayonnaise, and vinegar. Mix in the raisins, apple, walnuts, parsley, salt, and pepper. Pile on wheat bread or in a pita for a refreshing and sweet sandwich. Makes enough to fill 4 sandwiches.

Lunch Specials

How To Keep Lunches Cool

- ☞ Add a frozen juice box.
- ☞ Make your sandwich on frozen bread.
- ☞ Pack a bunch of frozen grapes to insulate the sandwich.
- ☞ Refrigerate a small thermos overnight.
- ☞ Buy a mini ice pack for the lunch box.
- ☞ Use an insulated lunch bag or box.

The Big Chicken

Spreads

From top to bottom: Real Peanut Butter; Quick Boursin; and Hummus

Hummus

This chickpea spread makes a wholesome vegetarian sandwich. On wheat bread, top a layer of hummus with grated carrot, bean sprouts, and cheese.

- 1 15-ounce can chickpeas, drained
- 1 to 2 crushed garlic cloves
- ¼ cup lemon juice
- ¼ cup tahini paste
- 2 tablespoons olive oil

Place all the ingredients, except the olive oil, in the bowl of a food processor or blender and puree. If necessary, add 1 to 2 tablespoons of water to make creamy. Pour the olive oil over the spread before refrigerating so the hummus does not dry out. Makes 1½ cups.

Baba Ghanouj

For a Mediterranean sandwich, cover a pita pocket with this smooth eggplant dish and add tomatoes, cucumbers, and olives.

- 1 large eggplant
- 1 crushed garlic clove
- 2 tablespoons tahini paste
- 2 tablespoons lemon juice
- ½ teaspoon salt
- 2 tablespoons olive oil

Preheat the oven to 350°. Remove the stem from the eggplant, poke the skin with a fork, and bake on a cookie sheet for 45 minutes, or until soft. Cool thoroughly. Scoop out the flesh and place it in a food processor or blender with the garlic clove, tahini, lemon juice, salt, and olive oil. Puree until smooth and refrigerate. Makes 1½ to 2 cups.

Real Peanut Butter

Nothing beats the all-natural taste of peanut butter when you make it at home with no preservatives or sugar.

- 2 cups unsalted roasted peanuts
- 1 tablespoon vegetable oil
  Salt to taste

Puree the shelled peanuts and vegetable oil in a food processor or blender until smooth, about 3 minutes. For chunky peanut butter, stir in ¼ cup chopped peanuts. Add salt to taste and store in the refrigerator. Makes 1 cup.

Real Cashew Butter:

Puree 2 cups unsalted, roasted, or plain cashews with 4 tablespoons of vegetable oil. Store in the refrigerator.

Real Almond Butter:

Puree 2 cups unsalted, blanched almonds with 2 tablespoons of vegetable oil; if necessary, add more oil. Store in the refrigerator.

Quick Boursin

This flavored cream cheese, mixed with fresh herbs, makes a wonderful sandwich spread.

- 1 4-ounce package cream cheese
- 2 tablespoons butter
- 2 tablespoons fresh chopped dill, basil, chives, or a combination
- 1 crushed garlic clove
  Salt and pepper to taste

Place the cream cheese and butter in a bowl or a food processor and let soften. Add the herbs and garlic and stir or puree until smooth. Season with salt and pepper. Makes ⅔ cup.

Mayo Mix-ins

Mix the following into ½ cup mayonnaise for an excellent sandwich spread:

Pesto Mayo: 2 tablespoons pesto

Curry Mayo: 1 tablespoon curry powder

Horseradish Mayo: 1 tablespoon horseradish

Garlic Mayo: 1 crushed garlic clove

Grilled-Cheese
Sandwich: The
Next Generation

Grilled-Cheese Sandwich: The Next Generation

This sandwich from *FamilyFun* contributor Mollie Katzen is a far cry from the grilled cheese on buttered white of our youths. Open-faced and open to experimentation, this healthy lunch is a favorite in her household.

½	cup olive oil
1	small red onion, chopped
1	medium stalk broccoli, in small florets
	Salt to taste
	Dried thyme
8	slices sourdough, rye, or wheat bread
2	cups grated Cheddar cheese

Heat 2 tablespoons of the olive oil in a frying pan over medium heat and wait 30 seconds. Add the onions and cook for 2 minutes. Add the broccoli, sprinkle with salt and 2 pinches of thyme, and cook, stirring, for 8 to 10 minutes. Transfer the vegetables to a bowl and set aside.

Using a pastry brush, paint the bread slices lightly on both sides with the remaining olive oil (a good job for kids). Heat the pan on medium-low, add a few bread slices, and cook until golden brown. Flip the bread and reduce the heat to low. Place a small pile of broccoli florets and chopped onion on the center of each piece of bread. Sprinkle cheese over the vegetables and cover the pan until the cheese melts. Let the cheese cool a bit before serving. Serves 4.

FunFact
When the Earl of Sandwich ordered meat brought to him between two slices of bread, he inadvertently invented the lunch-box standby.

Designosaur a Pizza

Young *FamilyFun* reader Jacob Sandmire of Sandy, Utah, gets such a kick out of helping his mom make dinosaur-shaped pizzas that he forgets the vegetables he's using for eyes and mouths are destined to be eaten. By the time the pizzas are done, the veggies are buried under melted cheese, and Jacob's raring to dig in. (Many grocers sell bread dough in the frozen food section, or you can make your own with the recipe on page 124.)

2 pounds bread dough
1 large dinosaur cookie cutter (available at kitchen supply and and craft stores)

Toppings:
½ cup pizza or spaghetti sauce
½ cup grated carrots
½ cup steamed broccoli florets
1½ to 2 cups grated mix of Colby and Monterey Jack cheeses
½ cup chopped ham or pepperoni
½ cup chopped green pepper
½ to 1 cup sliced black olives
½ cup chopped onions
½ cup sliced mushrooms
½ cup chopped tomatoes

Preheat the oven to 350°. Roll out, stretch, and press the dough ¼-inch thick, then cut it into dinosaurs. Line up the shapes on a lightly greased cookie sheet and let your kids spread on the sauce and toppings of their choice. Make eyes, mouths, and spikes down the backs with larger olive pieces. Bake for 15 to 20 minutes, or until the edges lightly brown. Makes 8 mini pizzas.

Croque Monsieur

For a welcome change to the everyday grilled cheese, try this classic French alternative.

2 slices wheat bread
2 teaspoons butter
2 slices American cheese
1 slice ham

Spread butter on one side of each piece of bread. In a frying pan over medium-low heat, place one piece of bread, butter side down, then layer with cheese, ham, then cheese. Top with the remaining slice of bread and grill until the cheese melts and the bread is lightly browned. Flip the sandwich over to brown the other side. Serves 1.

GRILLED CHEESE AND...

Jazz up your grilled cheese with the following:
- Sliced tomatoes
- Salsa
- Sliced onions
- Fresh dill or basil
- Sliced apple
- Sliced green pepper
- Grated carrot
- Finely diced cucumber
- Olives

Try some different cheeses for a whole new flavor:
- Mozzarella
- Brie
- Monterey Jack
- Muenster
- Swiss

Turkey Meatball Sub

For a low-fat alternative to the traditional meatball sub, try this turkey version. It will stand up to a slathering of tomato sauce, onions, peppers, and melted Mozzarella cheese.

Meatballs:
- 1 pound ground turkey
- 1 egg, beaten
- ¼ cup minced onion
- 1 teaspoon oregano
- 1 teaspoon basil
- Salt and pepper to taste
- 3 tablespoons bread crumbs

Subs:
- 3 to 4 sub rolls
- 1 small onion, sliced and sautéed (optional)
- 1 green pepper, sliced and sautéed (optional)
- 2 cups tomato sauce
- 1½ cups grated Mozzarella cheese (optional)

Preheat your oven to 350°. In a large bowl, break up the turkey meat. Blend the egg with the onions, oregano, basil, and salt and pepper and thoroughly mix into the turkey. Sprinkle with bread crumbs and mix. Roll the meat into 2-inch balls and bake on a jelly roll pan for about 25 minutes, turning occasionally until light brown and completely cooked. (Alternatively, you can pan-brown the 2-inch balls in a lightly oiled, large skillet, turning them until completely cooked. Drain on paper towels.)

To build a sub, set two to three meatballs into a roll and layer on the sautéed onion and green pepper. Spread with the tomato sauce and top with the grated Mozzarella. Warm in the oven until the cheese melts and then serve. Makes 3 to 4 subs.

Lunch Specials

Pizza Men

These two cheery designs are offered as a suggestion, not a blueprint — children tend to be inventive when creating faces! (See the recipe for Designosaur a Pizza, opposite, for other topping options that may inspire your kids.)

- 2 tablespoons tomato sauce
- 1 English muffin, split and toasted
- ⅓ to ¼ cup grated Mozzarella cheese
- 3 olives, cut in half
- 1 slice red pepper
- 1 slice green pepper

Spread tomato sauce on both English muffin halves. Sprinkle grated cheese all over one half. Add olive halves for eyes and a nose, and a red pepper slice for a mouth. On the other muffin half, use olive slices for eyes and a nose, a green pepper for a mouth, and the remaining cheese for hair. Broil in a toaster oven for 5 minutes. Makes 2 individual pizzas.

Pizza Men

How To Make Bread Crust Croutons

Don't toss those crusts — they make great croutons. Each day, place them into a sealable bag and store it in the refrigerator. At the end of the week, cube the collection of crusts, toss them with melted butter, and arrange them on a baking sheet. Sprinkle with herbs, such as oregano, parsley, and paprika. Bake in a 350° oven for 20 minutes, or until the crusts are lightly toasted. Serve over fresh green salad or as a soup garnish.

CELEBRATE CINCO DE MAYO!

On the fifth of May throw a Mexican fiesta. For ideas, see page 136.

Quesadilla

This is my favorite weekend lunch or light dinner. Essentially Mexican grilled-cheese sandwiches, these treats have tons of kid appeal. Quesadillas can really heat up inside, so slice them into wedges before serving to your kids.

> 2 6-inch flour or corn tortillas
> 2 tablespoons grated cheese
>   Salsa and/or sour cream
>   (optional)

Place 1 tortilla on an ungreased skillet over medium heat. Sprinkle lightly with grated cheese and top with a second tortilla. Cook for about 2 minutes on each side, or until the cheese melts. Let cool for 2 minutes, then cut into wedges, pie style. Serve with salsa and sour cream. Serves 1.

Spinach Quesadilla:

Add 1 to 2 tablespoons of chopped spinach, cooked and drained, between 2 layers of cheese.

Black Bean Quesadilla:

Layer refried beans or your own black bean filling between cheese layers. To make your own bean filling, sauté 2 tablespoons of cooked black beans with 2 teaspoons onion and taco seasoning.

Beef Quesadilla:

Top your quesadilla with leftover taco-seasoned meat.

Chicken Quesadilla:

Sauté shreds of chicken with taco seasoning or chili powder for a nutritious filling.

Veggie Quesadilla:

Sauté shredded carrot and zucchini or summer squash and season with chili powder. Then add 1 tablespoon of the mixture along with the cheese filling.

Mexican Tuna Melt

This mayo-free tuna salad is made with the flavors of Mexico — lime juice, avocado, and fresh cilantro.

> 2 6-ounce cans white tuna in water
>   Juice of 1 lime
> 1 tablespoon chopped fresh cilantro
> 1 tablespoon minced onion
> 1 avocado, chopped
> 1 plum tomato, chopped
>   Minced jalapeño to taste
> 4 bagels, sliced
> 8 slices Monterey Jack cheese

Gently toss the tuna, lime juice, cilantro, onion, avocado, tomato, and jalapeño in a bowl. Spoon the salad on top of the bagel halves and top with a slice of cheese. Toast in a toaster oven until the cheese melts. Serves 4.

Bumpy Road

Cheese and pepperoni are delicious toppings for slices of crusty French bread. Once broiled, the cheese melts and the pepperoni pokes up so that the treat resembles a bumpy road. You can also use chopped vegetables or crumbled bacon.

    2   6-inch pieces of French bread
        Grated cheese (a mix of Ched-
            dar and Mozzarella is good)
    ¼   cup diced pepperoni or Genoa
            salami
    ⅛   cup black olives (optional)

Preheat the oven or toaster oven to 375°. Slice the bread in half lengthwise to form the "roads." Generously layer cheese and salami over the olives on the bread slices. Bake for 5 to 10 minutes, or until the cheese has melted. Cool for 2 minutes before serving. Makes 4.

Falafel Flying Saucers

For out-of-this-world taste, let your kids help make these vegetarian sandwiches. (Our testers particularly liked shaping the "flying saucers.") Falafel is sold premixed in boxes and in bulk.

Falafel:
    1   cup falafel mix
    ⅔   to ¾ cup water
        Peanut oil
Dressing:
    ¾   cup plain yogurt
    ¼   cup tahini
    ½   lemon, juiced
Sandwich:
    1   tomato, diced
    1   cucumber, peeled and sliced
    1   small red onion, diced (optional)
    2   cups shredded lettuce
    1   carrot, grated (optional)

Falafel Flying Saucers

    ½   cup alfalfa sprouts (optional)
    2   to 3 8-inch pitas, sliced in half

Mix the falafel and water together and let sit for 15 minutes. In the meantime, prepare your choice of vegetables and make the dressing. For the dressing, combine the yogurt, tahini, and lemon juice (thin with water if necessary).

Heat ½ inch of the peanut oil in a frying pan. To shape the "flying saucers," roll 1½-inch balls of the falafel mix and flatten slightly. Fry in oil until lightly browned on each side, about 3 minutes. Drain on paper towels.

To assemble the sandwich, spread the dressing in half a pita, layer two to three falafel flying saucers with the vegetables, and top with more dressing. Serves 4 to 6.

Veggie Tic-Tac-Toe

Get your kids to munch down veggies with this edible tic-tac-toe. Use aspic cutters (tiny cookie cutters) to cut the vegetables into shapes.

Purple Passion Shake and Spiral Sandwiches

Help your kids prepare this tempting alternative to PB & J for their school lunch and they may become more adventurous eaters — at least at lunchtime.

⅓ cup vanilla yogurt

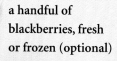
1 tablespoon fresh lemon juice

1 cup grape juice

a handful of blackberries, fresh or frozen (optional)

2 ice cubes

1 To mix the Purple Passion Shake, place the grape juice, yogurt, lemon juice, blackberries, and ice cubes in a blender and puree until smooth (it's okay if the ice is still in small pieces).

2 To make the Spiral Sandwich, ask the chef to snip around the edge of the pita bread to make two circles. Place the circles inside up on plates, a wooden board, or a clean countertop. (If you want, you can use flour tortillas instead of pita bread.)

Cooking Tip: Scissors are easier and safer for kids to use than knives. Keep a pair on hand for kitchen projects.

3 Place the softened cream cheese in a small bowl. Stir in the minced scallion, chives, or basil, or a combination of the three. Or, leave the cream cheese plain.

Cooking Tip: If you have leftover cream cheese, store it in an airtight container in the refrigerator. For a quick after-school snack, spread it on crackers and top with grated carrot.

4 Use a butter knife to spread a thin layer of cream cheese onto each pita half. Place about 3 thin slices of tomato, single file, on top of the cream cheese.

Cooking Tip: Your child can choose other ingredients to add to the roll-up, such as thin slices of turkey or smoked salmon.

1 piece of pita bread
or 2 flour tortillas

1 medium-size ripe
tomato, sliced into
thin rounds

8 spinach leaves,
clean and crisp

½ cup softened
cream cheese

1 scallion or 6 chives,
minced (optional)

3 basil leaves (optional)

5 Spread a little cream cheese onto each spinach leaf (this is a bit messy, but will help the sandwich hold together). Lay the frosted spinach leaves on top of the tomatoes.

Cooking Tip: Teach your child how to clean spinach: Pinch off the stems, place the leaves in a large bowl, and fill with cold water. Pick out the leaves and pat dry on a paper towel.

6 Roll up the sandwich, pressing tightly as you roll. You can either eat it whole or cut it into 1½-inch pieces, which will show off the spiral design on the inside.

Cooking Tip: Pita bread can tear easily, so remind the chef to roll slowly. It also helps to lightly warm the bread before assembling the sandwich.

7 This colorful sandwich and beverage combo can easily be packed and transported in a lunch box. Pour the shake into a widemouthed thermos and, if it's thick, pack a spoon. Serves 1.

Cooking Tip: Ask your kid to prepare snacks for their lunch boxes, too — raw vegetables cut into sticks and customized trail mixes (see page 73).

Chinese Sesame Noodles

FunFact
Noodles don't actually come from Italy — they were first made in China at least 3,000 years ago.

Chicken Nuggets

These nuggets may be packed for a school lunch as finger food, gathered on skewers, or stuffed in a pita pocket.

1 whole skinless, boneless chicken breast, cut into 1-inch cubes
2 teaspoons paprika
1 teaspoon salt
½ cup all-purpose flour
¼ cup sesame seeds
  Black pepper to taste
  Garlic salt or granules to taste (optional)
1 cup vegetable oil

Shake the chicken cubes (you can also use skinned drumsticks) in a sealable plastic bag with the seasonings. Heat the vegetable oil in a pan and fry the nuggets until golden brown. Drain well on paper towels to remove excess oil. These nuggets can be stored in the refrigerator and reheated in a microwave on paper towels. You can also send these off to school with a bit of Honey Mustard Dip or soy sauce for dipping. Wrap them in foil before packing in a lunch box. Serves 4.

Honey Mustard Dip:

In a small bowl, mix ¼ cup Dijon mustard, 1 tablespoon honey, and 1 tablespoon water with a fork until smooth. Serve with the Chicken Nuggets for dipping.

Oodles of Noodles

When you're serving spaghetti for dinner, cook extras. The noodles, spirals, and bow ties, with or without the sauce, make great leftovers for lunch. Add the following to plain pasta:

☞ **Parmesan cheese and butter**
☞ **Olive oil, basil, and diced tomato**
☞ **Raw vegetables and salad dressing**
☞ **Cubed roast chicken, salad dressing, and peppers**

Chinese Sesame Noodles

This dish may sound exotic, but it pleases peanut-lovers. (You can substitute Italian spaghetti for the noodles.)

¼ cup creamy peanut butter or sesame paste
½ cup hot water
⅓ cup soy sauce
2 teaspoons honey
1 crushed garlic clove
1 tablespoon chopped fresh ginger
1 pound cooked Chinese noodles
4 scallions, cut in ½-inch pieces
  Mung bean sprouts
  Chopped peanuts

In a large bowl, mix the peanut butter or sesame paste with hot water until creamy. Whisk in the soy sauce, honey, garlic, and ginger. Add the noodles. Top with scallions, sprouts, and peanuts. Serve warm or cold. Serves 6 to 8.

Miniature Quiches

With bits of red pepper and kernels of corn peeking through the custard, these child-size variations of the French dish make an attractive addition to a lunch buffet. Preparing the quiche pastry for the muffin tins takes a little extra time, but it's a fun way for young chefs to practice rolling, cutting, and shaping pie crusts. If you're in a rush, use store-bought pastry dough.

Pastry:

1½	cups all-purpose flour
1	teaspoon sugar
¼	teaspoon salt
½	cup cold butter
4	to 5 tablespoons ice-cold water

Filling:

2	teaspoons butter
½	small onion, minced
½	small sweet red pepper, minced
½	cup frozen corn
½	cup milk
1	egg
⅓	cup grated Cheddar cheese
	Salt and pepper to taste
	Paprika

To make the pastry, mix the dry ingredients in a medium bowl. Using a pastry cutter (or a fork and knife), cut the butter into the dry ingredients until the mixture resembles a coarse meal. Add the water, tablespoon by tablespoon, mixing well, until the dough holds together. Gently knead the dough, then gather it into a ball. Cover it in plastic wrap and chill for about 30 minutes.

While the dough chills, sauté the onion in the butter over medium heat for 5 minutes, or until translucent. Add the red pepper and corn and sauté for an additional 5 minutes, or until both the pepper and the corn are tender. Remove from the heat and set aside to cool. Meanwhile, in a medium bowl,

Miniature Quiches

whisk together the milk and egg, add the cheese, and salt and pepper to taste. Stir the red pepper and corn mixture into the milk and egg mixture until evenly combined.

Preheat the oven to 350°. To assemble the quiche, roll out the dough on a lightly floured surface to a ⅛-inch thickness. Using a widemouthed cup or glass (at least 4 inches in diameter), cut the dough into 12 circles. Place the circles into a 12-cup muffin tin, shaping the pastry to fit the mold and crimping the edges as you go. For crisper shells, prick the pie dough with a fork and prebake for about 5 to 10 minutes. (If the dough falls, gently press the sides back up.) Let them cool, then pour the quiche mixture almost to the top of each muffin cup. Place the tin on the middle rack of the oven. Bake for 20 to 25 minutes, or until the custard has puffed up and a toothpick inserted in the middle comes out clean. To remove them from the pan, run a sharp knife around the edge of each quiche. Sprinkle with paprika before serving. Makes 12.

Leftover Lunches

☞ Pizza slices
☞ Sliced London broil on toast
☞ Roast chicken: Toss cubed chicken with salad dressing and refrigerate in a plastic container. Pack along with a bag of greens for a quick chicken salad.
☞ Burritos: Make extra for dinner and seal in plastic wrap. Reheat in the microwave for lunch.

CHAPTER 4
After-School Snacks

WHEN WE PUT the word out in a recent issue of *FamilyFun* that we were looking to snack, recipes from our readers' kids poured in from across the country. We tested them all in our Northampton, Massachusetts, hometown and invited a panel of kids to give the recipes a yea or nay. To our surprise, it wasn't only the sweet stuff that scored the highest marks; it was the innovative, the silly, and the fun.

Because kids are the experts on snacking, we have taken our cue from them when selecting and developing recipes for this chapter. These suggestions should help your family bridge the snack gap — finding something between the parent-approved carrot stick and the child-approved marshmallow surprise. Con-

sider, too, some of the following rules:

Invention makes everything taste better. Even those dreaded good-for-you foods are a hit when cleverly disguised. Arrange fruits and vegetables in creative ways, such as the Skeleton Crudité on page 77, or let your kids garnish up the Smiling Banana on page 68.

Snacks should not take longer to make than to eat. Those that do may taste sublime, but practically speaking, they are just too labor-intensive to become a standard in your family's repertoire. The exceptions to this rule are cookies, granola bars, and other baked goods that can be made ahead in batches and stored.

Don't eat snacks with a fork. It's a proven fact that anything eaten with fingers tastes better.

Edible collage: *Page 84*

☞ **A bowl of cereal**

☞ **Orange wedges, blueberries, melon balls, frozen grapes, or other bite-size fruits**

☞ **Mini veggies, such as baby carrots, short celery sticks, broccoli florets, or cherry tomatoes**

☞ **Dried fruits – figs, apricots, apples, and raisins (let your kids pick favorites from the dry bins at the grocery store)**

☞ **Low-fat cookies and skim milk**

☞ **Cheese cut into fun shapes (use cookie cutters) on whole grain crackers**

☞ **Yogurt with smoosh-ins – granola, fruit, raisins, and carob chips**

Cucumber Dipping Sauce: Page 76

If you think your kids are snacking nonstop, don't worry, be happy. Because kids get a good percentage of their daily calories from snacks, these mini meals are an important part of their diet. When planning snacks, keep this in mind, trying not to serve too many sweets. (A few sugary items are okay, as long as they are figured into the overall intake for the day.) And if all they want is the sweet stuff, be sure they skip dessert after dinner and brush their teeth after snacking.

Designate a space for parentally approved snacks. Keep a drawer in the refrigerator, a canister on the counter, or a space in the freezer filled with snacks for your kids. (See Snacks in Seconds, at left, for ideas.) Whatever you provide should be something that you don't mind the kids having at any time of day without first asking you for permission. It's one of life's great simplifiers.

Turn the kids into snack chefs. Children who become creatively involved with food are less likely to engage in junk-food frenzies, and the best time for them to cook is after school or on a weekend afternoon, before the rush for dinner begins. Together, flip through the chapter for recipe ideas and do the grocery shopping as a team. You can then be cooking coach, overseeing the chef. (The no-bake recipes, such as Peanut Butter Balls and Spider Pretzels on page 67, are the fastest and safest.) The benefits of teaching kids to cook are tremendous — kids learn a sense of responsibility, are introduced to basic cooking skills, and feel a great deal of pride when they have something to show, and eat, for their efforts.

Healthy Snacks

Apple Rings

As a child, I painstakingly hung apples to dry by the fireplace until they turned leathery (a trick I learned at Old Sturbridge Village in Massachusetts). Drying apples naturally concentrates their sweetness and nutrition, which made them a hit for the Colonists and for me.

- 4 apples (McIntosh and Golden Delicious work well)
- 1 tablespoon lemon juice
- 3 tablespoons water
  Sturdy thread or twine

Peel, core, and slice the apples into rings about ⅛ inch thick. Mix the lemon juice and water in a shallow dish. To prevent discoloring, dip each ring into the mixture, then pat dry with a paper towel.

String the fruit through the center of each ring and hang in a dry, warm place (near a fireplace or sunny window is ideal). The rings will take 1 to 2 weeks to dry, depending on the room conditions. Kids can periodically taste them to determine if they are ready (dry rings will have a chewy, almost leathery texture).

To expedite the process, dry the apples in a warm oven. Instead of stringing the rings, place them on a wire cooling rack that rests on a baking tray (so the air can circulate). Put the tray in a 150° oven and allow the rings to dry for about 4 hours, turning once midway through. When the rings have no moisture left, remove them from the oven and eat, or cool before placing them in small bags for storing. Makes about 30 rings.

Apple Rings

Juicy Fruit Salad

Call this a soup or call it a salad, the Field sisters (Shanden, twelve, and Lauren, ten), of Petaluma, California, can't get enough of this clever fruit combo. They won 10th place in *FamilyFun*'s Snack-off contest.

- 1 cup shredded apples
- ½ cup diced strawberries
- ⅓ cup diced peaches
- ¼ cup chopped grapes
- ¾ cup orange juice
- 1 tablespoon lemon juice
  Juice of half a grapefruit

Stir the shredded apples, strawberries, peaches, and chopped grapes in a medium-size bowl. Pour the orange, lemon, and grapefruit juice over the fruit and stir well. Serves 3 to 4.

Snacking Apples

- McIntosh
- Empire
- Golden Delicious
- Cortland
- Winesap
- Jonathan

APPLE RINGS

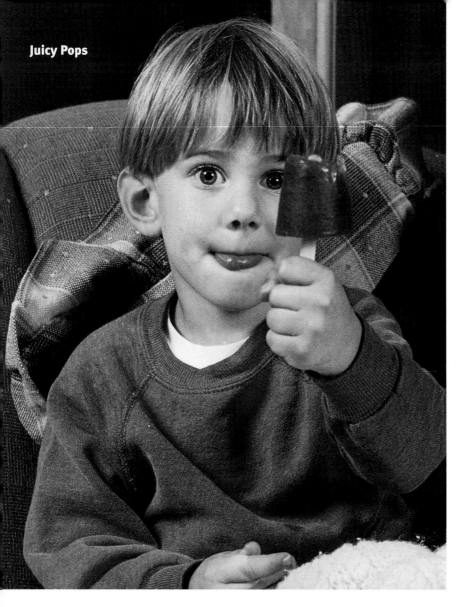

Juicy Pops

For this frozen treat with a surprise in the middle, choose a juice and fruit combination that you know will be a hit — orange juice with pineapple chunks or cranberry-apple juice with whole strawberries.

12 fruit pieces
36 ounces fruit juice

Press one piece of fruit onto the top of a Popsicle stick and place the stick, fruit side down, in a 3-ounce paper or plastic cup. Fill the cup with juice and cover with tinfoil, making sure to push the free end of the stick through the center of the foil (this will help the stick freeze upright). Freeze the pops for about 4 hours, or until solid. To serve, gently squeeze the sides of the plastic cup until the pop is loosened or peel away the paper cup. Makes 12.

Fast Fruit Freezes

In the steamy heat of summer, cool off with these healthy treats. Make them out of whatever fruit you have on hand — strawberries, pineapple, melon, bananas, or plums. To assemble, slide a Popsicle stick or toothpick into a piece of fruit. Cover with a sandwich bag or plastic wrap and freeze for at least 4 hours.

MINI FRUIT POPSICLES

When a bite is just enough, fill an ice tray with juice, cover with tinfoil, and stick a toothpick through the foil into the center of each cube. Freeze for about 3 hours, or until solid.

Smoothie Pops

FamilyFun reader Mallory Wright, age eleven, of San Luis Obispo, California, likes to make homemade vanilla ice cream, but smoothies on sticks are her real claim to fame.

5 strawberries, washed and hulled
1 medium banana
4 ice cubes, crushed
1 cup strawberry yogurt
½ cup milk
½ cup fruit juice

Mix all the ingredients in a blender until smooth. Pour into 3-ounce paper cups, cover with plastic wrap, and insert Popsicle sticks upright through the plastic. Freeze for 5 hours. Makes 9.

Peanut Butter Balls

Rolling up these no-cook treats gives kids a legitimate excuse for playing with their food. For a deluxe version, toss the finished balls in shredded coconut, carob chips, or chopped peanuts and call them "meteorites."

  1¼ cups confectioners' sugar
    1 cup creamy or chunky peanut butter
    1 cup powdered milk
    1 cup honey

In a medium-size bowl, combine all the ingredients. Roll the dough into 1-inch balls and set on waxed paper. Refrigerate until firm. Makes 30 to 36 balls.

Sawyer's Celery Logs

Fill celery with a crunchy mix and you'll be snacking healthy all afternoon. Sawyer Paull-Baird is a four-year-old smart eater from Milan, Michigan.

    2 stalks celery
    6 tablespoons cream cheese
  ¼ cup granola
      Raisins (optional)

Wash and dry the celery. Cut each stalk into three even lengths. Spread 1 tablespoon of cream cheese on each of the celery pieces and top with granola (press it down). Add raisins, if desired. Makes 6 pieces.

Spider Pretzel

It's easy to make this arachnid treat, and it looks positively lifelike crawling on the table.

For each:
    2 round crackers
    2 teaspoons creamy peanut butter
    8 small pretzel sticks
    2 raisins

Make a cracker sandwich with the peanut butter. Insert the pretzel "legs" into the filling. With a dab of peanut butter, set raisin eyes on top. Makes 1.

Rice Cakes and...

- ☛ Real Peanut, Almond, or Cashew Butter (see page 52) and jam
- ☛ Honey and sliced apple, pear, or peach
- ☛ Cream cheese and jelly
- ☛ Hummus (see page 52) and cucumber slices
- ☛ Cream cheese and tomato slices
- ☛ Peanut butter and honey
- ☛ Turkey slices and honey mustard

FunFact It takes about 540 peanuts to make a 12-ounce jar of peanut butter.

Quick Peanut Butter Snacks

Spread peanut butter in the center of a piece of celery and top it with several raisins to create Ants on a Log.

Stir peanut butter with a little honey to make a healthy dip for carrot or celery sticks, apple slices, and whole grain crackers.

Sandwich peanut butter between graham crackers or other crackers (this makes a nice surprise in your kids' lunch boxes).

Smiling Bananas

imaginative: add pumpkin seeds for teeth and fruit leather for a tongue. Combine dried apricots or mandarin slices with cherries and currants or raisins for the eyes and arrange pineapple rings for eyebrows. Banana or pineapple slices double as noses. For hair, mix the coconut and food coloring in a bowl, then style a hairdo. Makes 1.

A Mouse in the House

When your kindergartner bites into this after-school snack that doubles as a craft project, he'll squeak for more.

- 1 canned pear half
- 2 dried apricots
   String licorice
- 3 whole cloves
- 2 mini marshmallows
   Toothpicks

Place the pear facedown on a plate. For ears, insert toothpick halves into the apricots and stick them into the pears. Cut a mini marshmallow in half for eyes and use a whole one for a nose. Spear the marshmallows with cloves and attach them to the pear (remind your kids not to eat the cloves). The licorice tail can be curled around a child's finger and stuck where all tails go. Makes 1.

A Mouse in the House

Smiling Bananas

Introduce your kids to creative garnishing by letting them fashion goofy fruit faces with crisscross eyes, big smiles, or other silly expressions.

- 1 banana, peeled
   Pumpkin seeds
   Fruit leather
   Dried apricots or mandarin orange slices
   Maraschino cherries
   Raisins or currants
   Pineapple rings
- ¼ cup shredded coconut
- 3 to 4 drops food coloring

Cut the banana lengthwise and place one half on a bright colored plate for a smiling mouth. Now let your kids get

Fruity Kabobs

It's one of life's snack mysteries: Putting food on a stick improves the flavor. This colorful kabob alternates fresh summer fruits; for a more exotic version, try tropical fruits.

> Apples
> Bananas
> Pineapple, fresh or canned
> Assorted melons
> Kiwis

> Strawberries
> Star fruits
> Marshmallows (optional)
> Creamy peanut butter (optional)

Help your child cut the fruit into bite-size chunks, slices, or shapes (use plastic knives, cookie cutters, and melon ballers). To make one kabob, carefully push a skewer through the fruits, alternating colors and shapes. For a sweeter one, use marshmallows and spread a dollop of peanut butter on each one. Make as many as you wish.

Kitchen Craft: Fruit & Veggie Tees

Fruits and vegetables make wonderful snacks — and T-shirts. Serve half to your kids and use the other half to make wearable art.

☞ Wash and dry a light-colored cotton T-shirt. Insert a large piece of cardboard and stretch the shirt tightly around it to create a flat surface.

☞ Pour nontoxic fabric paints into pie plates. Cut open assorted fruits and vegetables (apples, onions, peppers, oranges) and invite your kids to pick their favorite designs. Blot the cut surfaces with a paper towel, then press into the paint (you might want to try a few test prints on newspaper). Print the shirts randomly or create patterns.

☞ Hang the shirts up to dry, then follow the fabric paint instructions for heat-setting the paint.

Crunchy Snacks

Tortilla Chips

Homemade Tortilla Chips

FamilyFun contributor Cynthia Caldwell's baked tortilla chips have been the hit of many family parties. Her advice: Don't toss leftover flour tortillas; turn them into chips.

> 2 8-inch flour tortillas
> 2 tablespoons olive oil
>   Coarse salt

Preheat your broiler. Cut each tortilla into 8 wedges and lightly brush both sides with the oil. Arrange them on a jelly roll pan. Broil, flipping once when they begin to brown. When brown on both sides, remove and lightly sprinkle with salt. Serves 1.

Parmesan Chips:

Instead of salt, sprinkle with 1 to 2 teaspoons grated Parmesan cheese.

Garlic Chips:

Crush 1 clove of garlic and add to oil before brushing on tortillas.

Herb Tortillas:

Add 1 tablespoon chopped fresh herbs (parsley, cilantro, basil, or dill) to the oil, then brush on the tortillas.

TORTILLA TIP
To recrisp store-bought chips, microwave on high for 10 to 40 seconds.

Crunchy Teaser

Here's a Chinese stick puzzle you can solve and eat. Instead of using the traditional wooden sticks, try carrot sticks. Arrange eighteen into nine triangles as shown. The challenge: remove three sticks to change the pattern into six triangles. Like any good brainteaser, this puzzler has several solutions. How many can your family find?

Nuke-able Nachos

The following makes enough for two to four kids, depending on their size and appetite. They will undoubtedly stretch and snap the gooey cheeses.

> 2 cups nacho chips
> 1 cup grated cheese (Monterey Jack, Cheddar, and/or Muenster)
> ½ cup diced tomatoes
>   Leftover hamburger, refried beans, onions, jalapeño peppers, and olives (optional)
>   Mild salsa and/or plain yogurt to taste

Place chips on a dinner plate. Sprinkle with the cheese, tomatoes, and the optional items if desired. Microwave on high for 1½ minutes. Serve with salsa and yogurt for dipping. Serves 2 to 3.

Potato Chip Nachos:

Substitute potato chips for tortilla chips.

70

How To Flavor Popcorn

Plain and simple popcorn was served at the first Thanksgiving, and 300 years later, Americans are still enjoying this wholesome snack. Leave a bowl on the counter for when your kids come home from school — serve it as is or spice it up. To 4 cups of popped popcorn, add a flavoring:

Cheese Popcorn: Mix ¼ cup grated Parmesan cheese with 1½ tablespoons melted butter or margarine and toss with popcorn.

Sweet Cinnamon Popcorn: Shake popcorn with cinnamon sugar.

Zesty Popcorn: Top popcorn with grated Parmesan, then spice it up with a dash of garlic salt.

Tex-Mex Popcorn: Add a pinch of chili powder or taco seasoning to melted butter, pour over popcorn, and toss.

Pizza Popcorn: Mix a pinch of oregano, basil, and parsley into melted butter before tossing.

Power Popcorn: Sprinkle with 1 tablespoon of nutritional yeast for a healthy alternative to salt and butter.

Red-Hot Popcorn: Add a dash or more of hot sauce to melted butter and toss with popcorn.

Corny Caramel: Heat caramel or butterscotch sauce, pour over popcorn, and stir until coated. Spread on waxed paper to dry or roll into balls.

Flavored Popcorn

Witch's Brew

This party mix comes from five-year-old Jacob Mulhern of Cottage Grove, Wisconsin. The secret is a cupboard-clearing frenzy just prior to stirring. Anything goes in this recipe.

    1   cup popped popcorn
    ¾   cup mini pretzels
    ½   cup each of mini marshmallows,
        chocolate chips, raisins, and
        Goldfish crackers

Stir all the ingredients together in a large bowl. Makes 3¾ cups.

Popcorn Art

Carry on the Native American tradition of making ornaments from popcorn. With a needle and thread, string popcorn and dried fruits (raisins, cherries, or cranberries) into bracelets and necklaces.

HOMEGROWN SWEET POTATOES

It doesn't take an experienced gardener to turn sweet potatoes into houseplants. Here's how your kids can help knobby spuds evolve into exotic vines.

Wash a sweet potato in water. Insert three wooden toothpicks around its middle, then lower the more pointed end into a widemouthed glass jar with the toothpicks resting on the rim. Fill with enough water to keep the bottom tip covered (periodically freshen the water).

Place in a warm spot, and in about a week's time, you will notice delicate white roots developing from the submerged end. Deep purple vines will emerge from the top a few days later (the vines grow quickly). You can keep this plant in water or pot it in a deep container, covering the tuber completely with loose, sandy soil.

Cinnamon Bagel Chips

You can use any variety of bagels for this snack, but our young taste-testers liked cinnamon-raisin the best. Parents should do the bagel slicing, which can be difficult to do safely.

> 2 bagels
> 1 tablespoon butter or margarine
> Cinnamon Sugar (see page 36)

Slice the bagels in half lengthwise, then lengthwise once again, and place them in a small plastic bag. After school, ask your child to lightly spread each piece with the butter or margarine and sprinkle generously with the Cinnamon Sugar. Toast in a toaster oven or on a cookie sheet under the broiler for about 5 minutes, or until crisp. Let cool, then break apart into chip-size pieces or leave whole. Makes 32 small chips or 8 large chips.

Sweet Potato Chips

Take it from Jade Littlefield, an eleven-year-old regular in the *FamilyFun* offices, "These chips are not like real chips. They're not crunchy, but they're kind of soft and salty and sweet at the same time. They're just *so* good."

> 3 sweet potatoes, peeled
> 1 tablespoon olive oil
> 1 tablespoon butter, melted
> Salt to taste

Preheat the oven to 450°. Thinly slice the sweet potatoes in a processor or with a vegetable grater and toss with the oil and butter. Spread them out in a thin layer on a jelly roll pan, sprinkle with salt, and bake them for about 20 minutes, or until crispy. Flip once during baking to crisp both sides. Serves 6.

Step 1: Slice the bagels into thin rounds with a serrated knife. Spread with butter and sprinkle with Cinnamon Sugar.

Step 2: Toast them under the broiler or in a toaster oven.

Hit-the-Trail Mixes

Whether you call it gorp, birdseed, or trail munchies, it's all the same — high-energy food that can be eaten on the run. Let your child fill a sealable plastic bag with a handful of his or her favorite dried fruits and nuts (buy them in bulk at a health food store). You'll need ½ cup of mix per child.

Gorp:

An acronym for "good old raisins and peanuts," gorp is a camping trip essential. Mix peanuts, raisins, and M&M's.

Rain Forest Munch:

The fruits of the rain forest give this combination its name. Mix dried pineapple, dried papaya, unsweetened coconut flakes, macadamia nuts, cashews, and chocolate chips.

Birdseed:

Here's a bird food for humans: combine hulled sunflower seeds, raisins, peanuts, and dried dates (the pellet-shaped ones, rolled in dried milk).

Morning Sunburst:

Mix up an all-fruit mix with dried apples, pineapples, cranberries, and cherries, as well as banana chips and raisins (eating 1 cup of this will fulfill two out of the five daily minimum servings of fruits and vegetables).

FunFact
A large sunflower, with a 2-foot-wide bloom, can produce up to 2,000 sunflower seeds.

Curveball Crunch

Half the fun of going to the ballpark is snacking on popcorn and peanuts, but it can get expensive. Here's an irresistible stadium treat to make at home.

8	cups popped popcorn
3	cups mini pretzels
1	cup roasted peanuts
2	tablespoons margarine or butter
½	cup brown sugar
1	tablespoon maple syrup

Measure the popcorn, pretzels, and peanuts into a large mixing bowl. Meanwhile, make a toffee syrup by melting the margarine or butter in a saucepan over low heat. Use a wooden spoon to stir in the brown sugar and continue stirring until the mixture bubbles. Remove from the heat and stir in the maple syrup. (The toffee should be smooth.)

Next, drizzle the toffee onto the dry mixture, tossing to distribute the glaze evenly. Once cool, immediately wrap portions in plastic. Makes 12 cups.

Trail Mix Extras

Variety is the key to a good trail mix; it enables kids to explore new tastes.

- **Banana chips**
- **Dried apricots or apples**
- **Corn nuts**
- **Mini pretzels**
- **Cereal**
- **Pumpkin, sunflower, or sesame seeds**
- **Walnuts**
- **Butterscotch or carob chips**

Curveball Crunch

Nachos, Salsa, and Guacamole

Mollie taught her kids how to make these south-of-the-border basics after a family vacation in Mexico. "In our family, food provides an opportunity for learning about history and culture."

2 medium-size ripe avocados

salt to taste

½ teaspoon cumin

2 teaspoons fresh lemon juice

1 to 2 medium-size garlic cloves, minced

1 Slice each avocado in half the long way and let the chef pull out the pits. A less messy trick (parents only) is to spear the pit with a knife and turn the handle slightly so the pit pops out.

2 Use a spoon to scoop out the avocado flesh and place it in a shallow dish (this makes mashing with a fork more manageable). Stir in the lemon juice and add the garlic, cumin, and salt to taste.

Cooking Tip: Buy ripe avocados that feel tender but not mushy. Save the pit to put in the leftover guacamole (this will prevent browning).

3 To make the salsa, cut the tomatoes into little pieces and put them in a medium-size bowl.

Cooking Tip: Cherry tomatoes are easier for a child to cut; give the young chef a small serrated knife to do the job. If you can't find ripe cherry tomatoes, use two medium-size tomatoes. Cut them open first, then squeeze out and discard the seeds.

4 Mince the fresh herbs and the scallions in a food processor. Add the tomatoes and puree. If you don't have a food processor, mince the herbs and scallions with a knife (a job for parents), then stir them into the tomatoes.

Cooking Tip: Explain that tomatoes grow on vines, herbs grow in small bushes, and avocados grow on trees.

2 cups cherry tomatoes

1-pound bag of tortilla chips

½ pound Monterey Jack or mild Cheddar cheese, or a combination

a handful of fresh basil, parsley, and cilantro

2 scallions

a cheese grater

5 Return the salsa to the bowl and add salt to taste. If the chef likes salsa *picante* (spicy), consider adding a little minced jalapeño (prepared by parents only).

Cooking Tip: For the guacamole and salsa, let the kids determine how much salt to add. (Some chips are saltier than others, so the nachos will taste more or less salty as a result.)

6 To make the nachos, preheat the oven to 375°. Spread the chips on a baking tray and sprinkle with the grated cheese. Bake until the cheese just melts (about 4 minutes).

Cooking Tip: If possible, use a mix of white and orange cheese — it looks pretty melted in a marbled pattern. If your oven has a window, it's fun for the kids to watch the cheese melt.

7 Cool the nachos slightly before transferring them to a plate. Serve with bowls of guacamole and salsa for dipping. Serves 4 kids.

Cooking Tip: Make these Mexican treats anytime — as an after-school project, a weekend lunch or birthday fiesta (round out the meal with beans, rice, and fresh tortillas), or an appetizer to a Mexican dinner.

Big Dips

Peanut Butter Dip

Cheese-Lover's Dip

Many finicky eaters live by the philosophy, "If I can dip it, I'll try it." This dip is fun to serve in a bowl shaped from a hollowed-out loaf of pumpernickel bread.

    2   8-ounce packages cream
            cheese, softened
    2   tablespoons mayonnaise
    1   tablespoon heavy cream
    1   tablespoon grated onion
    1   teaspoon Worcestershire sauce

Beat all the ingredients together until smooth and chill until ready to serve. Present with carrot and celery sticks, broccoli florets, or bagel chips. Makes 2 cups.

Great Dippers

☞ **Bread sticks**

☞ **Raw veggies**

☞ **Leftover chicken and steak**

☞ **Grilled vegetables**

☞ **Cheese cubes**

☞ **Apple slices**

☞ **Bagel chips**

☞ **Crackers**

☞ **Pretzels or potato chips**

☞ **Tortilla chips**

☞ **Pita bread, toasted**

Peanut Butter Dip

Tricia Vega of Port Chester, New York, says her children, Torrai and Briana, love this dip — a variation on an Asian recipe — with everything from grilled meats to raw vegetables or as a sauce on rice and noodles.

    ½   cup chicken broth
    ½   cup milk
    4   tablespoons peanut butter
    3   tablespoons grated green pepper
    1   teaspoon soy sauce
    1   crushed garlic clove
    ½   teaspoon sugar
        Salt and pepper to taste
    2   tablespoons chopped scallions
        (optional)

In a heavy saucepan, mix all the ingredients except the scallions and cook over low heat until the sauce thickens. Stir often for about 15 minutes. Sprinkle with scallions and serve hot surrounded by your choice of dippers. Makes 1 cup.

Cucumber Dipping Sauce

This healthy dip has a robust flavor that all of our adult taste-testers (and some of the kids) raved about. You can skip the garlic for a subtler flavor.

    1   medium cucumber, peeled, halved
            lengthwise, seeded, and cut into
            1-inch pieces
    ¼   cup chopped fresh parsley
    1   medium scallion, thinly sliced
    ¼   cup plain yogurt or cottage
            cheese
    2   tablespoons fresh lemon juice
    1   tablespoon cider vinegar or white
            wine
    1   crushed garlic clove
        Pepper to taste

Process all the ingredients in a blender or food processor until creamy and smooth. Store in the refrigerator for at least 10 minutes before serving. This dip is delicious when served with crackers. Makes ¾ cup.

Black Bean Dip

With this easy-to-make sauce, your family will be dipping into rich protein. Lap it up with tortilla chips, carrot sticks, or wedges of fresh flour tortillas.

1   19-ounce can black beans
1   tablespoon chili powder
1   teaspoon cumin powder
1   crushed garlic clove
    Minced jalapeño (optional)

Rinse and thoroughly drain the beans. Place them in the bowl of a food processor or a blender along with the chili powder, cumin powder, garlic clove, and a pinch of minced jalapeño (for a hotter taste). Process until smooth. Makes 1½ cups.

Skeleton Crudité

Served with Dip for Brains, a curry dip with peach jam, this vegetable platter cries out for a Halloween party. Choose the freshest vegetables you can and set to work creating an original like the skeleton at right.

Dip for Brains:
3   cups low-fat
        yogurt
1   cup mayonnaise
½   cup peach jam
1   tablespoon orange juice
½   teaspoon to 1
        tablespoon
        mild curry powder
½   teaspoon white pepper

Stir all the ingredients in a skull-size bowl or scooped-out head of lettuce and refrigerate. Makes 4¼ cups.

Red Bean Dip:
Substitute the black beans for pinto or red kidney beans.

White Bean Dip:
Substitute the black beans for cannellini beans.

Skeleton Crudité

Chunky Guacamole

Your kids can use a table knife to dice the avocado — the remaining ingredients just need to be measured and stirred.

> 3 ripe avocados, peeled and diced, one pit reserved
> 2 tablespoons fresh lime juice
> 1 cup Salsa Fresca

Sprinkle the chopped avocado with lime juice, stir in the salsa, and place the mixture in a bowl lined with lettuce leaves. If you don't plan to serve it immediately, place an avocado pit in the bowl to prevent browning and cover it tightly with plastic wrap. Store in the refrigerator. Makes 4 cups.

Salsa Fresca

Otherwise known as *pico de gallo* (beak of the rooster), this bright red salsa can be used as a dip as well as a topping. The key ingredient is fresh cilantro (aka coriander) — a flavor that makes any dish taste Mexican.

> 2 garlic cloves
> 4 jalapeño peppers, sliced in half, seeded, and veined
> 1 medium onion, quartered or 1 bunch of scallions, chopped
> ¼ cup cilantro leaves
> 2 large tomatoes or 6 small ones, cored and quartered

Chop the ingredients in the order listed above. Drop each ingredient into a food processor with the blades running, turning the machine off between additions (avoid liquefying the tomatoes). If you plan to store the sauce in the refrigerator, place it in a jar and pour a tablespoon of vegetable oil over the top. Makes 3 cups.

FunFact
One Aztec king drank up to 50 goblets of hot chocolate a day.

Chile Con Queso

This famous chip dip will whet your family's appetites for a Tex-Mex dinner. You can make it with bottled salsa or homemade Salsa Fresca.

> ¾ pound Monterey Jack or mild Cheddar cheese, cubed
> 1 cup salsa

In a 1-quart microwave-safe bowl, mix the cheese cubes and salsa. Cover and cook on medium for 5 minutes, or until the cheese melts (halfway through the cooking time, stir the mixture). Serve the dip in the bowl with a basket of tortilla chips. You can also offer sliced raw vegetables, such as red and green peppers or broccoli spears, for dipping. Makes 2¼ cups.

Mexican Hot Chocolate

Mexicans make their hot chocolate with tablets that are flavored with cinnamon and orange rind. For this unique flavor, combine ½ cup water and 2 ounces semisweet chocolate in a saucepan. Cook over medium heat, stirring, until melted. Bring to a boil for 2 minutes, then stir in 3 cups milk, and simmer for 5 to 7 minutes. Add a dash of cinnamon and grated orange rind. Serves 4.

Apple Yogurt Dip

To some kids, this after-school favorite seems suspiciously healthy, but the vanilla gives it a smack.

- ½ cup plain or vanilla yogurt
- ¼ teaspoon cinnamon
- ¼ teaspoon vanilla extract
- 1 medium apple, sliced

Combine the yogurt, cinnamon, and vanilla extract in a small bowl and use as dip for the slices of apple. Makes 1 cup.

Fall Fondue

The first picks of the apple season taste all the better when dipped in a gooey, caramel fondue.

- 50 caramel candies (just under 1 pound)
- 2 tablespoons milk
- 1 tablespoon butter
- 2 apples and/or pears
  Skewers
  Chopped nuts, mini marshmallows, coconut flakes, or chocolate chips (optional)

In the top of a double boiler over simmering water, melt the caramel candies with the milk and butter (warning: it's extremely hot). Whisk until smooth, pour into a bowl, and set aside for 5 minutes to cool. Meanwhile, cut the apples or pears into halves, insert skewers, and arrange on a plate for dipping into the fondue. If desired, roll the dipped fruit in the optional ingredients. Makes 2 cups.

Dipped Strawberries

This simple fare is an attractive addition to a buffet table. With no cooking required, kids can prepare the entire snack on their own.

- ¼ cup heavy cream
- ¼ cup sour cream
- 1 5-ounce high-quality chocolate bar
- ⅓ cup confectioners' sugar
- 2 pints strawberries, washed with stems left on

In a medium-size bowl, whisk the heavy cream and sour cream until the mixture is smooth. Refrigerate covered for at least 2 hours. Working over a piece of waxed paper, use a potato peeler to shave the chocolate bar. Transfer to a small bowl and set aside. Sift the confectioners' sugar over the waxed paper, then pour into a separate small bowl. Just before serving, pour the cream mixture into a small bowl, too. Arrange the strawberries around the three bowls on a platter and serve. Guests should first dip the strawberries into the cream, then the sugar, and finally into the chocolate. Serves 6 to 8.

Dipped Strawberries

Berries and Dip

On your next picnic, take along a pint of fresh washed berries, a container of brown sugar, and another of softened cream cheese (with an electric mixer, beat well with a bit of milk). First dip berries in cream cheese and then in sugar for a delicious treat.

Fall Fondue

Sweet Snacks

Choc-o-bananas

Choc-o-bananas

With no stove-top cooking or chopping required, this frozen banana recipe is truly for children. The chocolate hardens quickly, so work fast.

- 3 bananas
- 6 Popsicle sticks
- 3 1.5-ounce chocolate bars
- 1 tablespoon nut topping, crispy rice cereal, granola, or shredded coconut (optional)

Peel the bananas and remove any stringy fibers. Cut them in half, width-wise, and push a Popsicle stick through the cut end of each half. Cover them in plastic wrap and freeze for about 3 hours.

Place the chocolate bars in a microwave-proof bowl and cook on high for about 2 minutes, or until the chocolate melts (check after 1 minute). Stir in the nuts, cereal, or coconut. Using a butter knife, spread the chocolate mixture over the frozen bananas to coat them completely. Kids can roll them in more topping, but this is messy! Rest the pops on a plate covered with waxed paper and freeze until ready to serve. These keep in the freezer for 1 to 2 weeks. Makes 6.

Delectable Dominoes

Kids won't bother adding up the dots on these edible game pieces before popping them down the hatch. Spread graham crackers with a thin layer of cream cheese or peanut butter, then arrange chocolate, butterscotch, and white chocolate chip dots in domino patterns.

Chocolate Quicksand

There is really no need to measure the chocolate for this — just squirt to taste.

- 1 banana, peeled
- 1 cup vanilla or chocolate ice cream or frozen yogurt
- ½ cup milk
- ¼ cup chocolate syrup

In the morning, slice the banana, place it in a plastic lunch bag, and freeze. After school, place all the ingredients in a blender and process until smooth. Makes 1½ cups.

Chocolate Peanut
Butter Cups

Chocolate Peanut Butter Cups

A homemade version of one of the most popular treats of all time (you know which one we mean). The calorie count is high, so eat this one in moderation.

- 1 tablespoon chocolate chips
- 1 heaping tablespoon peanut butter (creamy or chunky)

Place half the chips in a double paper muffin cup and microwave on high for 1 minute. Stir, then repeat for 30 seconds, or until chips are completely melted. Place the cups in the freezer for 5 minutes. Spoon the peanut butter on top of the chocolate, then sprinkle with remaining chips. Microwave on high for another minute. Stir and swirl with a butter knife. Microwave for 30 seconds more, or until chips are completely melted. Freeze for 5 minutes; remove and eat. Makes 1 muffin cup so rich it can be shared.

Chocolate Peanut Butter Pizza

Nine-year-old Sherri Maunsell of Brandon, Manitoba, Canada, spends her summers cranking out chocolate candies. Here's one from the chocolate connoisseur that took first place in the *FamilyFun* Snack-off.

- 1 6-ounce package chocolate chips
- 1 6-ounce package peanut butter chips
- 2 ounces white baking chocolate Candies for decoration

Microwave the chips in a microwave-safe dish on high for 1 minute, stir, and microwave for 1 more minute. Grease a 12-inch pizza pan and spread on the melted chips with a spatula. Microwave the white chocolate for 1 to 2 minutes, or until melted, and drizzle over the pizza to look like cheese. Decorate with candy and refrigerate for 20 minutes. Cut into 12 wedges. Serves 12.

Almost S'mores

Lose the marshmallow, says Alexa Scally. Her minimalist creation introduces a nouveau classic that's a big hit at her preschool in Macomb, Michigan.

Graham crackers
Chocolate frosting

Break each cracker into four sections and spread frosting on two. Place the other two crackers on top to make sandwiches. Soften overnight in an airtight container, if desired. Make as many as you like.

Peanut Butter Clay

With this edible play dough, you can invite your kids to play with their food. Stir 1 cup creamy peanut butter, 1½ cups instant powdered milk, and 3 tablespoons honey in a medium-size bowl until the dough is smooth (if it's dry, add more honey; if it's too moist, add more powdered milk). Kids can form it into critters of their choice, from snakes to monsters, then decorate their artwork with peanuts, raisins, chocolate chips, and coconut. Store the unused dough in the refrigerator. Makes about 10 creatures, depending on their sizes.

Chilly Yogurt Sandwiches

For a quick frozen treat, put a scoop of frozen yogurt between two graham crackers, wrap in plastic, and freeze.

Chocolate Chip Ice-Cream Sandwiches

FamilyFun contributor Barbara Albright (former editor of *Chocolatier*) keeps a stash of these frozen delights in her freezer for a cool way to satisfy a chocolate attack. The small amount of corn syrup and vegetable oil in the dough prevents the cookies from becoming rock hard.

- 2⅓ cups all-purpose flour
- 1 teaspoon baking powder
- ½ teaspoon salt
- 1 cup unsalted butter, softened
- ⅔ cup firmly packed brown sugar
- ½ cup sugar
- 1 tablespoon vegetable oil
- 1 tablespoon light corn syrup
- 1 large egg
- 2 teaspoons vanilla extract
- 1 package (10 to 12 ounces) chocolate chips or M&M's
- ¾ cup chopped walnuts or pecans (optional)
- 5 to 7 cups vanilla ice cream

Preheat the oven to 325° and adjust the shelves to the upper third of your oven. Lightly butter large baking sheets. In a large bowl, stir the flour, baking powder, and salt. In a separate bowl, combine the butter, sugars, oil, and corn syrup. Mix in the egg and vanilla extract until blended, then gradually add the flour mixture. Stir in the chocolate chips and nuts, if desired.

Pat 2 tablespoons of dough into flat circles on the prepared baking sheets, leaving 2 inches between them. Bake for 14 to 16 minutes, or until lightly browned. Remove the sheets to wire racks and cool for about 5 minutes. Using a metal spatula, transfer the cookies to racks and cool completely. Repeat until all the dough is used.

Let the ice cream soften in the refrigerator for 30 minutes. Spread ½ cup of ice cream on the bottom of one cookie. Place a second cookie on top. Wrap each sandwich in plastic wrap or foil and freeze for 2 hours, or until firm. If the sandwiches are too hard, stand at room temperature before serving. Makes 16 to 20.

An Edible Fishbowl

Dig up that old fishbowl and give it a good scrub. Then try this "sea" food that Sandy Drummond and Betsy Rhein of Holland, Michigan, adapted from a creative Jell-O advertisement.

6   3-ounce packages of blueberry
      gelatin dessert
1   cup blueberries or grapes
      Gummy fish

Prepare the blueberry gelatin in a large mixing bowl according to package directions and refrigerate until partially set (for an aquarium with more waves, let the gelatin thoroughly set). Make a rocky ocean floor by pouring the blueberries or grapes into the fishbowl. Spoon the blue "water" over the fruit, arranging the gummy fish into the gelatin. Chill thoroughly. Let the kids fish for the snack with a ladle and be sure to restock the aquarium with extra candies. Makes 12 cups.

An Edible Fishbowl

Fluttery Creations

Young butterfly fans will flutter at the sight of sweet, gelatin butterflies. The idea came from *FamilyFun* contributor Jean Mitchel, who made them for her daughter's butterfly-themed birthday party.

2   3-ounce packages of cherry,
      blueberry, or lemon gelatin
      dessert
1   cup boiling water
      Twisted licorice
      Shoestring licorice
      Candy dots

In a medium-size bowl, dissolve the gelatin dessert with the boiling water. Pour the mixture into an 8-inch square pan and refrigerate for at least 3 hours. Using a 2½-inch butterfly cookie cutter (available at kitchen supply stores), carefully cut out the gelatin. Alternatively, cut a butterfly stencil out of waxed paper, place it on the gelatin, and cut around it with a sharp knife. If the butterflies are difficult to remove, dip the bottom of the pan in warm water for a few seconds.

Arrange a short length of twisted licorice in the center of the wings. For antennae, insert shoestring licorice into the heads. For added color, remove several candy dots from their paper and press them into the wings. Makes 9 butterflies.

Fluttery Creations

No-Hands Jell-O Eating Contest

Every player is a winner in this birthday party or backyard carnival contest. Prepare several packages of flavored gelatin as directed. Then the judge should put 1 cup per contestant in a bowl and instruct each player to sit on his hands. When the kids hear "Go," they race to clean their bowls. The first clean plate wins, and the winner gets a full tummy.

Ice-Cream Flowerpots

Crackling Peanut Butter Balls

Our kid testers loved this messier, higher protein version of the Rice Krispies Treats classic.

- ¼   cup margarine
- 1   10-ounce package marshmallows
- ⅓   cup creamy peanut butter
- 6   cups crispy rice cereal

Melt margarine in a large saucepan over low heat. Add marshmallows and stir quickly until they are all melted (mini marshmallows melt faster). Turn off the burner and stir in peanut butter until mixed. Add the cereal and stir until coated. Butter your hands and roll the mixture into tennis ball shapes. Dry on waxed paper for 5 minutes before eating (store leftovers in plastic wrap). Makes 24 to 36 balls.

EDIBLE COLLAGES

Skip the paper and glue and let your kids use graham crackers and honey to create artwork they can eat. Fill a variety of small paper cups with goodies, such as raisins, chocolate or carob chips, carrot curls, gumdrops, gummy dinosaurs, or colored cereal. Spread a thin layer of honey (this is the glue for the collage) over the surface of a graham cracker. Using items from the cups, your kids can make any design in the honey — a rainbow, a funny face, a Matisse-like collage. When the collages are complete, the kids can dig in or save them for dessert.

Ice-Cream Flowerpots

With an ice-cream treat that looks like a flowerpot, you can invite your kids to go ahead and eat the daisies.

- 2   tablespoons chocolate cookie crumbs
- 1   scoop chocolate ice cream
    Green sprinkles
    Gumdrops
    Cookies or peanut butter cups
    Candy spearmint leaf

To make the "dirt," place 1 tablespoon of the chocolate crumbs into the bottom of a clear plastic cup. Add a scoop of softened chocolate ice cream, followed by a second layer of cookie crumbs. For grass, sow green sprinkles on the top. Place a straw (cut to a 6-inch length) into the center of the flowerpot and freeze. Meanwhile, make a flower by sticking gumdrops and cookies or peanut butter cups together with toothpicks. To serve, press the flower into the straw. Add a candy spearmint leaf. Makes 1 pot.

How To Make Ice Cream out of Snow

If you're lucky enough to be snowed in, scoop up a bowl of fresh snow and make a batch of ice cream. Place 1 pint whipping cream in a blender with ½ cup of sugar and your choice of flavoring: 1 teaspoon vanilla extract, ¼ cup chocolate syrup, 1 sliced banana, ¼ cup berries, or a few tablespoons of peanut butter. Blend on high for 3 minutes, or until the cream thickens. Meanwhile, fill a large mixing bowl with very clean snow. Pour the cream mixture over the snow, fold in crushed cookies, candies, or chocolate chips. Eat fast: it tastes best fresh. Serves 4 to 6.

After-School Apple Cake

After-School Apple Cake

This moist, all-natural dessert was my mother's standby, and my siblings and I couldn't get enough of it.

- 6 apples (Cortland, Braeburn, and Empire work well)
- 2 teaspoons cinnamon
- ¾ cup vegetable oil
- 4 eggs
- 1¼ cups sugar
- 1 tablespoon baking powder
- 1 cup all-purpose flour
- 1 cup whole wheat flour

Preheat the oven to 350°. Grease and flour a 13- by 9- by 2-inch baking pan. Peel, core, and slice the apples, set them in a large bowl, and sprinkle with the cinnamon. In the bowl of an electric mixer, blend the oil, eggs, and sugar. Add the baking powder, flour, and wheat flour and blend until combined. Pour the batter over the apples, gently stirring until the apples are just coated. Pour this mix into the prepared baking pan, arranging the apples in an even layer, and bake for 35 to 45 minutes, or until a knife inserted in the center comes out clean. When the cake is cool, cut it into small squares. Makes 16 to 18 pieces.

Apple Skins a la Mode

If you polled a dozen adults on their favorite childhood dessert, eight would say apple crisp. The drawback was waiting an hour for it to come out of the oven. This version can be made in minutes in the microwave.

- 1 apple
- 1 tablespoon margarine or butter
  Cinnamon Sugar (see page 36)
  Granola and/or wheat germ
- 1 scoop frozen yogurt or ice cream

Quarter an apple, scoop out the seeds, and place skin side down in a microwave-safe bowl. Place a pat of butter on each quarter. Sprinkle with Cinnamon Sugar and granola or wheat germ. Microwave on high for 1 minute, or until the apple is soft. Top with ice cream or yogurt. Makes 1 large serving.

HOT WHITE COCOA

Not everyone is a chocolate-lover, so here's to vanilla fans. In a medium-size saucepan, heat 2 ounces of white baking squares and 1 cup of water over medium heat, stirring constantly. When melted, bring to a boil, then simmer for 3 minutes. Add 3 cups of milk and heat until warm. Remove from the heat and beat with a whisk until frothy. Ladle into mugs and garnish with white chocolate shavings or a peppermint stick. Serves 6.

Apple Skins a la Mode

CHAPTER 5

Soup's On!

TWO KINDS OF DAYS are soup days. The first is a long, winter Sunday when you are putzing around the house. A pot of soup made from scratch bubbles and steams on the stove. For hours, its promising aroma assures you that simple pleasures are still to be had. This is the way your grandmother ran a household, you think to yourself.

The other day is a weekday. You come home from work to a hungry, expectant crew. The living room floor is a battlefield of toys, you're tired, and there is no getting out of the fact that it's your night to cook. Because you are a brilliant parent, you've anticipated this moment and pull from the freezer a container of your weekend's leftover minestrone. As you kick back, tending to homework questions, the smell of soup wafts through the kitchen, seeping into the general mood of the house. Suddenly, life is full of comfort. You are as resourceful as a pioneer.

Make extras and freeze. It is basic human instinct to make too much soup, so freeze your leftovers in sealable plastic containers and label them well (soup keeps up to three months in the freezer). The morning you plan to eat the soup, put it in the refrigerator, and by the end of the day it will be thawed enough to warm on the stove top or in the microwave.

Always serve bread with soup. When accompanied by a warm wheat roll or a slice of fresh-baked bread, soup becomes a well-balanced and substantial meal. Check "Breads We Love" (see page 106) for ideas — and for the ultimate taste experience, bake a loaf or two of bread in the

Sweet Corn Chili: Page 104

At Home Soup Bar: *Page 92*

oven while your soup simmers on the stove. Add a small green salad to round out the meal.

Don't have time to make your own stock? Keep canned broth on hand. The basis of any good soup is stock. For most of the recipes in this chapter, you can either use the Real Chicken Stock (opposite) or substitute a low-salt canned stock (in the grocery store it is called broth, but it is essentially the same thing). You might want to sample a few brands to find the one that suits your family's taste the best. For a host of stir-in ideas, see our At Home Soup Bar on page 92.

Use scraps for stock. Don't toss your wilted carrots; store them in the freezer until you are ready to make soup. Then throw them into a pot along with the carcass of a roast chicken, a clove-studded onion, celery leaves, potatoes, a few peppercorns, salt to taste, and any other vegetables you happen to have. (Use the stinkier varieties, such as broccoli and cabbage, with a very light hand.) Pour water over everything and let it simmer for several hours; skim, strain, and you've got yourself a great stock.

Invite a friend for soup. If you're planning to have guests for dinner but you don't want to cook an elaborate meal, plan on serving soup. You'll only dirty one pot, and your guests will feel welcome and satisfied.

Real Chicken Stock

FamilyFun contributor Becky Okrent says her soup options are almost limitless when she has a freezer stash of this homemade stock.

- 1 4-pound whole chicken or 3 pounds chicken backs and wings
- 2 carrots, cut into thirds
- 2 stalks celery, cut into thirds
- 1 onion, halved
   Peppercorns and salt to taste

Cover the chicken (remember to remove the bag of giblets and add them to the stock) and vegetables with water in a soup pot and slowly bring to a boil. Season and boil for about 5 minutes, then skim off the surface scum, reduce the heat to simmer, and cook partially covered for 2 to 3 hours. (If using a whole chicken, remove the breast meat when it is tender and save it for salads and sandwiches.)

Allow the broth to cool to a warm temperature, remove the carcass or bones, and strain the broth with a sieve. Refrigerate and skim off the solidified fat. Makes 3 to 4 quarts.

Does Chicken Soup Really Cure a Cold?

☛ **Probably not, but the hot steam coming off the chicken soup can act as a decongestant, helping to temporarily open stuffed nasal passages.**

Real Chicken Stock

Split Pea Soup

On winter weekends, I fill my home with the aroma of this hearty soup.

- 2 tablespoons olive oil
- 1½ cups chopped onions
- 3 carrots, peeled and diced
- 1 crushed garlic clove
- 2 cups split peas, rinsed
- 5 cups water
- 1⅔ cups chicken or vegetable broth
- 1 tablespoon dill or thyme
   Salt and pepper to taste
   Chopped fresh parsley

Sauté the onions, carrots, and garlic in the oil in a soup pot until the onions are translucent. Add the split peas along with the water, broth, and dill. Cook uncovered for 2 hours, stirring three to four times per hour. Add more water or broth if your soup is too thick. Season with salt and pepper and garnish with parsley. Serves 6 to 8.

Top This

To a child, half the fun of soup is what's floating on top.
- ☛ **Oyster crackers**
- ☛ **Goldfish crackers**
- ☛ **Star-shaped Croutons (page 104)**
- ☛ **Cubes of crispy garlic bread**
- ☛ **Bagel chips**
- ☛ **Crumbled tortilla chips**
- ☛ **Bread crumbs**
- ☛ **Bacon bits**
- ☛ **Parmesan cheese**

1 pound boneless turkey breast (you may substitute chicken breasts), cut into 2 or 3 large pieces
4 medium carrots
1½ cups cooked wild and long-grain rice mix

In a large soup pot, combine the water, chicken stock, onion, celery, bay leaf, and salt and pepper. Bring to a rapid boil. Add the turkey breast pieces, reduce the heat to low, cover, and simmer for 30 minutes, or until the meat is tender and cooked through. Meanwhile, peel and dice the carrots. When the turkey is done, use a slotted spoon to remove it from the stock, along with the bay leaf, celery, and onion pieces. Reserve the celery and onion for another use.

Allow the turkey to cool slightly and then cut it into cubes. Return the turkey cubes to the stock, add the cooked wild rice and the diced carrots, and return the soup to a boil. Reduce the heat to medium and simmer for another 5 minutes. Serve on a bed tray with toast, if desired. Serves 6 to 8.

Wild Turkey Soup

A twist on the classic get-well food — chicken soup with rice — this recipe makes soup that's mild enough for your sick ones but appealing to an adult's palate, too.

1 quart water
1 quart chicken stock
1 small onion, peeled and halved
2 celery stalks, chopped
1 bay leaf
Salt and pepper to taste

FunFact
The first bowl of soup was made of hippopotamus bones, and it was served in 6,000 B.C.

An Enchanted Forest

When your bedridden child is stuck indoors, bring the outdoors to her by transforming her room into a magical forest. To make the forest canopy, tie a 4-foot-long branch or broom handle onto each post of her bed and secure with twine. Drape a sheet over the tops of the branches. A simple vine can be made by threading green construction paper leaves onto fishing line (use a regular sewing needle) and wrapping the vine around the branches. For extra greenery, place houseplants by her bedside. String tiny lights around the branches for a twilit forest. For a treat, serve Wild Turkey Soup.

Colorful Tortilla Soup

This tortilla soup, cooked up by *FamilyFun* reader Bonnie Alexander of Dallas, turns dinner into a Mexican fiesta. Her choose-your-own-add-ins approach produces a family meal that can be different every time it's served.

Soup:

- 4 13¾-ounce cans chicken broth or 6¾ cups homemade stock
- 1 13-ounce can corn
- 2 to 3 Roma tomatoes, chopped
- 3 tablespoons salsa

Add-ins:

- 2 boneless chicken breasts
- 4 tablespoons soy sauce
- 10 corn tortillas
   Vegetable oil for frying
- 1 ripe avocado
- 1 tablespoon lemon juice
- 2 cups grated Monterey Jack cheese
- ½ bunch cilantro, chopped

In a large soup pot, mix the broth, corn, tomatoes, and salsa. Bring to a boil, cover, and lower the heat to warm.

To prepare the add-ins, begin by marinating the chicken breasts in soy sauce for 15 minutes to 1 hour. Cut the tortillas into 1-inch strips. Fry five strips at a time in 1 inch of oil until golden brown. Drain well on paper towels and set aside in a warm oven. Grill or sauté the chicken, slice it into strips, and set aside, covered. Cube the avocado and sprinkle with lemon juice. Place the remaining toppings in bowls on the table. Each diner fills a soup bowl with his or her own choice of add-ins, then ladles the hot broth over them. Serves 6 to 8.

Low-Salt Variation: Use half low-sodium chicken broth and half water.

Colorful Tortilla Soup

Thai Coconut Soup

The combination of lime juice, ginger, and coconut milk creates a unique Thai flavor. The coconut milk can be found in the international section of grocery stores. (Be sure you don't buy coconut cream.)

- 1⅔ cups or 13¾-ounce can chicken broth
- 1 cup water
- 2 to 3 tablespoons lime juice
- 1 teaspoon chopped fresh ginger
- ¼ teaspoon salt
- 2 teaspoons sugar (optional)
- 1 14-ounce can coconut milk
- 1 uncooked chicken breast, cut into thin slices
   Fresh cilantro leaves
   Crushed red pepper (optional)

Mix the chicken broth with the water, lime juice, ginger, salt, and sugar. Cook for 5 minutes, then add the coconut milk and chicken breast. Cook for 5 more minutes. Serve topped with cilantro and a pinch of crushed red pepper. Serves 4.

Mind Your Manners

Rather than constantly reminding her children of the dos and don'ts of table manners, Cindi Tripken of Lexington, North Carolina, has adopted a humorous approach. If the children forget to place their napkins in their laps, they must place it on their heads for two bites of food. If they put their elbows on the table, the person who catches them tugs on his ear as a signal. The absurd works better than harping.

At Home Soup Bar

Making soup doesn't have to take all day. With creativity, you can make a quick, satisfying dinner. Just heat up 1 cup per person of any broth listed here, stir in ½ cup of vegetables, meat, or grains (or a combination) and ½ teaspoon of flavorings, then pour into bowls.

Stocks & Broths
Chicken broth
(canned or homemade)
Beef broth
Vegetable broth
Bouillon cubes
Consommé
Ramen noodle soup mix

Meats & Proteins
Canned beans (black, pinto, cannellini, or chickpeas)
Chicken or turkey
Beef strips
Shrimp or fish

Vegetables
Diced tomato
Diced carrots
Strips of fresh spinach
Diced green pepper
Frozen corn or peas
Diced celery and onion
Sliced mushrooms
Snow peas

Grains
Leftover cooked rice
(white, brown, wild)
Pasta, such as tortellini
Pastina (pasta stars)
Couscous

Flavorings
Crushed garlic
Fresh parsley, dill, basil, and ginger
Lemon or lime juice
Minced jalapeño
Chili powder

Thickeners
Mashed potatoes
Milk or cream

Toppings
Croutons
Grated cheese or sour cream
Snipped chives

Soup Shortcuts
☞ Always have broth on hand. Either stir up a batch of Real Chicken Stock (page 89) or pick up cans when they are on sale.
☞ Get your kids to help you wash, chop, and dice the vegetables.
☞ Keep fresh parsley in your refrigerator and frozen vegetables in the freezer to add to broth.

Quick Chicken Soup:
In a saucepan, warm chicken broth. Add diced vegetables. (For a creamy soup, mix in mashed potatoes.) Cook for 5 minutes, or until the vegetables are soft. Add cubes of cooked chicken and sprinkle with fresh herbs, salt, and pepper.

Hot and Sour Soup:
Add lemon juice, minced jalapeño pepper, peas, sliced mushrooms, soy sauce, ginger, and black pepper to any kind of broth. Bring to a boil, then serve.

Chicken Noodle Soup:
To chicken broth, add noodles cooked al dente, strips of cooked chicken, and fresh snow peas. Cook for 2 minutes, then pour into bowls.

Tortellini Soup:
Warm chicken broth, add cheese tortellini cooked al dente, snipped chives, and strips of fresh spinach.

Chicken and Stars:
Heat chicken broth, add 1 tablespoon pastina (available in the pasta section of most grocery stores), diced carrots and celery, and chicken cubes. Simmer until the stars are cooked.

Quick Fish Chowder:
Add cooked codfish, diced potatoes, celery, onion, and a little cream to fish or chicken broth. Cook for 5 minutes.

Chicken Soup with Rice:
Warm chicken broth and add leftover rice, diced carrots, and cubes of cooked chicken.

Ramen Noodle Soup:

Prepare ramen noodle soup mix according to directions. Then add your favorite vegetables, such as frozen peas, sliced mushrooms, and a diced tomato.

French Onion Soup:

Sauté onions in a soup pot, add beef broth, and cook until the onions are tender. Pour into ovenproof bowls and top with croutons or toast. Sprinkle with grated cheese and broil until the cheese melts.

Soup on the Grill:

In the heat of the summer, move your cooking outdoors by making soup on the grill. Add broth to a soup pot and bring to a boil on a grill over hot coals. Toss in grilled veggies, cubes of grilled chicken or steak, and fresh herbs from the garden.

Quick Chili:

Heat beef broth, add canned pinto beans, diced tomato, and chili powder. Enhance the flavor with frozen corn niblets, jalepeño pepper, a squeeze of lime juice, diced green pepper and onion, and crushed garlic.

Clear Tomato Soup:

Bring chicken broth to a boil and add an equal measure of tomato juice or fresh tomatoes.

Matzo Ball Soup:

Follow the box directions for matzo ball mix, but add some extra flavoring (onion powder, black pepper, celery seed, or nutmeg). Simmer chicken broth with diced carrots and celery and chopped onion, then add the matzo balls.

Fresh Herbs Make a Difference

A snippet of fresh parsley, dill, or chives is the perfect garnish and flavor enhancer for soup. Keep a clean pair of scissors in the kitchen and put your kids in charge of the snipping. When you buy or pick the herbs, place them in a glass of water like a bouquet and leave on the counter. They'll stay fresh and be ready to add to any dish.

Salad Bar Soup

SALAD BAR SOUP

For a quick dinner after a busy day, I head to the supermarket salad bar and pick up about 1 cup of prepared vegetables, such as chopped carrots, diced onions, fresh spinach leaves, diced tomato, and sliced mushrooms, as well as a can of chicken broth. At home, I divide the vegetables into soup bowls. Heat up the chicken broth, then pour the hot broth over the vegetables (the veggies will lightly cook from the heat of the broth).

STONE SOUP

Before you and your children make soup, read *Stone Soup* by Marcia Brown. Originally published in 1947, this is a classic tale of hungry soldiers who come into a village and trick the peasants into sharing the food they had hidden. The soldiers place a large iron pot over a fire in the town square and ask first for some water to fill the pot and then for "three round, smooth stones." Then a little salt and pepper is called for, and "If there were carrots, it would be so much better." You might do well to cook along with the soldiers' recipe, allowing the children to add ingredients as called for by the soldiers and provided by the peasants, omitting the beef and, of course, the stones. "We shall never go hungry, now that we know how to make soup from stones," say the villagers. "Oh, it's all in knowing how," say the soldiers.

FunFact
Early spoons were thin, concave pieces of wood to dip into foods that were too thick to drink.

Sneak-It-to-Em Broccoli Soup

Sneak-It-to-Em Broccoli Soup

If your kids turn up their noses at vegetables, tempt them with this creamy, light green soup. You can substitute leftover mashed potatoes or a baked potato for the instant powder, as well as other green vegetables in equal measure.

1   cup homemade or canned chicken stock
1   cup water
1   onion, thinly sliced
1   10-ounce package frozen broccoli, or 2½ cups fresh broccoli, chopped
1   teaspoon salt
4   cups milk
4   tablespoons instant mashed potato powder
3   tablespoons butter
    Pinch of ground nutmeg

In a soup pot, heat the stock and water over medium heat, add the onion, broccoli, and salt and cook for 10 minutes, or until tender. Puree half the vegetables with half of the liquid in a blender or processor until smooth, then repeat with the other half (be sure to vent the steam). Heat the milk in a large saucepan until bubbles form on the edges. Stir in the mashed potato powder, butter, and nutmeg and simmer for 3 minutes. Stir in the pureed broccoli and onion, taste for seasoning, and ladle into individual bowls. This soup keeps well overnight and can be frozen. Serves 4 to 6.

Sweet Sausage Minestrone

This everything-but-the-kitchen-sink soup has something for everyone. Serve with bread to sop up every last bite.

- 1 large onion, chopped
- 1 tablespoon olive oil
- 1 red pepper, chopped
- 1 green pepper, chopped
- 1 crushed garlic clove
- 1 13¾-ounce can beef broth
- 3 cups water
- 1 28-ounce can crushed tomatoes
- 2 cups coarsely chopped cabbage
- 6 Italian sweet sausages (about 1 pound)
- 1 tablespoon basil
- 1 tablespoon oregano
- 1 teaspoon salt
- ¼ teaspoon pepper
- 1 15-ounce can cannellini beans, drained
- ½ cup sliced olives
- 1 8½-ounce can artichoke hearts
- 1 1-pound package fresh tortellini
  Chopped fresh parsley
  Parmesan cheese

In a soup pot, sauté the onions in the oil until translucent. Add the peppers *Soup's On!*

and garlic and sauté for 5 minutes. Add the broth, water, tomatoes, cabbage, sausages, and seasonings. Bring to a boil, then cook over medium-low heat for 20 minutes. Remove the sausage, cut into ½-inch rounds, and return to the pot. Add the beans, olives, and artichoke hearts and cook for 5 minutes. Just before serving, add the tortellini and cook in the soup until al dente. Garnish with the fresh parsley and Parmesan cheese. Serves 8 to 10.

Sweet Sausage Minestrone

Give the gift of soup

Warm the heart of a teacher or neighbor with all the fixings for homemade soup. Pour 6 to 8 bags of different dried beans into a large mixing bowl and let your child stir them up. Measure 2 cups into each of 9 pint-size canning jars. Fold index cards in half to create gift cards and copy the following recipe. Punch a hole in the card, slip a ribbon through the hole, and tie it around the lid with a big bow.

FULL OF BEANS SOUP

Soak the beans in water overnight. Drain and place them in a soup pot with 4 crushed garlic cloves and 10 cups of water or stock. Bring it to a boil, then simmer for 1½ hours. Add 2 diced carrots and simmer for 1 more hour. Add 2 cups crushed tomatoes, 2 cups chopped onions, 1 diced green pepper, 1 teaspoon parsley, ¼ cup lime juice, and 1 teaspoon chili powder. Simmer for 3 hours. Makes 1½ quarts.

Pot-au-feu

Pot-au-feu

Contributor Becky Okrent discovered this French dish when a friend served it at a fancy dinner party. She says, "It always makes guests feel like members of a congenial family."

3 to 4 pounds lean beef, bottom round or rump
1 pound short ribs of beef
1 pound shinbone or other soup bones
1 peeled yellow onion stuck with 3 cloves
1 garlic clove
6 whole peppercorns
1 to 2 tablespoons salt
6 sprigs fresh parsley
1 bunch celery, sliced into 2-inch lengths with leaves reserved
2 bay leaves
1 teaspoon thyme
12 carrots, peeled and sliced into 2-inch lengths
4 medium potatoes, peeled and quartered
2 small turnips, peeled and quartered
3 to 4 leeks, washed and cut into 2-inch lengths (optional)
1 cup fresh or frozen peas

Place the meat and soup bones in a large soup pot and cover with cold water. Add the onion, garlic, peppercorns, salt, parsley, celery leaves, bay leaves, and thyme. Bring to a boil. After 5 minutes, skim off any foam that has risen to the surface. Cover and simmer for 2 hours.

Skim off the foam again and add all of the remaining vegetables, except the peas, and cook for 20 to 30 minutes, or until just tender; add the peas 10 minutes before you're ready to remove the dish from the heat. (Pot-au-feu gains flavor as it ages and can be stored in the refrigerator up to two days.)

Serve the dish in soup bowls or use the broth for soup and serve the meat and vegetables separately, as the French do. In any case, you will want to slice the meat thin, remove the bones, and offer mustard or catsup to the kids. This dish is also good served with a vinaigrette or a sauce made from two parts sour cream and one part horseradish with a dash of Worcestershire sauce. Serves 8.

Peanut Butter Soup

If your kids are fans of peanut butter, they'll enjoy this nutritious soup inspired by the traditional African dish, groundnut stew.

- 2　medium onions, chopped
- 1　crushed garlic clove
- 1　tablespoon vegetable oil
- 1　28-ounce can crushed tomatoes
- 1　13¾-ounce can chicken broth
- 4　cups water
- 2　large yams, peeled and cubed
- 1　cup creamy peanut butter
- ¼　teaspoon cayenne pepper
- ¼　teaspoon salt
- 2　cups cooked chicken pieces
- ½　cup crushed peanuts

In a soup pot, sauté the onions and garlic in the oil over medium heat for 5 minutes. Add the tomatoes, broth, water, and yams. Cook over medium-low heat for 25 minutes, or until the yams feel soft. Stir in the peanut butter, cayenne pepper, and salt. Cool for 30 minutes. Puree the soup in a blender or food processor, then pour it back into the saucepan and warm. Sprinkle with the chicken and peanuts. Serves 6 to 8.

Hot Dog Soup

Skip the catsup and mustard and serve your kids hot dogs with lentils (the dogs will help them down the protein-loaded beans).

- 1　pound hot dogs, cut into 1-inch pieces
- 1　tablespoon vegetable oil
- 1　cup chopped onion
- 1　cup chopped celery
- 2　cups ½-inch carrot slices
- 2　crushed garlic cloves
- 6　cups water
- 2　13¾-ounce cans chicken stock
- 1　pound lentils
- 1　teaspoon salt
- ½　teaspoon pepper
- ½　teaspoon basil

In a soup pot, sauté the hot dogs in the oil until browned. Remove and sauté the onion, celery, carrots, and garlic for about 5 to 10 minutes. Add the water, stock, lentils, salt, pepper, and basil. Bring to a boil, then reduce the heat to low and simmer for 1 to 1½ hours. Adjust the seasonings, add hot dogs, and serve. Serves 8 to 10.

Handprint Apron

When her daughter, Heather, was in pre-school, *FamilyFun* reader Nancy Ojeda of Houston helped the class make a handprint apron for their teacher. On their way to the bus, the four-year-olds lined up in the parking lot, dipped their hands in paper plates of fabric paint, and pressed them on a solid-colored apron. "It went like clock-work," she said. When they were done, the apron was covered with sixteen little handprints and the teacher's name was written with a fabric pen. Nancy appreciated how easy it was to make the gift: What did the kids like? "Oh, the mess!"

Peanut Butter Soup

97

Cold Soups

Purple Soup

and pepper for 1 hour. In batches, puree the soup in a food processor or blender. Pour into a large bowl and stir in the cream. Chill until ready to serve. Garnish with chives. Serves 6 to 8.

Purple Soup

Otherwise known as borscht, a Russian peasant soup, this cold soup is a great source of vitamin C. The purple color is a big plus with kids.

Soup:
1	large red onion, chopped
2½	cups chopped red cabbage
1	teaspoon caraway seed
2	crushed garlic cloves
2	tablespoons butter
5	beets, peeled and quartered
4	cups water
2	cups vegetable stock
2	tablespoons red wine vinegar
¼	teaspoon black pepper
1½	teaspoons salt
½	cup sour cream

Toppings:
1	hard-boiled egg, thinly sliced
¼	cup chopped fresh dill
¼	cup sour cream

In a soup pot, sauté the onion, cabbage, caraway seed, and garlic in the butter for about 5 minutes. Add the beets, water, and stock, then cover and cook until the beets are tender, about 45 minutes. Add the vinegar, pepper, and salt and puree the soup in a food processor or blender. Pour into a large bowl and chill. When you are ready to serve the soup, stir in the sour cream. Garnish with slices of hard-boiled egg, fresh dill, and sour cream. Serves 6 to 8.

Sprout Some Leeks

This spring, grow leeks for Vichyssoise. Pick up a set of starters at a garden center and plant them in sandy soil, 2 to 4 inches deep and 6 inches apart. Water frequently, and within 60 days they'll be ready. Less sandy than store-bought, your leeks will only need a rinse before going into the pot.

Vichyssoise

The light flavors of potatoes and leeks combine in a refreshing white soup — a favorite recipe in my repertoire because it is surprisingly easy to make.

5	cups peeled and coarsely chopped potatoes
3	cups thinly sliced leeks (use the white and 2 inches of the green)
1⅔	cups chicken or vegetable stock
5	cups water
1	teaspoon salt
½	teaspoon white pepper
½	cup heavy cream
	Chopped chives

In a soup pot, simmer the potatoes and leeks with the stock, water, salt,

Strawberry Yogurt Soup

FamilyFun contributor Emily Todd brings this soup on picnics: it's quick, it's refreshing, and it can be made the night before, poured into a wide-mouthed thermos, and chilled in the refrigerator. Her claim? "The results will do you proud."

- 1 32-ounce container of nonfat plain yogurt
- 1¾ cups white grape juice
- 3 tablespoons sugar
- 2 tablespoons fresh lemon juice
- ⅛ teaspoon cinnamon
- 1 pint fresh strawberries
- 1 kiwi, sliced (optional)

In a large bowl, whisk together the yogurt and white grape juice. Add the sugar, lemon juice, and cinnamon and mix until thoroughly blended. Pour into a plastic container, cover, and chill for several hours or overnight.

Before serving, wash, hull, and slice the strawberries. Spoon several berries into a large cup or bowl and pour the yogurt mixture over them. Garnish with kiwi slices, if desired. Serves 6 to 8.

Strawberry Yogurt Soup

Soup Stories

In *Mean Soup* by Betsy Everit (Harcourt Brace & Co.), Horace learns soup soothes his anger.

Growing Vegetable Soup by Lois Ehlert (Harcourt Brace Jovanovich) tells of a family who farms the vegetables they make into soup.

Marisa makes dumplings to celebrate a new year in *Dumpling Soup* by Jama Kim Rattigan (Little, Brown).

Mollie Katzen's TEACHING KIDS TO COOK

Quick Tomato Soup with Crunchy Croutons

Mollie calls this a "quick but real" soup — it's simple for kids to make, boasts a start-to-finish time of 20 minutes, and contains no mysterious stocks.

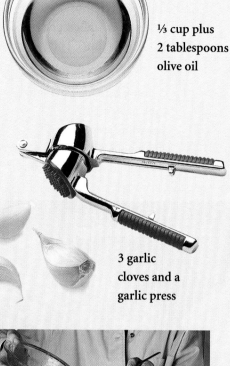

1 Preheat the oven to 350°. Pour the ⅓ cup olive oil into a bowl and add 1 crushed garlic clove. Place the bread on a cutting board and have your child lightly brush both sides with the olive oil.

6 to 8 slices of French or Italian bread (sourdough works wonderfully)

⅓ cup plus 2 tablespoons olive oil

3 garlic cloves and a garlic press

2 Next, cut the bread into cubes (kids ages eight and up can do this). Place the cubes on a baking sheet and bake. Crunchiness is a matter of taste: keep an eye on the croutons and let your child determine when they are ready (5 to 10 minutes).

Cooking Tip: Parents should be in charge of putting the baking sheet into the oven and taking it out.

3 Ask the chef to heat the remaining 2 tablespoons of olive oil (or 2 tablespoons butter) in a medium-size saucepan. Add the minced onion, the two other crushed garlic cloves, and ½ teaspoon salt. Cook and stir over medium-low heat for about 10 minutes, or until the onions become very soft and smell really good.

4 Open the can of tomatoes (a job for the cooking coach, not the child) and place the tomatoes and their juice into a food processor or blender. Add the cooked onions and garlic and puree until smooth.

Cooking Tip: Blades on food processors and blenders are sharp, so parents should remove the food from either type of machine.

28-ounce can whole, peeled tomatoes and a can opener

Kitchen scissors

1 cup minced onion

1 cup milk

Salt and black pepper

Fresh basil (optional)

Fresh dill (optional)

5 Pour the pureed mixture into a saucepan. Heat it slowly, stirring occasionally. When it's warm, have the chef drizzle in the milk.

Cooking Tip: During the summer, substitute 3 pounds of fresh tomatoes. Core them, cut in chunks, cook in a covered saucepan over medium heat for 15 minutes, and proceed with the recipe.

6 Ladle the soup into serving bowls. If desired, add a few shakes of salt and pepper to taste. If you can find fresh dill or basil, it's fun for kids to snip tiny bits into the soup with scissors.

Cooking Tip: Be sure the kids smell the fresh herbs first — smelling ingredients is an important part of learning to cook.

7 Put the croutons into a big bowl in the middle of the table and let everyone float a handful in their bowls of soup. Serves 4.

Cooking Tip: When Mollie tested this recipe with her kids, the croutons were clearly the most popular, so she recommends you make extras and keep them around for salads and, of course, snacking.

Soup's On!

Cold Zucchini Soup

My mother-in-law gave me this rich, creamy soup recipe, a staple in our house during the zucchini season.

- 1 large white onion, diced
- 1 tablespoon olive oil
- 1 large zucchini, cut into 1-inch chunks
- 3 cups chicken broth
- 1 tablespoon dill
- 1 cup light cream
  Salt and pepper to taste
  Fresh dill (optional)

In a soup pot, sauté the onion in the olive oil until translucent. Add the zucchini, broth, and dill and cook until the zucchini is soft, about 20 minutes. In batches, puree the soup in a food processor or blender. Pour into a bowl, stir in the cream, and season with salt and pepper. Chill for at least 3 hours. Top with fresh dill. Serves 6 to 8.

Cold Zucchini Soup

Summertime Gazpacho

At the peak of my summer harvest, I like to make this tomato-based cold soup. Just about any fresh herb from my garden gets tossed in — parsley, dill, basil, or cilantro.

- 4 tomatoes, chopped
- 1 cucumber, peeled and chopped
- 1 small onion, diced
- 2 cups tomato juice
- 1 crushed garlic clove
- 1 tablespoon olive oil
- 2 tablespoons red wine vinegar or lime juice
- ½ cup chopped herbs, including fresh dill, parsley, cilantro, and chives
  Salt and pepper to taste
  Lime slices or cilantro sprigs

In a food processor or blender, place half the tomatoes, half the cucumber, half the onion, and the tomato juice, garlic, oil, and vinegar. Puree until smooth. Pour the mixture into a large bowl, then stir in the remaining tomatoes, cucumber, and onion. Add the herbs and salt and pepper to taste. Chill for at least 2 hours, then serve with a lime slice or cilantro sprig for garnish. Serves 4 to 6.

Stews & Chowders

Beef Burgundy

Serve this warm, traditional stew over wide, buttered noodles. It can be prepared a few days ahead, so even the cook can relax before dinner. Garlic bread tastes great on the side.

- 6 bacon strips
- 2 pounds lean beef, cubed
  Salt and pepper to taste
  Flour for dredging
- 2 to 3 tablespoons butter
- 1 onion, chopped
- 1 crushed garlic clove
- ¼ teaspoon ground cloves
- ½ teaspoon thyme
- ½ teaspoon marjoram
- 2 bay leaves, crumbled
- 1 cup red wine
- 1 cup beef broth
- 1 14½-ounce can stewed tomatoes
- 2 cups carrots, peeled and cut into 2-inch pieces
- ½ 16-ounce package frozen pearl onions
  Chopped fresh parsley

In a three-quart, covered casserole on the stove top, slowly cook the bacon. Remove the strips, drain, and reserve for another use.

Season the beef lightly with salt and pepper. Lightly dredge the beef in flour and brown in small batches in the bacon fat, adding a little butter if the pan becomes dry. Remove the beef and pan juices and set aside. Add a tablespoon of butter to the pan and sauté the onion until translucent. Add the garlic.

Return the beef and juices to the pan. Sprinkle with the cloves, thyme, marjoram, and bay leaves. Add the wine, beef broth, and tomatoes. (If needed, add more broth or water to cover.)

Bring the mixture to a boil, stir, then reduce the heat. Add the carrots, cover, and cook for 1½ hours. Cool and refrigerate for at least 1 hour. Before serving, add the frozen onions and reheat for 45 minutes. Sprinkle with chopped fresh parsley. Serves 6 to 8.

Beef Burgundy

Soup Supper

During National Soup Month (January), share the joy and simplicity of making soup. Help your kids make Quick Tomato Soup (page 100) or let them pick any soup in this chapter.

Sweet Corn Chili

Kids will appreciate this not-too-spicy chili topped with grated Cheddar cheese, chopped scallions, and a dollop of sour cream.

1½   pounds ground beef
1½   cups chopped onions
 3   tablespoons oil
 2   green peppers, chopped
 3   crushed garlic cloves
 2   tablespoons chili powder (or
       more to taste)
 1   teaspoon cumin
 1   teaspoon oregano
 1   teaspoon salt
 ½   teaspoon black pepper
 1   28-ounce can crushed tomatoes
 1   28-ounce can whole tomatoes
 2   15-ounce cans kidney beans,
       drained
 1   28-ounce package frozen corn

Brown the beef in a frying pan over medium heat. Meanwhile, in a soup pot, sauté the onions in the oil over medium heat for about 5 minutes, or until translucent. Add the green pepper and garlic and cook for a few more minutes. Once the meat browns, drain the fat and add the meat to the onion mixture. Lower the heat, add the seasonings, tomatoes, beans, and corn. Stir well, cover, and simmer for ½ hour. Serves 8 to 10.

Star-shaped Croutons

With a small star-shaped cookie cutter, cut out croutons from 5 thin slices of bread. (Give the crusts a spin in your food processor for fresh bread crumbs.) Brush both sides with olive oil and sprinkle with herbs and seasonings, such as basil, garlic, oregano, and cayenne pepper. Place croutons on a jelly roll pan and bake for 6 to 10 minutes in an oven preheated to 375°, or until light brown. (Check midway through baking to see if they need to be flipped.)

Corn Chowder

This light and flavorful corn chowder is a crowd-pleaser — especially when served in mugs alongside warm rolls.

 2   medium onions, finely chopped
 2   crushed garlic cloves
 2   teaspoons thyme
 ½   teaspoon salt
 ¼   teaspoon black or white pepper
 3   tablespoons butter
 3   tablespoons flour
 1   cup chicken broth
 1   cup water
 2   potatoes, cubed
 1   bay leaf
 2   10-ounce packages frozen corn
 1   red pepper, diced
1½   cups milk
 1   cup half and half
 4   scallions, sliced into ¼-inch pieces
 ½   cup chopped fresh parsley
 3   slices bacon, cooked and crumbled
       (optional)

In a large soup pot over medium heat, sauté the onions, garlic, and spices in butter until the onions are translucent. Sprinkle with the flour and stir well. Add the chicken broth, water, potatoes, and bay leaf and cook for 15 minutes over medium to low heat, stirring occasionally. Add the corn, red pepper, milk, and half and half and simmer for another 15 minutes. Five minutes before serving, add the scallions and parsley. Pour the chowder into mugs and top with crumbled bacon. Serves 6.

Lamb and Black Bean Chili

The flavor of chili improves with age, so prepare this recipe a day in advance and reheat it in the microwave oven, advises contributor Becky Okrent. Microwaving cuts the cooking time way down for this chili.

1	pound lean ground lamb
2	tablespoons vegetable oil
1	large green pepper, chopped
1	medium onion, diced
2	crushed garlic cloves
4	teaspoons chili powder
1	teaspoon ground cumin
1	teaspoon oregano
¼	teaspoon cayenne pepper
2	16-ounce cans black beans with their liquid, or 4 cups cooked black beans
1	16-ounce can peeled, whole tomatoes with their liquid
	Fresh cilantro, minced
1	jalapeño pepper, minced
	Salt and pepper to taste

Crumble the ground lamb with a fork in a 2- to 3-quart microwave-safe casserole. Cook on high for 5 minutes, stirring once halfway through the cooking time. Transfer the meat to a strainer to drain excess fat and wipe the inside of the casserole with a paper towel. Return the meat to the casserole dish and add the oil, green pepper, onion, and garlic. Cover and cook on high for 5 minutes, stirring once. Add the chili powder, cumin, oregano, cayenne, beans, tomatoes, and cilantro and mix well. Cover tightly and cook on high for 15 minutes. Stir in the

Lamb and Black Bean Chili

minced jalapeño and cook on high, uncovered, for an additional 10 minutes. Add salt and pepper to taste. Serve with rice and warmed tortillas, offering garnishes, such as sour cream, grated Cheddar or Monterey Jack cheese, chopped tomatoes, red onion, or diced avocado with lime juice. Serves 6 to 8.

KIDS' SANGRIA

Rather than using the traditional sangria ingredient of red wine, this recipe calls for cranberry-raspberry juice. Pour 4 cups of the fruit juice into a large pitcher. Thinly slice 3 oranges and 2 limes, remove any seeds, and add the slices to the pitcher. Serve over ice.

FunFact
Americans slurp up more than 10 billion bowls of soup each year. That's about 38 bowls per person.

CHAPTER 6

Breads We Love

FOR A WHILE NOW, I have been on a bread crusade. It seems like everyone I know thinks baking bread is too time-consuming, something that you just don't do anymore. Why make it when you can buy a loaf at the bakery down the block? Now, don't get me wrong. I'm also too busy to bake bread every week. But I am determined to let people know how easy and rewarding it is to make a loaf of bread from scratch every once in a while.

It used to be that everyone knew how to bake yeast bread. Mixing the flour, kneading the dough, and letting it rise were part of daily life. Over the years, we have grown further away from our food sources — and now too many children are growing up thinking bread comes from a plastic bag in the grocery store. Baking something so basic and wholesome is worth the effort, even if you only do it once a year. When you bite into a warm slice of any of the breads in this chapter it will hit deep down, connecting you to a time gone by. **Bake bread when you are home for the afternoon.** Contrary to what your mother may have told you, it doesn't take very long to bake bread. You do need to be around the house for several hours, but the work of mixing and kneading can be done in as little as thirty minutes. While the bread rises, you can take a break and go for a walk — or leave dough covered in the refrigerator overnight and punch it down in the morning.

Best Ever Banana Bread: *Page 109*

The World's Simplest Bread Dough: *Page 117*

Bread Shortcuts

☞ Always have all-purpose and whole wheat flour as well as yeast on hand (yeast keeps for several months in the refrigerator or at room temperature).

☞ For fresh muffins and quick breads in the morning, prepare the dry ingredients the night before and store in the refrigerator. In the morning, add the liquids and bake.

☞ Freeze homemade bread and then thaw at room temperature in a sealed plastic bag to avoid moisture loss.

☞ Prepare a batch of Quick Biscuit Mix (see page 112) and store it in a canister in the refrigerator for fresh biscuits in minutes.

Put bread back on the table. In the rush to lower fat and cut down on calories, don't cut back on your bread intake. It is not the thing that holds the sandwich together that racks up the calories, but the fillings — the mayonnaise, dressing, and so on. In fact, nutritionists say it's important to maintain your grain intake at six to eleven daily servings.

Make extra loaves and freeze. When you make the effort to bake bread, you might as well double the recipe. Freeze extra loaves in plastic bags for a welcome treat on a busy day.

Make bread in all shapes and sizes. Shaping yeast bread dough can be as creative as working with clay. Quick breads can't be twisted into the same pretzels and rolls, but you can pour the batter into different size pans and experiment with muffins (mini, regular, or giant).

Pass on the art of bread baking. After about the age of four, any child can help bake bread, though he might not be interested in or able to do every step. That's okay. Just play it by ear and be prepared to pick up the slack.

Quick Breads

Corn Bread

Thanks to the Native Americans, the early American settlers learned how to grow corn, and a version of this bread was born.

- 1 cup all-purpose flour
- 1 cup cornmeal
- 2 teaspoons baking powder
- ½ teaspoon baking soda
- ¼ cup brown sugar
- ½ cup milk
- ½ cup plain yogurt
- 1 egg, lightly beaten
- ¼ cup butter, melted

Preheat the oven to 425° and grease an 8-inch square baking pan. In a large bowl, mix the flour, cornmeal, baking powder, baking soda, and brown sugar. In a separate bowl, whisk the milk, yogurt, egg, and melted butter together. Gradually add this mixture to the dry ingredients and stir until just combined. Pour into the prepared pan and bake for 15 to 20 minutes. Serves 6 to 8.

Corn Sticks:

Add an additional ¼ cup milk to the batter. Spoon into preheated and greased cast-iron corn stick molds. Makes 21 corn sticks.

Best Ever Banana Bread

Before you haul your overripe bananas to the compost, turn them into banana bread; the riper the banana, the sweeter the bread. Unlike a yeast bread, this quick bread tastes best a day old.

- ½ cup vegetable shortening
- 1¼ cups sugar
- 2 eggs
- 5 overripe bananas
- 2 cups all-purpose flour
- 1 teaspoon salt
- 2 teaspoons baking soda
- 2 tablespoons wheat germ
- 1 cup chopped nuts (optional)

Preheat the oven to 350° and grease two 8½-inch loaf pans. Cream the shortening and sugar in the bowl of an electric mixer. Add the eggs and bananas and blend until the bananas are thoroughly mashed. In a separate bowl, sift the flour, salt, and baking soda and stir in the wheat germ and nuts, if desired. Add the dry ingredients to the banana mixture and blend until just mixed. Pour the batter into the prepared pans, dividing it evenly. Bake for 50 minutes, or until the top springs back when gently pressed. Makes 2 loaves.

Fruit Freeze

Store overripe bananas for another day's baking by peeling and then freezing them in a sealable plastic bag. Defrost for 1 to 1½ hours before mixing into bread batter.

FunFact
The average American eats 52 pounds of bread every year (that's about 41 loaves).

Corn Sticks

whisk, beat the eggs, then blend in the oil. Use a spatula to mix the dry ingredients into the egg mixture in several additions, then fold in the zucchini and the orange peel. Divide the batter evenly between the two pans and bake for 50 minutes, or until the top springs back when pressed lightly with a finger. The bread may cool in the pans for 5 to 15 minutes before being turned out onto a rack or plate. Makes 2 loaves.

Sweet Zucchini Muffins:

Divide the batter into two lightly greased 12-cup muffin tins and bake for 17 to 22 minutes, or until the top springs back when lightly pressed. Makes 24 muffins.

Zucchini Tips

☞ **Because the thin skin of a zucchini is easily penetrated by soil, the best way to clean one is to soak it in cold water for about 20 minutes, then rub it briskly with your hands or a cloth under running water. Scrub the zuke but do not peel it; the flecks of dark green look beautiful in bread or muffins.**

☞ **If you have a food processor and an abundance of zucchini, use the grater attachment to process cupfuls of zucchini. Store measured amounts in plastic bags in the freezer for making bread or adding to soups.**

Sweet Zucchini Bread

According to *FamilyFun* contributor Becky Okrent, the key ingredient in her favorite zucchini bread is "unfortunately, sugar." The tastiest breads use quite a bit, but you can adjust the sugar according to your tastes. She usually makes one loaf of zucchini bread and a batch of muffins from this recipe.

  2   cups all-purpose flour
  1   cup whole wheat flour
  2   cups sugar
  1   tablespoon baking powder
  ½   teaspoon baking soda
  ¼   teaspoon salt
  4   eggs, beaten
  1   cup vegetable oil
  3   cups grated zucchini
      Peel of 1 washed orange, minced

Preheat the oven to 375°. Butter two 8½-inch loaf pans and dust with flour or wheat germ. Mix the all-purpose flour, whole wheat flour, sugar, baking powder, baking soda, and salt in a large bowl. With an electric mixer or wire

Zuke Boats

Set some zukes a-sail in celebration of your zucchini harvest. To build your boats, cut one zucchini in half lengthwise and hollow out each half with a spoon, making "dugout canoes." Then, tape small paper sails onto sticks or straws and poke them into the boats. Send the vessels across a bathtub, pool, or pond.

Lemon-Poppy Seed Bread

After you bake this tea bread (or batch of mini muffins), you can use the remaining frozen lemonade concentrate to mix up a batch of lemonade to serve at teatime.

- 2 cups all-purpose flour
- ½ teaspoon baking powder
- 1 teaspoon baking soda
- ½ teaspoon salt
- ½ cup vegetable oil
- 1 cup sugar
- 2 eggs
- 1 teaspoon vanilla extract
- 3 tablespoons frozen lemonade concentrate
- ½ cup buttermilk
- 2 tablespoons poppy seeds

Preheat the oven to 350° and grease one 8½-inch or two 5-inch loaf pans. Sift the flour, baking powder, baking soda, and salt. In the bowl of a mixer, cream the oil and sugar. Beat in the eggs, vanilla extract, and 1 tablespoon of the lemonade concentrate. Add alternately the buttermilk and dry ingredients to the egg mixture. Fold in the poppy seeds and pour the batter into your prepared loaf pans. Place on a rack in the middle of the oven and bake for 40 to 45 minutes, or until the top springs back when lightly pressed.

When they're done and the loaves are still warm from the oven, prick them with a fork and drizzle with the remaining lemonade concentrate. Wrap breads in foil. They'll keep for a week in the refrigerator or months in the freezer. Makes 1 large or 2 small loaves.

Poppy Seed Mini Muffins:

Pour batter into lightly greased mini muffin tins and bake for 14 to 16 minutes. Makes 36 mini muffins.

Puffed Popovers

Make sure everyone is seated at the table before you take these treats out of the oven — and then eat them fast.

- 2 eggs
- 1 cup milk
- ¼ teaspoon salt
- 1 cup all-purpose flour
- 1 tablespoon butter

In a large bowl, beat the eggs, milk, salt, and flour until smooth. Allow the batter to sit for about 30 minutes. Preheat the oven to 350°. Divide the butter into the 12 cups of a muffin tin. Set the tin in the oven to melt the butter. Pour the batter into the cups while the pan is still hot and bake for 35 minutes. Serve immediately. Makes 12.

A Crust You Can Trust

When making muffins, it's better to grease your tins than to use liners. You'll get a crispier crust, and you won't have to worry about the papers sticking to the muffins when you peel them off.

Quick Biscuits

Quick Biscuit Mix

Making your own mix means you can have biscuits for dinner at the drop of a hat — and they're worlds better than those made from a store-bought mix.

    6   cups all-purpose flour
    3   tablespoons baking powder
    3   teaspoons salt
    1½ cups butter or margarine

Sift the flour, baking powder, and salt on waxed paper a few times, then transfer to a medium-size mixing bowl. Cut in the butter or margarine, working the dough until it resembles a coarse meal. Store the mixture in covered Mason jars in the refrigerator for up to 2 months. Makes about 7 cups of mix, enough for 36 biscuits.

Quick Biscuits:

If your oven has a light, your kids can watch the biscuits rise.

    ¼   cup buttermilk, plain yogurt,
        or sour cream
    1   cup Quick Biscuit Mix (above)

Preheat the oven to 450°. Add the buttermilk, plain yogurt, or sour cream to the biscuit mix. If the dough is too sticky, add more biscuit mix. Turn the dough out onto a lightly floured surface and knead lightly. Roll out to about ½-inch thickness and cut into 2-inch circles. Press the scraps together, roll, and repeat until all the dough is used. Bake on an ungreased cookie sheet for 12 minutes. Makes 6 biscuits.

Cheese Wedge Biscuits

When our taste-testers bit into these moist biscuits, they all said "Cheese!" The key ingredient is grated Cheddar.

    2   cups all-purpose flour
    1   tablespoon baking powder
    ¼   teaspoon salt
    5   tablespoons butter
    ⅔   cup milk
    ½   cup grated Cheddar cheese

Preheat the oven to 425°. Combine the flour, baking powder, and salt in the bowl of a food processor or electric mixer. Add the butter in chunks and blend until the mixture resembles a coarse meal. Add the milk and mix until just combined. Turn the dough out onto a lightly floured surface and pat into a round, about ⅓ inch thick. Place the round in a 9-inch pie plate and cut into wedges. Cover evenly with the cheese and bake for 15 minutes, or until lightly toasted on the top. If the cheese hasn't browned, broil for 1 minute. Makes 6 large wedges.

How To Warm Biscuits

☞ To reheat biscuits and rolls, place them in a dampened paper bag in a warm oven (set below 200°) for 5 to 10 minutes.

Crazy Cheese Straws

Your kids won't be able to sip through these totally twisty straws, but they can gobble them up at dinner. You can buy the frozen puff pastry in the freezer section of your grocery store.

    1   sheet frozen puff pastry, about
            12 by 14 inches
    1   egg white
    2   teaspoons water
    1½ teaspoons grated Parmesan cheese

Let the frozen puff pastry thaw for about 30 minutes, then lay it on a floured surface. Preheat the oven to 400°. In a small bowl, mix the egg white and water. Use a pastry brush to "paint" the mixture onto one side of the pastry. Sprinkle with the Parmesan cheese and cut the pastry into strips, ½ inch wide and as long as the pastry. Place the strips on an ungreased cookie sheet and gently twist several times (a good job for kids). Press the ends onto the cookie sheet so the strips don't unravel. Bake for 10 minutes, or until golden brown. Makes 15 to 20 straws.

Irish Soda Bread

In Ireland, this bread is better known as Dairy Bread (it's loaded with butter-milk), and it's eaten every day. Raisins or currants are added to our cakelike American version.

    3   cups all-purpose flour
    2   cups whole wheat flour
    2   teaspoons baking soda
    1   tablespoon baking powder
    2   tablespoons brown sugar
    2   to 2¼ cups buttermilk
    ½   cup currants or raisins (optional)

Preheat the oven to 400°. In a large mixing bowl, combine the all-purpose

Crazy Cheese Straws

flour, wheat flour, baking soda, baking powder, and brown sugar. Add the buttermilk and stir until the mixture forms a soft dough.

Turn the dough out onto a lightly floured surface and knead just to blend the ingredients. If desired, add currants or raisins to the dough. Divide the dough into two portions and form each into a rounded loaf.

Place on a greased baking sheet and bake for 45 minutes, or until golden brown. Cool on racks for 10 minutes, then serve. Makes 2 loaves.

On St. Patrick's Day

Make an authentic Irish sandwich with corned beef on Irish Soda Bread with steamed cabbage or sauerkraut and Cheddar cheese.

Navaho Fry Bread

These fry breads act like edible plates. Use as a scoop for chili or serve piled with Tex-Mex toppings — refried beans, chili, cheese, tomatoes, olives, onions, sour cream, even salsas.

- 1 cup all-purpose flour
- 1 cup white wheat flour (see page 118)
- 1 cup cornmeal
- 2 teaspoons baking powder
- 1 teaspoon salt
- 1 cup water
- ½ cup milk
- 1 tablespoon vegetable oil
- 4 cups peanut or vegetable oil for deep-frying

In a large mixing bowl, stir the all-purpose and white wheat flours, cornmeal, baking powder, and salt. Add the water and milk and stir until a moist dough forms (if your dough is too soft, add more flour). On a lightly floured surface, knead the dough into a mound and return to the bowl. Coat with the tablespoon of vegetable oil and cover the bowl with a damp cloth. Let sit for 15 to 30 minutes.

Meanwhile, fill a deep fryer or soup pot with the oil (it should be at least 3 inches deep). Just before you roll out the dough, turn up the heat on the oil.

Pinch off a tangerine-size ball of dough and roll it into a disk on a well-floured surface. It should be about ⅛ inch thick (the thinner the dough, the crispier the fry bread). Place the round into the oil and fry for 2 minutes, watching carefully for the dough to turn a deep golden brown. Remove the bread with a spatula, drain, gently pat off the excess oil, and cool on a rack covered with paper towels. After the first one, adjust the temperature, thickness of the dough, and frying time. Repeat for the rest of the dough. Makes 6 to 8 large fry breads.

Homemade Tortillas

This delicious recipe is adapted from *The Well-Filled Tortilla* by Victoria Wise and Susanna Hoffman (Workman Publishing Company).

- 3 to 4 cups all-purpose flour
- ⅓ cup vegetable oil
- 1 teaspoon salt
- 1 cup warm water

In a medium-size bowl, mix the flour and vegetable oil until it crumbles. Dissolve the salt in the warm water and pour it over the flour mixture, then use your fingers to combine the dough (if your dough is too soft, add more flour). Knead the dough on an unfloured surface until elastic, about 4 minutes. Place it back in the bowl, cover with a damp cloth, and let it rest for at least 1 hour. Divide it into 12 balls and roll each one into a thin, 8-inch round (make sure the edges are as thin as the middle). Place one tortilla at a time on an ungreased skillet over medium-high heat and cook each side for 1 to 3 minutes. Makes 12.

SNAKE ON A STICK

To make this novel campfire treat, mix 2 cups all-purpose flour, 3 tablespoons buttermilk powder, 1½ teaspoons cream of tartar, and ½ teaspoon baking soda in a large bowl. Rub in ¼ cup margarine or butter until it resembles a coarse meal. At the campfire, stir in ¾ cup water. Roll the dough into a long, thin snake and twist it around the peeled end of a green stick. Pinch the dough ends and roast it over a campfire until brown and cooked through. Slip it off the stick and enjoy.

Yeast Breads

Teddy Bear Bread, Pretzels, and Crescent Rolls: *Pages 119–120*

CHAPTER 7

Dinner's Ready

YOUR JOB as the family chef can be as demanding as that of a chef in a three-star restaurant. You have to find a winning recipe, shop for the ingredients, and cook for an audience that won't eat anything too soft or too green. And after all that, you still risk having your creation wrapped in a napkin or slipped to the dog. So how do you please those picky diners and make sure they eat a well-balanced meal?

Culinary school probably won't make your job any easier, but the selection of recipes in this chapter, all approved by kids, just might help. Adapting them to suit your family's very particular tastes is the next step. Try giving our recipes a taste-test, then amend away — add an avocado, cut back on the curry — then jot down in the margins of this book what works for you and what doesn't.

Make it fast. You don't want to spend an hour cleaning up after a thirty-minute meal, so choose recipes that can be made in one pan or try a no-cook recipe, such as the Peanut Butter Dip on page 76 or the Rainbow Buffet on page 157.

Make the meal innovative. As *FamilyFun* reader Patricia Vega so aptly puts it, sometimes what the whole family really goes for are the "foods that don't seem like they're supposed to be for dinner." Look for recipe ideas in other chapters in this book — breakfast, lunch, or snacks — and serve them. Or, shake up the standard Monday through Friday fare by giving each meal a theme (see page 130 for inspiration). Try a Mexican Fiesta, page 136, serve a no-fork dinner with foods you can eat with your hands, or cook a meal based on a children's story.

At Home Burger Joint: *Page 134*

Jazz up the dinner table. Dinner doesn't always have to be served at the table. Eat your supper outside during warmer weather or spread a tablecloth on the family room floor and have an indoor picnic in the winter. If you're staying put, set the table in a new way: use paper plates, fold your napkins into pockets for silverware (see page 15), or take a cue from *FamilyFun* reader Nancy Weber and try a designer table setting (see page 15).

Give the kids options. You can avoid making a different meal for every person at the table by serving dishes with optional mix-ins. Recipes such as the Terrific Taco Filling on page 136, or Chicken Curry on page 144 can be dressed up and customized with toppings and fillings.

Turn off the tube; turn on the answering machine. On the nights that your family can all eat together, eliminate the biggest distractions — the television and telephone — and enjoy each other's company. Go around the table and share one good and one bad thing that happened that day, tell a new joke, or answer the questions in the Table Topics game on page 11.

Serve restaurant foods at home. If your kids like the foods they eat in restaurants, recreate the dishes at home. You'll find several Americanized versions of international foods in this chapter as well as some diner favorites.

Beef Fajitas: Page 137

Meats

Back-to-Basics London Broil

Dress up the all-American steak with one of our accompanying sauces. For a true back-to-basics dinner, support your town butcher — you'll often get the best cut of beef while contributing to an important local trade.

> 2 pounds London broil or
>   flank steak, 1 inch thick
>   Coarse salt and black pepper
>   Vegetable oil

   Preheat your broiler or prepare the coals for grilling. Oil the broiling pan or grill before laying on the steaks. Rub the meat with the coarse salt and a bit of pepper. Cook 3 inches from the flame for 4 to 6 minutes per side for medium. To serve, slice the meat on the diagonal, following the grain. Serves 4 to 6.

Dijon-Herb Butter:

In a food processor or by hand, mix 6 tablespoons butter with 2 tablespoons mustard and 1 minced shallot. Add 8 chopped sprigs of parsley and 8 chopped chives. Pat into a log on waxed paper, refrigerate, and slice into rounds. Dot on warm steak.

Lemon Pepper:

Before you cook the steak, coat both sides with store-bought lemon pepper.

Veggie Smother:

Sauté 8 ounces of sliced mushrooms, 1 medium chopped onion, 1 sliced green pepper, and 1 crushed garlic clove in 1 tablespoon of butter or olive oil. Spoon over the warm steak just before serving.

Parsley Pesto:

In a food processor, blend 2 cups fresh parsley, 1 crushed garlic clove, and 2 tablespoons sunflower seeds with ⅓ cup olive oil. Add 3 tablespoons Parmesan cheese and ½ teaspoon salt. Dot on warm steak.

Horseradish Dipping Sauce:

Mix ½ cup sour cream with ¼ cup prepared horseradish and a dash of Worcestershire sauce.

Last-Minute Marinade:

Marinate the steak in Dijon Vinaigrette (page 174), Soy-Honey Dressing (page 174), or any Italian salad dressing for at least 1 hour prior to cooking.

Back-to-Basics London Broil
with Dijon-Herb Butter

Cube Steak Sandwich

For a quick, inexpensive dinner or lunch, panfry cube steaks for 2 to 3 minutes per side. Place them on bulky rolls and sauté a sliced onion in the pan drippings. Top the steak with the onions and, if desired, Creamy Dreamy Blue Cheese dressing (see page 174).

Homemade Catsup

Blanch 8 large tomatoes in boiling water until the skins split (about ½ to 2 minutes), then plunge into cold water and peel. Slice the tomatoes in half, remove the seeds, and cut into quarters. Place quarters in a large saucepan with 1 cup of water and simmer for 20 minutes, or until soft. Drain any excess liquid and set aside. Puree the tomatoes with 1 chopped onion and 1 garlic clove in a blender or food processor (add reserved liquid, if necessary). Return to the saucepan and add ½ cup white vinegar and 1 tablespoon salt. Cook over medium heat for 5 minutes, stirring constantly. Add ¼ cup brown sugar, 1 teaspoon pepper, and ¼ teaspoon each of cinnamon, ground cloves, and mustard powder. Continue cooking, stirring occasionally, for 1½ hours, or until thick. Transfer to a jar and cool before refrigerating. Makes about 2½ cups.

Mean and Lean Meat Loaf

In diners across America, meat loaf is often part of the blue plate special, so named because the meal was once served on a blue plate divided into three sections for meat, potatoes, and vegetables. This recipe comes from Rosie's Diner in Rockford, Michigan. If you're lucky enough to live near Rosie's, your family can play a round of diner-theme miniature golf at the diner while you wait for your blue plate special.

Meat loaf:
- 2   pounds lean ground beef
- 2   eggs, beaten
- 1   cup rolled oats
- ½   cup chopped onion
- ½   cup catsup
- ¼   cup chopped green pepper
- 2   tablespoons steak sauce
- 1   teaspoon black pepper
- ½   teaspoon salt
- ½   teaspoon basil
- ½   teaspoon garlic powder

Sauce:
- ½   cup catsup
- 3   tablespoons packed brown sugar
- 1   teaspoon ground mustard

Preheat your oven to 350° and grease an 8½-inch loaf pan. In a large bowl, combine the ground beef and eggs. Add the oats, onion, catsup, pepper, steak sauce, black pepper, salt, basil, and garlic powder and mix well. Transfer to the loaf pan and smooth the top.

In a small bowl, whisk the catsup, brown sugar, and mustard together, then spread it over the meat loaf before baking. Bake for 1 to 1½ hours, or until the inside reaches 160°. Let the meat loaf sit for 10 minutes before slicing. Serves 4 to 6.

Steak on a Stick

FamilyFun reader Louann Sherbach of Wantagh, New York, has to cook a pound and a half of steak to satisfy her family: Sara, fourteen; twins Matt and Alison, eleven; and Kimberly, nine.

- 1½   pounds London broil or flank steak, about ¼ inch thick
- ½   cup soy sauce
- ¼   cup vegetable oil (optional)
- ¼   cup water
- 2   tablespoons molasses
- 2   teaspoons dry mustard
- 1   teaspoon powdered ginger
- ½   teaspoon garlic powder

Cut the steak on the diagonal in ¼-inch slices and place them in a sealable bag. Mix the remaining ingredients in a bowl, then pour into the bag. Seal the bag with no air pockets, shake, and marinate in the refrigerator for at least 4 hours, or freeze until ready to use.

When you're ready to cook, skewer the meat ribbon style with 3 to 4 pieces on a skewer (soaked bamboo skewers work well). Broil or grill the meat, about 3 minutes on each side. Makes 10 to 16 skewers.

Steak on a Stick

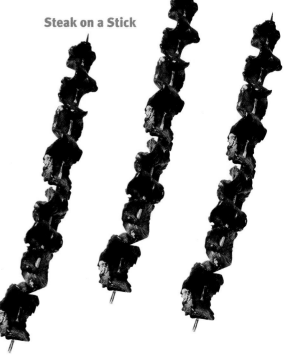

Where's the Beef Stir-fry

A little beef goes a long way when it's stir-fried with Chinese cabbage, green beans, or broccoli. You can marinate the beef and prepare the vegetables in advance.

½   pound boneless top round or flank steak, trimmed and sliced on the diagonal into thin, 2-inch-long strips

Marinade:

2   teaspoons cornstarch

2   teaspoons soy sauce

2   teaspoons dry sherry

2   tablespoons sesame seeds, toasted in a skillet until they start to pop (but don't burn)

1   teaspoon sugar

Vegetables:

½   pound Chinese cabbage, trimmed string beans, or broccoli florets

½   red pepper, cut into strips

Sauce:

6   tablespoons chicken broth

2   tablespoons oyster sauce

2   teaspoons cornstarch

1   tablespoon soy sauce

1   tablespoon dry sherry

½   teaspoon sugar

1   crushed garlic clove

1   tablespoon minced fresh ginger

For the pan:

2   tablespoons peanut oil

Mix the marinade ingredients in a shallow dish, toss in the beef, and marinate while you prepare the vegetables. If you are using Chinese cabbage, blanch it for about 3 minutes in boiling water, drain, and cool; slice diagonally into strips. For string beans, blanch 2 minutes, drop into ice water to stop the cooking, drain, and cut in half. For broccoli, blanch florets for 2 minutes, drain, and cool. (At this point, you can

Where's the Beef Stir-fry

cover and refrigerate the vegetables for up to 12 hours. Just bring them to room temperature before proceeding with the recipe.) In a small bowl, combine the sauce ingredients, except the garlic and ginger. Set aside.

Heat 1 tablespoon of the peanut oil in a wok or large nonstick frying pan. When the oil just smokes, add the cabbage, beans, or broccoli and the red pepper and stir-fry for 1 minute; remove to a plate. Add the remaining oil to your pan, heat, then toss in the strips of beef, stirring for 1 minute. Sprinkle on the garlic and ginger and stir for 1 more minute. Return the vegetables to your pan. Restir the sauce and add it to the pan. Stir until the sauce thickens slightly and the ingredients are coated evenly. Remove from the heat and serve with rice. Serves 3 to 4.

AS EASY AS STIR-FRY

☛ For best results, use a nonstick skillet or wok. Coat with oil, cooking spray, broth, wine, vinegar, or water.

☛ Heat oil until it's very hot. Test with a drop of water — if oil snaps, it is ready.

☛ Cut meat into small, uniform pieces before heating the skillet.

☛ Keep food in almost constant motion to avoid overcooking.

At Home Burger Joint

Perfect Burgers Every Time

For all burgers, start with a ¾-inch-thick patty. Don't pack the meat too hard (you want to leave some air) or handle it too much. For a more flavorful burger, mix 1 pound lean ground beef, lamb, or turkey with 4 drops Worcestershire sauce, 1 teaspoon crushed oregano, and salt and pepper, then form into patties. Broil or grill the burgers, turning once.

☛ Hamburger: For well done, 10 minutes; for medium, 8 minutes

☛ Lamb burger: 12 minutes

☛ Turkey burger: 10 minutes

The Burgers & Dogs

Ground beef
Ground turkey
Ground chicken
Ground lamb
Fish patties
Vegetarian burgers
Hot dogs
Tofu pups

The Breads

Bulky rolls
Dinner rolls
Biscuits
Sliced bread
Pita bread
English muffins
Hot dog buns
Bagels

The Spreads

The Basics: Catsup, mayonnaise, mustard, and relish
Quick Boursin (page 52)
Tartar sauce
Horseradish Mayo (page 52)
Cucumber Dipping Sauce (page 76)
Russian dressing
Cranberry sauce
Salsa
Garlic Mayo (page 52)

The Toppings

Sautéed mushrooms
Onions, grilled, sautéed, or raw
Sliced tomatoes
Diced green peppers
Crispy bacon
Sliced avocado
Roasted red peppers
Chili
Sauerkraut
Lettuce
Spinach leaves
Fresh herbs

The Cheeses

Cheddar
Monterey Jack
American
Mozzarella
Colby
Brie
Provolone
Muenster
Parmesan
Swiss

Bacon Burger Deluxe:

Grilled hamburger topped with bacon, Swiss cheese, tomato, and grilled onions and mushrooms on a bulky roll.

The Ultimate Turkey Burger:

For a lighter burger, use lean ground turkey rather than ground beef. Top with lettuce, tomato, and mayo.

Mini Burgers:

Form a burger about half the diameter of an average burger and ¾ inch thick, cook it for 8 minutes, and sandwich it in a biscuit.

Thanksgiving Burger:

Top a turkey burger with cranberry sauce and stuffing and serve on dinner rolls.

Deep-Sea Delight:

Prepare a fish patty and serve with tartar sauce on a bulky roll.

Cowboy Special:

Top a hamburger with chili and melted Cheddar on a bulky roll.

Fancy Pantsy:

Serve any burger with melted Brie on a toasted English muffin.

Mexican Burger:

Pile any burger with salsa, avocado, tomato, red onion, and Monterey Jack.

Greek Goddess:

Lamb burger topped with fresh mint, tomato, red onion, and Cucumber Dipping Sauce (page 76).

Tofu Melt:

Load a grilled tofu pup with Russian dressing, sauerkraut, and Swiss cheese and broil until the cheese melts.

Double Decker:

Cook two ½-inch-thick patties and layer them on a roll with your favorite toppings.

Kansas Dog:

Hot dog on a roll with mustard and American cheese.

More Than Mushrooms:

Sauté sliced mushrooms with onions and heap them on a burger.

California Burger:

Prepare a vegetarian burger (available in health food stores) according to package directions. Serve on a whole wheat bun with avocado, red peppers, and Garlic Mayo (page 52).

The Great Grill:

Grill your burger and favorite vegetables (sliced onions, peppers, cherry tomatoes). Toast a bun on the grill and sandwich all the goodies in the bun.

Cheeseburger in Paradise:

Melt Muenster and Cheddar cheese on a beef or turkey burger. Add sliced tomatoes, pickles, and onions. Decorate with a mini umbrella.

Bacon Burger Deluxe

Dinner's Ready

Smiling Tostadas

Terrific Taco Filling

You can buy a package of taco shells or make your own by laying corn tortillas on the rack in an oven preheated to 300°. When they have softened, fold them over the oven rack grills so that they hang down, then heat until crisp, about 5 minutes.

½ tablespoon vegetable oil
½ cup chopped onion
1 pound lean ground beef
2 crushed garlic cloves
⅓ cup tomato juice, beef stock, water, or wine
2 tablespoons chili powder
½ teaspoon cumin
   Salt and pepper to taste

Heat the oil in a skillet over medium heat. Add the onion and sauté until translucent. Break up the ground beef with a fork and add it to the skillet. Stir in the garlic and continue stirring until the meat browns; drain out any excess fat. Stir in the tomato juice, chili powder, cumin, and salt and pepper. Continue cooking, stirring occasionally, until the mixture is heated through and the tastes are well combined. Spoon the beef mixture into prepared taco shells and top with your favorite accompaniments: shredded lettuce, olives, avocado, tomatoes, cheese. Makes 2½ to 3 cups.

Chicken Taco Filling:

For a leaner version, substitute ground chicken for the ground beef.

Turkey Taco Filling:

Substitute ground turkey for the beef.

Beef Fajitas

This help-yourself meal, a Texas original, combines sizzling steak, onions, and peppers in a warm tortilla. Using skirt steak is traditional, but if you can't get this from your butcher, substitute flank steak.

- 1 tablespoon vegetable oil
- 2 pounds skirt steak or flank steak
- 4 small onions
- 2 red, green, or yellow peppers
- 8 to 10 flour tortillas
    Salsa Fresca (see page 78)
    Tomatillo Salsa (see recipe below)
    Chunky Guacamole (see page 78)

Heat the oil in a large nonstick frying pan over medium-high heat. Cook the steak on both sides, about 12 minutes for medium, and remove from the pan. Slice the onions and peppers and sauté until soft. Warm your tortillas in a skillet. Thinly slice the steak on the diagonal and arrange on a platter with the vegetables. Serve with salsas, guacamole, and the tortillas. Serves 4 to 6.

Grilled Fajitas:

Peel the onions and cut them in half; slice the peppers in half, too. Rub the vegetables with olive oil and place on your grill. Cook for several minutes, then push them aside. Cook the steak on both sides. Warm the tortillas on the grill. Slice the grilled vegetables and steak and serve with the tortillas.

Chicken Fajitas:

Substitute 2 boneless, skinless chicken breasts for the skirt steak.

Veggie Fajitas:

Substitute mixed vegetables — peppers, onions, carrots, zucchini, and squash — for the skirt steak.

How To Make Smiling Tostadas

☞ These open-faced sandwiches begin with a crispy shell. You can either purchase the shells or briefly fry corn tortillas in 2 tablespoons of oil. Spread the shell with taco filling or refried beans and grated cheese, then arrange shredded lettuce for hair, olive slices for eyes, a carrot slice for a nose, and tomato pieces for lips.

Tomatillo Salsa

Tomatillos, also known as Mexican tomatoes, have a wonderful, mild lemon flavor and make an excellent sauce for any Mexican dish. Husk and rinse 1 pound of fresh tomatillos. In a large saucepan over medium heat, combine the tomatillos, 1 small jalapeño, seeded, veined, and chopped, 1 cup chopped onion, 1 cup water, and 3 to 4 crushed garlic cloves. Bring to a boil, reduce the heat to low, and simmer, covered, for about 15 minutes. In a blender or food processor, puree the juice of 1 lime, ¼ cup Italian parsley, and ¼ cup fresh cilantro. Add the tomatillo mixture, one third at a time, and process until smooth. Cool in the refrigerator. Makes 3½ cups.

Dinner's Ready

Mexican Fiesta

TOOLS OF THE GRILLING TRADE

☛ For best results, use long-handled utensils — fork, spatula, basting brush, and tongs.

☛ Keep a table nearby to hold serving platters, an oven mitt, and marinades and sauces.

☛ Use vegetable spray to coat the racks before grilling to prevent foods from sticking.

☛ For cooking fish and vegetables, invest in a wire-mesh hinged basket.

☛ An instant-read meat thermometer will help you judge the temperature or doneness of meat.

☛ A wire brush makes cleaning the racks after grilling a cinch.

TIPS OF THE GRILLING TRADE

☛ Always heat the rack for 5 minutes over coals before cooking.

☛ Brush on thick or sweet sauces during the last 5 minutes of grilling to prevent burning.

☛ Try not to pierce meat often, as juices will be lost.

☛ For kabobs, soak wooden skewers in water for 30 minutes prior to piercing with meats and vegetables.

Lamb and Vegetable Shish Kabobs

Lamb and Vegetable Shish Kabobs

For an authentic Middle Eastern meal, serve these delicious kabobs with Tabbouleh (see page 177), Cucumber Dipping Sauce (see page 76), couscous, and warm pita bread.

Marinade:
1   cup olive oil
⅓   cup fresh lemon juice
2   crushed garlic cloves
1   teaspoon salt
1   teaspoon coarse black pepper

Meat:
3   pounds lean lamb from the leg or shoulder with the fat removed, cut into 1½- to 2-inch cubes

Vegetables:
12   whole cherry tomatoes
1   green, yellow, or red pepper, cut into 1½-inch squares
1   dozen large mushroom caps
1   small eggplant, peeled and cut into 1½-inch cubes
1   dozen small white onions, peeled and parboiled for 5 to 10 minutes until just tender

Combine the ingredients for the marinade in a glass mixing bowl. Add the meat and marinate for 2 hours, turning frequently, or overnight in the refrigerator.

Prepare the coals for grilling. Using ten 14-inch skewers, pierce the meat and vegetables; leave about 2 inches of space at the handle and the tip. (If you pack the skewers tightly, you will get rarer meat; leave more space for well done.) When the coals are hot, arrange the kabobs on the grill, about 3 inches from the heat. Brush them with the marinade and turn frequently. Start testing for doneness after about 12 minutes. The kabobs will continue to cook a bit off the flame, so be careful not to overcook them. Serves 6 to 8.

Beef and Vegetable Kabobs:
Substitute cubes of beef for the lamb.

Vegetable Kabobs:
Skip the lamb; use just the vegetables.

Pork Chops with Apples

When *FamilyFun* contributor Becky Okrent needs dinner on the table *fast*, she cooks up this one-skillet dinner.

- 4   medium apples, peeled, cored, and cubed
-     Juice of 1 lemon
- ¼   teaspoon nutmeg
- 1   to 2 tablespoons vegetable oil
- 4   pork chops
-     Salt and pepper
- ¼   cup apple cider or juice
- 1   tablespoon butter (optional)

Sprinkle the apples with the lemon juice and nutmeg. Warm a 10-inch or larger skillet over medium-high heat and add enough oil to keep the pork from sticking. When the skillet is hot, add the chops and a pinch of salt and pepper. After about 6 minutes, turn the chops to brown the other side. After 5 minutes, push the chops aside and add the apples. Cover the pan and cook for about 2 minutes. Remove the cooked pork chops from the pan to a warmed serving platter (at this point, the center of the pork chops should be white, and the juices should run clear).

Continue cooking the apples until soft, about 3 minutes. Deglaze the pan with the cider or juice by turning up the heat, stirring the juice and apples, and scraping up the browned bits. To make a richer sauce, swirl in 1 tablespoon butter. Remove the pan from the heat and pour the apples and sauce over the pork chops. Serves 4.

Pork Chops with Mint Pesto:

In a food processor, blend 2 cups fresh mint, ⅓ cup olive oil, 1 garlic clove, and ¼ teaspoon salt. Serve atop pan-fried pork chops (follow the method above but skip the apples and sauce).

Dinner's Ready

Baked Ham with Chutney-Mustard Glaze

This succulent ham can be eaten right away or cooked in advance, covered, and refrigerated, and then served as part of a buffet (an ideal main course for a Party on the Move at right).

- 1   5-pound smoked, boneless ham, fully cooked
- ⅔   cup fresh fruit chutney
- ⅓   cup Dijon mustard
- ⅓   cup white wine

Preheat the oven to 375°. Line a roasting pan with foil. Set the ham into the pan, and with a sharp knife, score the top of the meat in a grid pattern (about ¼ inch deep).

Blend the remaining ingredients in a bowl until smooth, adding more wine if necessary for a spreadable consistency. With a brush, evenly spread the glaze over the top and sides of the ham. Bake for 45 minutes to 1 hour, basting several times. Cool completely, if desired, and slice thin before serving. Serves 12.

A Party on the Move

Progressive dinners are popular for a reason: you get to throw a party, but you don't have to do all the cooking (and cleaning up). To plan a party, ask a few neighborhood families to serve a course in their homes. Arrange for the party group to visit one house for appetizers, another for the main course, and a third for dessert. Families can plan their part of the meal around favorite foods and share the recipes with their guests. Or have an international theme or "kids' choice" dishes prepared by young chefs.

Pork Chops with Apples

Poultry

Veggie Roast Chicken

Plain and Simple Roast Chicken

On weeknights, dinner in my household is a rushed affair, so once a month, I try to roast a chicken and make an old-fashioned Sunday dinner. We bring out the cloth napkins and candles and eat slowly, enjoying each other's company. This crispy-skin recipe welcomes your embellishments.

- 1 4- to 5-pound roasting chicken
   Half a lemon
- 1 large onion, sliced
- 2 tablespoons olive oil
- 1 teaspoon thyme
   ½ teaspoon coarse salt
   ¼ teaspoon pepper

Preheat the oven to 400°. Remove the giblets, thoroughly rinse the chicken, and pat dry. Squeeze the juice from the lemon half over the chicken, then stuff the half into the cavity. Close the cavity with small skewers and tie the legs together with string. Make a bed of onion slices in the bottom of the pan and place the chicken, breast side up, on the onions. Drizzle with the olive oil, sprinkle with the thyme, salt, and pepper and bake for 1¼ to 1½ hours, basting frequently, until the juices from behind the leg run clear. Let rest 5 minutes, then carve. Serves 4 to 6.

Veggie Roast Chicken:
Surround the chicken with peeled carrots and pearl onions, unpeeled new potatoes, and whole mushrooms. Serve with the roasted vegetables on the side.

Orange-Ginger Chicken:
Arrange orange slices on the bird, sprinkle with minced fresh ginger, and pour ½ cup orange juice over the top.

Apple-Hazelnut Chicken:
Place cored apple halves and peeled pearl onions in the roasting pan. Arrange apple slices on the bird and dash with cinnamon. Drizzle apple brandy over the bird for a full flavor. Ten minutes before the chicken is done, add 1 cup hazelnuts to the pan.

Lemon-Rosemary Chicken:
Place lemon slices on the chicken and sprinkle generously with rosemary and a little olive oil.

Stuffed Chicken:
Just before roasting, loosely stuff the chicken with your favorite stuffing or the recipe on page 231. Increase the cooking time by 25 minutes.

Potato Chip Chicken Fingers

These irresistible fingers get their crunch not from deep-frying but from potato chips. Experiment with chip flavors, from barbecue to sour cream and chive.

- 1   whole boneless, skinless chicken breast
- 5   to 6 ounces potato chips, plain, barbecue, or sour cream
- 1   egg
- 2   tablespoons milk

Preheat the oven to 400°. Cut the chicken into finger-size pieces. Fill a large, sealable plastic bag with the potato chips, seal the bag, and crush the chips with the back of a wooden spoon.

In a small bowl, whisk the egg and milk. Dip the chicken pieces into the egg mixture, then into the bag. Shake gently to cover. Place on an ungreased cookie sheet. Bake for 20 minutes, flipping once during the cooking time. Serve with barbecue sauce, salsa, or Honey Mustard Dip (page 60). Serves 4.

Bat Wings

Soy sauce and honey transform ordinary chicken wings into exotic bat wings — a special Halloween treat.

- ½   cup honey
- 1   cup soy sauce
- 1   cup water
- 2   crushed garlic cloves
- 2   dozen chicken wings

Combine the honey, soy sauce, water, and garlic in a large baking dish, reserving ⅔ cup in a bowl for the sauce. Toss in chicken wings and marinate for at least 1 hour. Broil for 10 minutes on each side, allowing the wings to char slightly. Present with sauce. Serves 8.

MOM'S RESTAURANT

FamilyFun reader Sue Jones, of Altamont, New York, created an "at home" restaurant that has her family jumping for leftovers. She dreamed it up because it didn't make sense for her to prepare a new meal when the refrigerator was already overcrowded. On the other hand, when the response to "What's for dinner?" was "Leftovers!" her family predictably groaned. So Sue inventoried her refrigerator and made a menu for Mom's Restaurant. (She used her computer to write the menu, but a handwritten one will suffice.)

At dinnertime, she met her family at the entrance to the dining room, apron on, menus in hand, and asked, "How many in your party?" The first response

was a giggle. Then they said, "Three." When Sue returned with a notepad, they were ready to place an order.

If your kids really take to this idea, you might suggest they occasionally play waiter and head chef themselves, deciding what kind of restaurant to have (fast food, ethnic, or gourmet), and what to make for an upcoming meal. If they add prices to their menu and you request an itemized bill, the kids will also have to do some quick math.

Nuked Nuggets

Chicken nuggets, made in the microwave and served with peanut dip, make a quick and satisfying snack or pita filler, as well as a complete meal. Use toothpicks or longer wooden skewers to spear the nuggets (wooden skewers are available at most grocery stores).

¼	cup soy sauce
1	tablespoon brown sugar
2	tablespoons orange juice
1	tablespoon sesame or vegetable oil
1	to 2 garlic cloves, crushed
1½	pounds boneless, skinless chicken breasts, cut into 1-inch cubes
	Peanut Butter Dip (page 76) or the Chinese Sesame Noodle sauce (page 60)

Combine the soy sauce, brown sugar, orange juice, oil, and garlic in a deep bowl or casserole. Toss the chicken cubes in the marinade, cover, and refrigerate for 30 minutes to 12 hours.

Spear the chicken on toothpicks or wooden skewers, leaving a small space between each piece. Arrange the skewers like the spokes of a wheel on a microwave-safe plate, cover with plastic wrap, and cook on high for 6 to 10 minutes, or until cooked through.

Warm the Peanut Butter Dip or Chinese Sesame Noodle Sauce on high for 1 to 2 minutes. Pour a little over the chicken and serve the rest on the side for dipping. Serves 4.

Microwave Safety

Today's kids are more comfortable with new technology than we ever were. But before your kids zap their popcorn, review these safety tips.

☞ Remind your children which dishes are microwave safe: most ceramic, glass, and heavy plastic containers are fine, but metal and tinfoil should never be used. Avoid using plates with decorative trims that contain metal.

☞ Keep a separate drawer for microwave-safe containers, plastic wrap, waxed paper, and paper towels.

☞ Keep the microwave oven out of reach until your children can use it without your supervision.

☞ Introduce children to microwave cooking by supervising simple assignments, such as preparing frozen veggies or convenience foods.

☞ Pierce foods that have a membrane or skin, such as potatoes and eggplants, and never cook an egg in its shell.

☞ Microwave dishes may not seem hot, but you should always use pot holders.

☞ Uncover dishes by lifting the side away from your face so that the escaping steam will not harm you.

☞ Let microwaved foods stand for 2 minutes before serving. If food has been heated unevenly (which happens when the food hasn't been properly stirred), it may feel cool on the outside yet be scalding hot on the inside.

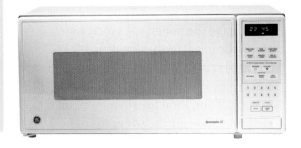

Maple Glazed Chicken

While this sweet-skinned chicken is roasting in the oven, prepare Couscous with Peas (see page 178) for a fast, creative dinner.

¼   cup maple syrup
4   teaspoons lemon juice or cider vinegar
2   tablespoons butter
4   whole chicken legs
    Salt and pepper

Preheat the oven to 450°. Combine the maple syrup, lemon juice, and butter in a small saucepan and simmer for 5 minutes. Line a baking dish with foil and grease. Pat the chicken dry (and trim excess skin, if desired) and lay it on the foil. Season with salt and pepper. Bake for 10 minutes, then pour the glaze over the pieces. Basting occasionally, cook for another 15 minutes, or until the meat is cooked throughout and the juices run clear. Serves 4.

How To Make Home-style TV Dinners

☛ **You can prepare frozen dinners your family will love for a fraction of the store-bought cost. Fill a couple of sectioned plastic plates with leftovers (roast chicken, potatoes, and vegetables are ideal). Add a few drops of water to each section, cover with plastic wrap, and freeze. To prepare, make a small slit in the plastic above each section and microwave for 6 to 8 minutes. Let stand for 1 minute before removing the plastic.**

Chicken Yumsticks

Drumsticks, or any raw chicken for that matter, should be used within two days of purchasing or should be frozen. Make an extra batch of these flavorful sticks for brown-bag lunches.

⅓   cup Italian-style bread crumbs
⅓   cup grated Parmesan cheese
⅛   teaspoon black pepper
8   chicken drumsticks
⅓   cup plain yogurt

Preheat the oven to 375° and butter a 13- by 9- by 2-inch baking sheet. In a shallow dish or pie plate, mix the bread crumbs, Parmesan cheese, and pepper. Using a pastry brush, carefully coat each drumstick with the plain yogurt. Next, roll each one in the bread crumb mixture until it is evenly coated.

Arrange the drumsticks on the prepared sheet and bake for 45 minutes, or until the juices run clear when the meat is pierced with a fork. Serve warm or wrap and refrigerate for up to two days. Serves 4.

The Dish-Drying Game

Doing the dishes at *FamilyFun* reader Glenda Urlich's house has always been a dirty (and unpopular) job. To make it enjoyable, they started to play a guessing game. The parent overseeing the dishwashing thinks of a certain dish or utensil that's being washed, and the child who picks up that item to dry gets to take a break. When the next child discovers the next chosen dish, he sits out, and the first child resumes drying. Their kids love this distraction, and the dishes are done before they know it.

Cindy's Steak and Chicken Stir-fry

2 to 3 stalks celery, sliced
1 pound frozen chopped broccoli
   (or use fresh)
½ head of green cabbage, chopped
4 cups cooked rice

Cut the chicken and steak into bite-size pieces and place in a large bowl. Cover with the teriyaki sauce and marinate for at least 6 to 8 hours in the refrigerator. Drain the meat with a slotted spoon before stir-frying to avoid a soupy quality in the final meal.

In a large wok or deep skillet, heat the oil and stir-fry the meat until brown. Add the cut vegetables in order of cooking: carrots, celery, broccoli, then cabbage. Stir until tender but not over-cooked. Serve over rice. Serves 4 to 6.

Chicken Curry

For an authentic Indian meal, I like to serve this dish with chapatis, basmati rice, and little bowls of condiments, such as chopped peanuts or cashew nuts, grated coconut, plain yogurt, and chutney. (Chapatis are available in the frozen food section of health food stores; basmati rice can be found in the rice section of most grocery stores.)

1 tablespoon vegetable oil
1 onion, chopped
1 whole boneless, skinless chicken
   breast, cut into 2-inch chunks
2 tablespoons butter or margarine
2 tablespoons curry powder
1 crushed garlic clove
1 14-ounce can coconut milk, or
   ½ cup chicken broth or milk, or
   1 cup plain yogurt and ½ cup
   applesauce
½ cup golden raisins (optional)
½ cup frozen peas (optional)

Heat the vegetable oil in a large frying pan over high heat. Add the onion and chicken and cook for 5 minutes, or until the chicken is browned on all

Cindy's Steak and Chicken Stir-fry

The Miles family of Canon City, Colorado, loves stir-fry and that's just fine with mom Cindy: it's easy to prepare, it tastes good, and it gets her three-year-old son, Paden, to eat his broccoli. Cindy saves time by cutting the meat the day before and marinating it in the refrigerator overnight.

2 to 4 boneless chicken breasts
1 to 1½ pounds round steak
2¼ cups teriyaki barbecue sauce (or
   your family's favorite barbecue
   or teriyaki/soy sauce mixture)
2 tablespoons sesame oil
2 to 4 carrots, diced or sliced

FunFact
The name *chopsticks* is our attempt to say the Chinese word *Kuai-za*, meaning quick ones.

Moo Goo Gai Pan

sides. Place the chicken and onion in a bowl. Pour out any leftover oil and use a paper towel to wipe the pan clean.

Melt the butter in the pan over low heat. Add the curry powder and garlic and cook for 3 minutes. Stir in the coconut milk and raisins. Return the chicken to the pan, cover, and simmer for 10 to 12 minutes (be sure the heat is very low or the sauce will curdle). Add the peas in the last 2 minutes of cooking. Serves 4.

Moo Goo Gai Pan

This Chinese dish calls for cooked chicken — and it's a wonderful way to use the remains of a roast chicken. If you don't have leftovers, poach a chicken breast for 20 minutes, then cool and cut into bite-size cubes.

- 2 tablespoons peanut oil
- ½ pound Chinese cabbage or bok choy
- ½ cup button mushrooms, thinly sliced
- 12 snow peas (or more)
- 4 water chestnuts, thinly sliced
- ¼ cup bamboo shoots, thinly sliced
- ¼ cup water
- 1 whole cooked chicken breast, cubed
- 1 teaspoon cornstarch mixed with 3 tablespoons water
  Dash of pepper
- ¼ teaspoon sugar
- 1 to 2 tablespoons soy sauce

Heat the oil in a frying pan or wok over high heat. Just as the oil begins to smoke, add all the vegetables and stir-fry for 30 seconds. Add the ¼ cup water. Cover and cook for 2 minutes. Add the chicken, cornstarch mixture, pepper, sugar, and soy sauce. Stir until the sauce has thickened and the ingredients are coated evenly and cooked throughout. Dish out over rice. Serves 2 to 4.

DINNER WITH FLAIR

When "Oh, Mom, not again," became a frequent chorus at her dinner table, *FamilyFun* reader Rachael Muro created theme dinners. Each family member takes a turn preparing a meal with a theme. Everyone must dress appropriately and bring music or activities to share. The Muros have dined Asian style (with robes and chopsticks), read cowboy poetry at their country and western meal, and dined on Dr. Seuss's *Green Eggs & Ham* (see page 21).

Turkey Breast Scallopini

Turkey Breast Scallopini

This recipe calls for turkey cutlets, which are boneless, skinless portions of turkey breast. You can use them interchangeably with any recipe that calls for chicken breasts.

　4　turkey breast cutlets
　¼　cup grated Parmesan cheese
　¼　cup bread crumbs
　3　tablespoons butter
　　　Juice of half a lemon or orange

Pat the turkey cutlets dry. Mix the cheese and bread crumbs on a plate and coat the cutlets in the mix. Heat 2 tablespoons of the butter in a skillet on medium and add the cutlets. Brown on both sides, about 3 minutes per side, and transfer to a platter. Deglaze the pan by turning the heat to high, adding the lemon juice, and scraping the browned bits into the sauce. Turn off the heat and stir in the remaining butter. Pour the sauce over the turkey and serve immediately. Serves 4.

Turkey Sloppy Joes

FamilyFun contributor Cynthia Caldwell adapted this lean version of the beef classic from her mother's "mean" sloppy joe recipe.

　1　tablespoon vegetable oil
　1　medium onion, minced
　1　green pepper, minced
　1　pound ground turkey
　¼　cup tomato paste
　2　tablespoons chili sauce
　2　teaspoons Worcestershire sauce
　2　tablespoons sweet pickle relish
　¼　teaspoon salt
　¼　teaspoon pepper
　¼　to ⅓ cup water
　4　to 6 bulky rolls

In a large frying pan over medium-high heat, sauté the onion and pepper in the oil for 5 minutes, or until soft. Add the turkey and cook until lightly browned. Add the remaining ingredients, except for the water, and cook until well combined. Add enough water to make the meat "sloppy." Pile onto bulky rolls and serve. Serves 4 to 6.

Fish & Seafood

Salmon Steaks with Quick Dill Sauce

As the Japanese have known for years, fish is a light and healthy dinner option, worthy of being served at least once a week. Whether you're shopping at your local grocer's or a fish market, always look for the freshest fish. It should have a firm, moist flesh and a sweet smell — never a fishy smell, which is a sure sign of aging. Salmon is great with this sauce, but any fresh filet you choose will work.

Quick Dill Sauce:

- ½ cup sour cream
- ¼ cup mayonnaise
- 2 tablespoons milk
- 1½ teaspoons dill
- 1 small crushed garlic clove
  Salt and pepper

Fish:

- 4 6-ounce salmon steaks, 1 inch thick
  Half a lemon

In a small bowl, whisk the sour cream, mayonnaise, and milk until creamy. Add the dill, garlic, and salt and pepper to taste. Stir well; set aside.

Preheat your broiler or prepare the coals for grilling. Rinse the salmon steaks and pat them dry. Squeeze the lemon over the steaks and sprinkle with salt and pepper. Broil or grill the steaks 3 inches from the heat for 8 to 10 minutes, or until the meat has turned from a bright pink to a pale orange. Serves 4 to 6.

Salmon Steak with Quick Dill Sauce

Fast Fish Filets

The microwave turns seafood into fast food that is nutritious and delicious.

- 2 to 3 fish filets, any white fish
  Salt and pepper
  Juice of half a lemon
- 1½ tablespoons chopped fresh herbs, such as dill, parsley, mint, cilantro, or sage
- 4 thin lemon slices
  Toppings (see right)

Rinse the filets and pat dry. Salt and pepper both sides and lay them like the spokes of a wheel in a glass pie pan with the thickest portions on the edges. Sprinkle with the lemon juice and herbs and top with the lemon slices. Cover and cook on high for 3 to 6 minutes, or until the fish flakes. Add toppings. Serves 4.

Fish Filets and...

- Tartar Sauce: Mix ½ cup mayonnaise with 2 to 3 tablespoons relish.
- Quick Cocktail Sauce: Mix ½ cup catsup with 2 tablespoons horseradish.
- Salsa Fresca: See page 78.
- Quick Dill Sauce: See recipe at left.
- Teriyaki sauce: Buy at your grocer's.

Panfried Fish-in-a-Flash

Fish-in-a-Flash Mix

This fish coating works well with almost any filet — scrod, sole, even trout. For extra crunch, use cornmeal instead of the flour.

- ½   cup all-purpose flour
- 2   teaspoons parsley
- 1   teaspoon dried minced onions
- 1   teaspoon garlic powder
- 1   teaspoon basil
- ½   teaspoon salt
- ¼   teaspoon dried lemon peel
- ¼   teaspoon pepper
-     Pinch of cayenne pepper

Shake all the ingredients in a large, sealable plastic bag. Makes 1 cup.

Panfried Fish-in-a-Flash:

Gently shake two to three 8-ounce fish filets in the bag of Fish-in-a-Flash Mix. Heat 1 tablespoon butter in a heavy frying pan set on the stove over medium-high heat or on a grill 1 inch above the hot coals. Cook the filets for 6 minutes, flip, and continue cooking until the flesh flakes. Serves 4 to 6.

Citrus Swordfish

This flavorful marinade is ideal for any firm fish (swordfish, tuna, or hake).

- ¼   cup olive oil
- 4   crushed garlic cloves
- 2   teaspoons ground cumin
- ¼   cup chopped fresh Italian parsley or cilantro
-     Juice from 2 lemons
-     Salt and pepper to taste
- 1   to 2 pounds swordfish

In the bowl of a food processor, combine the oil, garlic, cumin, parsley, and lemon juice. Puree until smooth and add salt and pepper to taste. (You can also do this by hand with a whisk in a large mixing bowl.)

Place the fish in a shallow dish with the sauce and marinate for several hours or overnight. Toss occasionally. Preheat your broiler or prepare the coals for grilling. Broil or grill the fish 3 inches from the flames for 6 to 8 minutes, flip, and continue cooking until it flakes. Serves 4 to 6.

Grilled Shrimp

I haven't met the child who doesn't like shrimp, especially when it's marinated and grilled, as in this recipe. Shrimp can be pricey, so serve it as part of a buffet with rice, vegetables, and salads.

- ¾ cup olive oil
- 2 crushed garlic cloves
- 1 cup dry white wine
- 1 teaspoon salt
- 1 teaspoon black pepper
- ¼ cup finely chopped Italian parsley
- 2 pounds raw shrimp, peeled and deveined

Combine the oil, garlic, wine, salt, pepper, and parsley in a glass bowl. Add the shrimp, cover, and marinate in the refrigerator for 2 to 3 hours or overnight, turning occasionally.

Prepare your coals for grilling and place the shrimp on the grill, about 2 inches from the heat (a grilling basket makes it easier to turn shrimp on the grill). Grill for about 3 minutes per side, depending on the size of the shrimp. Serves 4 to 6.

Grilled Shrimp

How To Boil Lobsters

Theories on how to boil, steam, or grill lobsters are outnumbered only by the amount of spots on a lobster shell. To prepare either of our methods, look for lobsters that are lively, with wiggly legs, moving claws, and a tail that goes into a curl when you pick it up. At home, store in the coldest part of your refrigerator and cook that day.

Boiling Method

2 tablespoons salt
2 to 4 lobsters, 1¼ pounds each
4 tablespoons butter, melted
1 lemon, cut in quarters, for garnish

Fill a large pot three quarters of the way with fresh water and bring it to a rolling boil. Add salt. Rinse each lobster with cold water, then plunge it head first and upside down into the pot. After the water has returned to a fast boil, reduce the heat and cook, covered, for 12 minutes. Remove each lobster with tongs and serve immediately with melted butter for dipping and lemon wedges. Serves 4.

Stove-top Clambake

Fresh seaweed, about 4 pounds, thoroughly washed of sand
1½ quarts fresh water

4 large potatoes, rolled in foil
2 lobsters, 2 pounds each
4 ears fresh corn, silk removed but husk intact, wrapped in foil
28 to 36 steamer clams, scrubbed
8 tablespoons butter, melted

In a 20-quart pot, place a layer of seaweed. Pour in the water and bring to a boil. In 12-minute increments, add the potatoes and another layer of seaweed, the corn and a layer of seaweed, the lobsters and a layer of seaweed, and finally the clams. Cover the pot during the cooking periods. When the clams have opened fully, serve the medley on large platters with melted butter and pot liquid on the side. Serves 4.

Chinese Fried Rice takeout style

If you wish your kids were more enthusiastic about eating vegetables, help them make this stir-fry. The Chinese have been cooking vegetables for thousands of years, and they know how to make them taste good.

2 eggs

2 cups chopped broccoli

1 teaspoon plus 1 tablespoon peanut or canola oil

2 medium carrots, chopped

salt and black pepper

1 Ask your child to break the eggs into a small bowl (remind her to whack them hard). Beat the eggs with a fork.

2 Heat an electric skillet (or a wok or regular skillet) for about a minute. Keeping the heat high, add 1 teaspoon of the oil and then the eggs. Scramble the eggs until cooked through, then transfer to a plate. Chop into little pieces and set aside.

Cooking Tip: Have someone hand ingredients to the cook, so the process can go smoothly and safely.

3 Clean the skillet, then heat it again over high heat. Add about 1 tablespoon of the oil, plus the chopped carrots, broccoli, and a few shakes of salt. Keep the heat high and stir for about 2 minutes.

Cooking Tip: Let the chef choose the vegetables, the amounts, and the size to cut them (show chefs ages eight and up how to use a paring knife).

4 Add the zucchini and crush the garlic cloves into the pan. Continue to stir-fry over high heat for another 2 minutes. Add the peas, scallions, and water chestnuts and stir-fry for 1 or 2 minutes longer. Turn the heat down to medium.

Cooking Tip: For a high-protein dish, add ½ pound of diced, firm tofu along with the zucchini.

CHAPTER 8
Side Dishes & Salads

MASHED POTATOES and peas were the only side dishes I liked as a child. The potatoes could hold a swimming pool of gravy, and garden-fresh peas tasted as sweet as candy. But mine is a family of vegetable-lovers, and we were raised eating carrots, corn, and beans from our garden, freshly picked in the summer and frozen, then steamed in the winter.

When I refused to eat anything but my mashed potatoes and peas, my grandmother would quietly sit at the table, hands folded, napkin in lap, waiting for me to finish, as if it would be impolite to let a child sit at the table alone. Eventually, I caught on that she wasn't going to excuse herself until all my turnips disappeared. One day in sixth grade, I decided to break the silence. So I said, "Grandma, the only reason why you like vegetables is because your taste buds are all worn down." Exasperated and no doubt a bit offended, she finally left me to cope with the turnips alone.

Getting kids to eat the required five servings of vegetables a day has tried many an adult's patience. Kids come up with a host of creative excuses — some as rude as my comment to my grandmother. But there are a few tips we could learn from her generation (like growing our own vegetables) and a few new approaches we might want to consider (beginning with the premise that forcing kids to eat their vegetables rarely changes their attitude toward food). The following ideas should be a start:

Eat fresh produce in season. For the best-tasting, and often the least expensive, vegetables, shop with the season in mind. Look for seasonal produce at your grocer's

Waldorf Salad: *Page 173*

selves where food actually comes from. Generally, they have the greatest success with the large-seeded vegetables (peas, squash, and watermelon) because they are easy to handle, and with the early risers (radishes and cucumbers) because they hold the kids' interest. If your children participate in the whole process — planting through harvesting — they will be more likely to sample the goods.

Serve raw vegetables instead of cooked. Cooked vegetables have a stronger flavor to kids than they do to adults, so try serving raw vegetables for a change. Carrot sticks, cucumber slices, and a spinach salad may go down the hatch easier than their cooked counterparts. You might also offer a dip for their veggies (see pages 76 through 78).

Make a meal of side dishes. For a satisfying, light dinner, serve two or more side dishes. Try Baked Potatoes a la Mode (see page 182) and Carrot Coins (page 166) with any of the salads in the At Home Salad Bar (page 176). If you don't want to skip the main course, cook two vegetables instead of one.

Serve fruits instead of vegetables. If your child balks at string beans or peas, serve him apples, pears, or strawberries. Although they taste sweeter, fruits are often just as nutritious.

Vegetables Kids Love

Serve vegetables you know your kids will eat — and introduce a new one once a week for variety.

☛ Raw, peeled baby carrots or carrot sticks
☛ Snow peas (see page 169)
☛ Broccoli Trees (see page 166)
☛ Sliced cucumbers
☛ Corn on the cob (see page 168)

or shop at a farmers' market, where your kids can meet the people who grow the vegetables. Pick up your family's favorites and some never-seen-before varieties, from white eggplants to purple potatoes, to prepare at home. If you want to receive a weekly supply of vegetables, join a food bank. Stock up and freeze the abundant supplies — out-of-season, frozen vegetables actually taste better than fresh ones shipped too far.

Grow your own. Planting a garden gives kids a chance to see for them-

164

Asparagus with Sesame-Orange Dipping Sauce

Although asparagus is available from January to June, the biggest, freshest supply hits the markets in early spring (March and April). This dish can be served warm or cold, depending on your family's preference.

  1   pound asparagus, trimmed
  ½   teaspoon salt

Sauce:

  2   tablespoons orange juice
  1   teaspoon orange rind, finely grated
  ¼   cup olive oil
  1   teaspoon sesame oil
      Sea salt to taste
      Freshly ground pepper to taste

Find a saucepan wide enough to hold the asparagus spears lengthwise and set it over medium-high heat. Fill about three quarters with water, add the salt, and bring to a boil. Plunge the spears into the boiling water, return to a boil, and cook until the spears are just tender when pierced with a fork, about 2 to 6 minutes depending on thickness (do not overcook). Rinse under cold running water to stop cooking and then drain on a clean kitchen towel.

To prepare the sauce, whisk together the orange juice, orange rind, olive oil, sesame oil, and coarse salt and pepper until they are well blended. Arrange the asparagus on a large serving platter with dipping sauce on the side. Serves 4.

Asparagus with Sesame-Orange Dipping Sauce

Sesame Broccoli

When cooked in the microwave oven, broccoli keeps its bright green color and crispiness. For even more crunch, I add sesame seeds.

  2   tablespoons sesame seeds
  1   head broccoli, cut into florets with the tough stems removed
  2   tablespoons water
      Salt and pepper to taste

Spread the sesame seeds on a paper towel. Microwave on high for 3 to 4 minutes, or until the seeds turn light brown. Set aside. Place the broccoli in a microwave-safe casserole with the stems pointing out. Add the water, cover tightly, and cook on high for about 4 minutes. Uncover and let stand for 2 minutes before draining and tossing with the sesame seeds and seasoning. Serves 4.

Veggie Toppers

Give your vegetables extra flavor with a sprinkle of the following:

☞ **Toasted chopped nuts, such as almonds, walnuts, and peanuts**
☞ **Crumbled bacon**
☞ **Toasted sesame seeds**
☞ **Bread crumbs**
☞ **Chopped fresh herbs (see Herb Flavorings on page 167)**
☞ **Grated Parmesan or Cheddar cheese**
☞ **Chopped hard-boiled egg**

Carrot Coins

The Shilling family of Fayetteville, West Virginia, started an annual tradition by accident. The first year their son planted carrots, they never got around to harvesting them all. After the first snowman of the season was built, a dash to the refrigerator brought a moan: "No carrots for the nose, Mom." Then mom, Terri, remembered the ones left in the ground, and sure enough, she dug down through the snow and frozen ground and pulled up beautiful carrots. Now, every spring the Shillings plant a special area of carrots to be saved for snowmen's noses.

Carrot Coins

Cynthia Caldwell, a regular *FamilyFun* contributor, learned to make these when she was a Girl Scout. She has passed her love of carrot coins on to her daughter, Isabelle.

- 3 to 4 carrots
- ½ cup water
- 2 tablespoons brown sugar
- 1 tablespoon butter
- 1 teaspoon cider vinegar
  Salt and pepper to taste

Peel and slice the carrots into thin rounds or coins. Place them in a medium-size frying pan with the water. Cover and cook over medium-high heat for 6 to 7 minutes, or until the water has nearly evaporated and the carrots are soft. Uncover and add the sugar, butter, and cider vinegar. Turn up the heat and sauté, stirring for 2 to 3 minutes. A copper-colored glaze will form over the carrots. Season with salt and pepper and serve. Serves 3 to 5.

Flower Power Carrots:

For a special occasion, cut slightly wider carrots into coins. Using an aspic cutter (tiny cookie cutter), cut each coin into a flower.

Oven-Roasted String Beans

When it's too cold to grill, I roast my vegetables for a great smoky flavor.

- 2 pounds green and/or yellow string beans, washed and trimmed
- 1 tablespoon olive oil
  Salt

Toss the beans with oil and spread them out on a cookie sheet. Sprinkle with salt. Roast in a 450° preheated oven for 10 minutes. Serves 8.

Oven-Roasted Asparagus:

Substitute 2 pounds asparagus for the beans and roast for 8 minutes. Serves 8.

Broccoli Trees

Watch the vegetables disappear as your kids create and eat a forest of broccoli. Prepare a dip by combining ¼ cup light sour cream, ⅓ cup mayonnaise, ½ teaspoon sugar, 1 tablespoon lemon juice, and 1 tablespoon chopped fresh basil leaves. To make the trees, cut 3 cups broccoli florets and peel 4 carrots. Cut each carrot widthwise and then lengthwise into 4 pieces. Assemble on a plate by laying 3 carrot pieces for a trunk with the broccoli florets as the leaves. Spread dip under the trunks for the forest floor. Makes 5 trees.

Grilled Vegetables

If you want your kids to eat all their veggies, try grilling. Grilled green beans taste as good as french fries, and red onions turn as sugary as a dessert. The easiest way to grill large amounts is to use grilling baskets, which make turning vegetables hassle-free. A spatula and patience will suffice as well. Wash and prepare all the vegetables and then toss them with olive oil (leaving the water on them ensures that not too much oil will stick). Prepare the hot coals and set the grill about 3 inches from the heat. The cooking times are flexible — just be sure to turn, turn, turn.

Grilled Vegetables

Green and Yellow String Beans:

Trim the beans; rinse and toss with olive oil, salt, and pepper. Grill for 8 minutes, or until crisp but brown.

Red, Yellow, and Green Peppers:

Wash, seed, and slice the peppers into quarters. Toss or rub with oil and cook for 8 minutes.

Baby Carrots:

Wash the carrots, toss with oil, and grill for about 8 minutes.

New Potatoes:

If you don't grow your own, look for a selection of red or yellow fingerlings at a farmers' market. Scrub them, cut into halves, and toss with oil, salt, pepper, and rosemary. Grill for 10 to 15 minutes, or until browned.

Red Onions:

Peel the outer skin and rub with olive oil. Grill for 15 minutes, or until tender. Use this same method for small leeks and white and yellow onions. If

they're large, halve them, and grill with the cut side down.

Eggplant:

Slice lengthwise into 1-inch-thick slices and sprinkle with salt. Let sit for a half hour. Pat dry, then rub with oil and grill until tender, about 15 minutes.

Summer Squash:

Select the smallest varieties available and grill them whole or halved. If whole, cook until tender; if halved, cook until browned, about 6 minutes.

Tomatoes:

Place whole, washed tomatoes on the grill (cherry tomatoes taste wonderful). Cook until they are charred on the outside, about 6 minutes.

Beets:

Trim the bottoms and leave about 1 inch of the greens' stems. Rub the beets with oil and grill for 15 minutes, or until tender.

Herb Flavorings

Basil: Beans, peas, peppers, potatoes, spinach, squash, and tomatoes

Dill: Beans, cabbage, cucumbers, potatoes, and squash

Oregano: Beans, eggplant, mushrooms, potatoes, squash, and tomatoes

Rosemary: Cabbage, tomatoes, cauliflower, potatoes, and squash

Sage: Asparagus, beans, corn, carrots, and peas

Tarragon: Asparagus, beans, beets, broccoli, cabbage, cauliflower, cucumbers, mushrooms, peas, squash, and tomatoes

Thyme: Artichokes, beans, broccoli, carrots, corn, leeks, onions, peas, potatoes, and tomatoes

Butternut Squash

Butternut squash, which keeps well through the winter, has a nutty flavor that melds well with herbs and spices. "This scalloped pie warms us twice," says *FamilyFun* contributor Vivi Mannuzza. "Once as it bakes and again as we devour it." You can increase or decrease the butter and flavorings to suit your family's taste.

- 2 tablespoons butter
- 1 3- to 4-pound butternut squash
- 1 onion, thinly sliced
- ¼ teaspoon each of thyme, sage, rosemary, marjoram, oregano, basil, garlic powder, salt, and ground black pepper
- 1 to 2 cups fresh bread crumbs

Preheat the oven to 375°. Lightly butter a 9- by 13-inch baking pan and set the remaining butter aside. Split the squash in half lengthwise, scrape out the insides, and crosscut slices about ⅛ inch thick. Trim off the hard skin.

Layer the squash and onion slices (this part is a fun job for kids). Sprinkle each layer with the herbs and spices, and dot with the remaining butter. Top with the bread crumbs.

Cover with foil and bake for 30 to 40 minutes, or until tender when a fork is inserted. Uncover and bake for another 5 minutes, or until the bread crumbs are toasted. Serves 6 to 8.

Roasted Corn on the Cob

Corn never tastes better than when it's still on the cob, and cooking it doesn't get much easier than when you roast it in its husk on the grill.

- 1 dozen ears unhusked corn
- 1 stick butter
- Salt and pepper

Without removing the husks or silk, soak the corn in water for 15 minutes. Remove from the water and place ears directly on the grill or coals. Rotate them with a pair of tongs while grilling so that all the sides are evenly cooked. The corn should be ready in 8 to 16 minutes, depending on how hot the fire is. Remove from the grill and peel carefully because the ears will be very hot. The husks and silks should come off easily. Spread butter on the corn and season with salt and pepper. Serves 12.

Stir-Fried Snow Peas

Chinese flavorings — soy sauce, ginger, and garlic — make any vegetable more appetizing to kids. Put your kids to work stripping the stems off the snow peas.

- 2 teaspoons sesame oil
- ½ to 1 teaspoon fresh minced ginger
- 1 pound fresh snow peas, rinsed and stems removed
- 1 8-ounce can water chestnuts, sliced
- 1 tablespoon soy sauce

In a frying pan or wok, warm the sesame oil over medium-high heat. Add the ginger, snow peas, water chestnuts, and soy sauce, and stir-fry for about 3 to 5 minutes, or until the peas turn bright green. Serves 4 to 6.

Candy Corn

With this recipe, you can magically turn ordinary corn into candy corn. The trick is a tablespoon of sugar. The novelty may be enough to get your kids to eat their corn.

- 1 10-ounce package frozen corn
- 3 tablespoons butter
- 1 to 2 tablespoons brown sugar
- ¼ cup diced, sweet red pepper (optional)
- 2 scallions, chopped (optional)

Cook the frozen corn according to package directions. Melt the butter in a saucepan over medium-low heat, add the brown sugar, and stir until smooth (be careful the mixture doesn't burn). Drain the corn and add it to the brown sugar mixture with the red pepper and scallions. Cook for 2 minutes, stirring constantly. Serve hot or cold. Serves 4.

Spaghetti Squash

Dragging a fork down the middle of a spaghetti squash transforms the squash to a mess of playful strings. This yellow squash can be found in your local grocery store during the fall and winter.

- 1 medium spaghetti squash
  Salt and pepper to taste
- 2 tablespoons butter
  Parmesan cheese

Preheat the oven to 375°. Cut the squash in half lengthwise, sprinkle the halves lightly with salt and pepper, and place in an ovenproof glass pan. Add about ½ inch of water. Cover with foil and bake for about 1 hour, or until the squash is cooked through.

To serve, add 1 tablespoon of the butter to each half and scrape the stringy flesh with a fork to make "spaghetti." Garnish with the cheese. Serves 6 to 8.

Garlic Spaghetti Squash:

Sprinkle the cooked squash with sautéed garlic and bread crumbs.

Candy Corn

Build a Vegetable Bug

If you want to teach kids about the anatomy of insects, the High Desert Museum of Bend, Oregon, says build bugs. Take a close look at backyard insects (sweep a net through tall grass or spread out a sheet on your lawn). In the kitchen, set out large vegetables for insect bodies (squash, potatoes, and bell peppers) and smaller vegetables for heads, legs, wings, and antennae (cherry tomatoes, corn kernels, beans, radishes, and carrots). Then, offer your kids toothpicks and an edible "glue" (cream cheese) to create a replica of the real bugs or their own fantasy creations. Have an insect book handy for inspiration.

Popeye's Super Side Dish

If there was ever a way to get kids to eat their spinach, these chewy, cheesy treats are it. When speared with fancy toothpicks, they become wonderful hors d'oeuvres.

- 2 10-ounce packages frozen chopped spinach, thawed and squeezed dry
- 2 cups herb stuffing mix, crushed to make fine crumbs
- 1 cup grated Parmesan cheese
- ½ cup butter or margarine, melted
- 4 scallions, finely chopped
- 3 eggs, lightly beaten
  Dash of nutmeg

Preheat the oven to 350°. In a large bowl, combine the spinach, stuffing mix, Parmesan, butter, scallions, eggs, and nutmeg and mix well. Shape the mixture into 1-inch balls (you may find this works better if you dampen your hands with water first). Bake the balls on ungreased cookie sheets for 20 to 30 minutes. Makes about 40 1-inch balls.

Oven-Baked Cherry Tomatoes

FamilyFun contributor Katherine Eastman says this side dish couldn't get any easier — there is hardly any preparation. She uses a combination of yellow and red cherry tomatoes, but all red works equally well.

- 2 cups red and/or yellow cherry tomatoes (about 1 pound)
- ¼ cup diced red onion
- 1 crushed garlic clove
- 2 teaspoons basil
  Salt and pepper to taste
- 2 teaspoons olive oil
- 2 teaspoons red wine vinegar
- 1 tablespoon parsley

Preheat your oven to 350°. Lightly grease a baking dish large enough to spread the cherry tomatoes over the bottom. Stem the tomatoes and place them in the baking dish. Sprinkle the onion, garlic, basil, and salt and pepper over the tomatoes, then drizzle with the olive oil and vinegar.

Bake until the tomatoes are soft, 20 to 30 minutes. Garnish with the parsley and serve warm. Serves 6 to 8.

Oven-Baked Cherry Tomatoes

Zucchini Pancakes

A first cousin to potato pancakes, these hearty flapjacks turn a lovely green from the zucchini skins. Garnish with apple slices and a dollop of sour cream.

1	pound zucchini, grated
1	bunch scallions, minced
1	egg, lightly beaten
½	cup all-purpose flour
⅓	cup grated Parmesan cheese
	Ground black pepper to taste
	Vegetable oil for frying
2	large apples, cored and thinly sliced (optional)

With a fork, gently mix the zucchini, scallions, egg, flour, cheese, and pepper. Place a large skillet over medium-high heat and add the oil, ¼ inch deep. Place a heaping forkful of the zucchini mixture into the pan and press into a circle about ⅓ inch thick. Cook until brown and crispy on both sides, pressing down with the back of your spatula several times to squeeze out excess moisture; repeat with the remaining batter.

For a sweet topping, sauté the apples in the skillet and serve over the warm zucchini pancakes. Serves 4 to 6.

Side Dishes & Salads

When your family can't stand the sight of one more zucchini, celebrate the bounty with a zany carnival. Invite friends to bring a homemade zucchini dish, then launch into the festivities.

Squash creatures: Decorate zukes with tempera paints, buttons, toothpicks, and other household items.

Rolling races: Raise one end of a sheet of plywood to make a platform, then roll the zukes down the slope and see whose vegetable tumbles the farthest.

Green bowling pins: Cut off one end of ten zukes to create flat bottoms, stand them up like pins, and strike with a soft ball.

Drop the zuke in the bottle: Have kids stand on a chair and try to drop a zuke into a widemouthed jar.

House building: Offer the kids plastic knives and let them create houses out of your largest zucchinis.

Storytelling: Tell favorite stories with zucchinis as the heroes.

Salads

Cucumbers with Yogurt-Dill Dressing

A generation ago, most parents made this refreshing dish with sour cream. This version, made with low-fat yogurt, is lighter and equally delightful.

3   to 5 cucumbers, thinly sliced
    Salt
1½ cups low-fat yogurt, drained of excess liquid
1   cup chopped fresh dill
¼   teaspoon ground cumin
    Chopped fresh mint (optional)
    Black or white pepper to taste

Lightly salt the sliced cucumbers and drain in a colander. Mix the yogurt, dill, and cumin in a serving bowl, then toss in the cucumbers. Refrigerate until ready to serve. Garnish with mint and pepper. Serves 8 to 10.

Tomatoes with Basil and Mozzarella

It's almost impossible to find tasty tomatoes out of season, so when they're at their seasonal best, this dish can be served as often as you like. I prefer to use fresh Mozzarella, which is packed in water and available in the deli section of most grocers.

6   or more large ripe tomatoes, sliced fairly thick
1   pound whole or part skim milk Mozzarella, sliced the same thickness as the tomatoes
    Handful of fresh basil leaves rinsed, patted dry, and minced
¼   cup olive oil
    Salt and pepper to taste

Alternate the tomato and Mozzarella slices on a large serving platter. Sprinkle with the basil and drizzle with the olive oil. Prepare in advance, then season with salt and pepper just before serving. Serves 8 to 10.

Tomatoes with Basil and Mozzarella, Couscous with Peas, Cucumbers with Yogurt-Dill Dressing: *Page 172, 178*

One-Bean Salad

Tossed in a light vinaigrette, this dish is for kids (and adults) who pick out the good beans in three-bean salads. For the chickpeas (garbanzos), you can substitute any bean you prefer — kidney, black, or pinto.

2   19-ounce cans of garbanzo
      beans, rinsed and drained
2   scallions, chopped
1   red onion, diced
1   tomato, chopped
1   crushed garlic clove
¼   cup red wine vinegar
¾   cup olive oil
½   cup chopped fresh parsley
¼   teaspoon salt
⅛   teaspoon black pepper

In a large bowl, combine all the ingredients and stir well. Cover and refrigerate before serving. Serves 6 to 8.

One-Bean Salad

Festive Corn Salad

Serve this bright yellow and green salad with tacos, fajitas, or any Mexican dish. For a bite, add minced jalapeño.

2   15-ounce cans whole corn kernels
1   green pepper, finely chopped
1   red onion, chopped
1   tomato, chopped
      Half a bunch of parsley, chopped
¼   cup cider vinegar
2   tablespoons olive oil
      Salt and pepper to taste

In a medium bowl, mix the corn, pepper, onion, tomato, and parsley. Toss with the vinegar and oil, then sprinkle on the salt and pepper. Serve immediately or refrigerate until ready to serve. Serves 8 to 10.

Waldorf Salad

This salad dresses up a plate nicely. Use fresh ingredients and toss well to coat the apples and prevent them from browning.

2   to 3 cups chopped apple
1   cup Cheddar cheese chunks
1   cup green or red grapes
½   cup diced celery
½   cup walnut pieces
½   cup raisins
⅓   cup mayonnaise
1   tablespoon fresh lemon juice

In a large bowl, toss all the ingredients and stir well to coat with the mayonnaise and lemon juice. Refrigerate until ready to serve. Serves 6 to 8.

Polar Picnics

With winters as cold as they are in Wisconsin, *FamilyFun* reader Patti Barnes of West Bend has found it hard to think of indoor activities to keep her kids happy. Last winter, she and her three-year-old son, Danny, hit on a solution — an indoor picnic. Patti put a red-checkered, vinyl tablecloth over her carpeting in the living room. She filled a basket with summer foods — salads, fruit, chips, and other goodies. Then they put on music and had a feast. As Patti says, "As long as kids think it's a party, they make their own fun."

Salad Dressings

Honey-Poppy
Seed Dressing

Creamy Dreamy Blue Cheese

Once you learn how easy it is to make this dressing, you'll never buy it again. It is best prepared a day in advance.

- ½ cup sour cream
- ¼ cup mayonnaise
- 2 tablespoons milk
- 1 tablespoon lemon juice
  Salt and black pepper to taste
- ¼ cup crumbled blue cheese

Using a fork, mix the sour cream, mayonnaise, milk, and lemon until smooth. Add the salt, pepper, and blue cheese. Refrigerate. Makes about 1¼ cups.

Soy-Honey Dressing

A versatile mixture, this can be used as a salad dressing, marinade, or dip.

- 4 tablespoons light soy sauce
- 3 tablespoons water
- 3 tablespoons honey
- 1 tablespoon sesame oil
- 2 tablespoons rice wine vinegar
- 1 tablespoon dry or cooking sherry
- 1 tablespoon crushed garlic
- 1 teaspoon minced fresh ginger
- 2 scallions, white part only, chopped

Combine all the ingredients and store in the refrigerator. Makes 1 cup.

Dijon Vinaigrette

Kids can do all the measuring and mixing for this classic dressing.

- ⅓ cup red wine vinegar
- ½ cup olive oil
- ½ cup vegetable oil
- ⅛ teaspoon coarse black pepper
- 1 crushed garlic clove
- ½ teaspoon thyme
- 2 teaspoons Dijon mustard
- ¼ teaspoon salt

Combine all the ingredients in a clean jar with a tight-fitting lid. Shake well. Makes 1⅓ cups.

Honey-Poppy Seed Dressing

A sweet dressing with a crunch, this is the hit of my household.

- 1 cup oil
- ⅓ cup vinegar
- 2 tablespoons water
- 2 tablespoons honey
- 1 to 2 tablespoons poppy seeds

Blend the oil, vinegar, water, and honey in a blender until creamy, then stir in the poppy seeds. Store in the refrigerator. Makes 1½ cups.

Pineapple Boats

The key to this fruit salad is in the presentation. Be sure to buy a fresh pineapple (the bottom should be slightly yellow and a leaf should pull out easily.)

1	pineapple, cut in half lengthwise
	Juice from half a lemon
1½	cups seedless grapes
2	kiwis, peeled and sliced
2	11-ounce cans mandarin oranges
12	strawberries, hulled and sliced
1	sliced banana (optional)
½	cup chopped walnuts (optional)

Remove the core of the pineapple halves, carve out the remaining fruit, cut it in bite-size chunks, and place them in a large bowl. Squeeze the lemon over the shells and chunks to prevent browning. To the bowl, add the grapes, kiwis, oranges without the juice, strawberries, banana, and walnuts. Toss well, then spoon into the pineapple shells. Chill covered until serving time. Serves 6 to 8.

Carrot Stick Salad

This uncomplicated salad, which comes from *FamilyFun* contributor Emily Todd, combines several foods kids like: carrots, pineapple chunks, and raisins. Although the result might seem like dressed-up carrot sticks to adults, kids recognize its true worth. To julienne the carrots, cut them with a sharp knife into matchstick-thin strips (a job for patient adults).

1	pound carrots, julienned
1	8¼-ounce can pineapple chunks in syrup (about 1 cup)
1	cup raisins
¾	cup walnuts (optional)

In a medium-size bowl, toss together the carrots, pineapple, and raisins. Add the walnuts, if desired. Cover and refrigerate until you're ready to serve. Serves 6.

Fabulous Fruit Sauce

FamilyFun contributor Mollie Katzen makes a quick raspberry sauce to drizzle over fruit, and her kids love it. To make it, puree 1½ cups fresh or frozen raspberries and 2 tablespoons orange juice concentrate (if you are using fresh or unsweetened berries, add 2 to 3 tablespoons sugar or honey as well). Pour the mixture into a strainer placed over a bowl. Stir with a spoon, pressing the smooth liquid through. Taste and adjust as necessary, adding more sugar, or lemon or lime juice to your liking.

At Home Salad Bar

Salad Bases

Lettuces (oak leaf, romaine, iceberg, butternut, arugula, or mesclun mix)
Spinach
Red cabbage

Vegetables & Fruits

Broccoli and cauliflower florets
Green beans
Grated carrots
Peas
Olives
Cherry tomatoes
Cucumber slices
Artichoke hearts

Sliced mushrooms
Bean sprouts
Radishes
Onion or scallion
Red or green peppers
Jalapeños
Sliced avocado
Sliced apples

Proteins

Hard-boiled eggs
Chickpeas
Crumbled bacon
Cubes of ham
Luncheon meat strips
Cubes of turkey or chicken
Crab meat, tuna fish, or shrimp
Anchovies

Feta cheese
Cubes of Swiss cheese
Cottage cheese

Dressings

Dijon Vinaigrette (see page 174)
Creamy Dreamy Blue Cheese (see page 174)
Caesar salad dressing
Thousand Island
Olive oil
Vinegar or lemon juice

Toppings

Croutons
Sesame seeds
Parmesan cheese
Walnuts
Fresh herbs

Salad Shortcuts

☛ Give the kids the assignment of washing and drying the lettuces, and tearing the leaves into a salad bowl. Store in the refrigerator, covered with a dish towel.

☛ Keep homemade dressing in the fridge; see page 174 for ideas.

☛ Make croutons from bread scraps (see page 55) and store in an airtight container.

☛ When dinner is chicken or steak, make extras. The following night, use the leftovers to make a main-course salad.

Garden Salad:

Top lettuce with onion slices, diced carrots, and green peppers; drizzle with any dressing you like.

Greek Salad:

Tear lettuce onto a platter and top with cucumber slices, tomato wedges, red onion slices, olives, crumbled feta, and anchovies, if desired. Drizzle with olive oil and red wine vinegar.

Salade Niçoise:

On a bed of lettuce, arrange chunks of white tuna, tomato wedges, hard-boiled egg slices, olives, steamed green beans, and anchovies. Top with Dijon Vinaigrette dressing (see page 174).

Chicken Caesar Salad:

Toss lettuce with bottled Caesar salad dressing and a handful of Parmesan cheese. Arrange on salad plates and top with sliced chicken and croutons.

Quick Rice Salad:

Mix cooked white rice with diced carrots, onion, and green pepper and toss with Italian dressing.

Blue Cheese, Apple, and Walnut Salad:

Top lettuce with apple slices, crumbled blue cheese, walnuts, and store-bought raspberry vinaigrette.

Shrimp and Avocado Salad:

Tear butternut lettuce onto a salad plate and top with slices of avocado and cooked, peeled shrimp. Drizzle with olive oil and finish with a spritz of lemon juice.

Quick and Easy Coleslaw:

Mix shredded cabbage and carrots with mayonnaise, a splash of vinegar, and a pinch of sugar.

Tabbouleh:

Buy a package of tabbouleh wheat salad mix and prepare according to the directions. Add chopped fresh tomatoes, diced red onion, peas, cucumber chunks, chickpeas, and mint.

Smiling Salad:

Arrange a bed of lettuce on a plate with two hard-boiled egg eyes, a carrot slice mouth, and a radish nose.

Black Bean Salad:

Toss canned, drained black beans with diced red pepper, corn, and diced onion. Toss with 2 parts vinegar and 1 part oil and fresh chopped cilantro.

Mushroom, Spinach, and Red Onion:

Toss fresh spinach with sliced mushrooms, red onion, croutons, and Dijon Vinaigrette (see page 174).

Chef's Salad:

Cut ham, Swiss cheese, and turkey into cubes and arrange on a platter of lettuce with tomatoes, cucumbers, and hard-boiled eggs. Top with creamy Italian or a light vinaigrette.

Mesclun Salad Deluxe:

Buy mesclun salad mix (a mix of baby greens) in the produce section of your grocer's. Top with radishes, onion, pepper, grated carrots, and cherry tomatoes.

Garbage Bag Salad

For a potluck salad lunch, ask everyone to bring a prepared part of a salad — cleaned and torn lettuce, sliced radishes, cherry tomatoes, diced celery, shredded carrots, artichoke hearts, sliced peppers and cucumbers, diced red onion, broccoli florets, hard-boiled eggs, croutons, and even chickpeas. Throw everything into a clean garbage bag, shake well, and serve on salad plates with garlic bread. Then, pass the dressings.

Mesclun Salad Deluxe

Rices & Grains

Couscous
with Peas

Couscous with Peas

Originating in North Africa, this fine, grainlike cereal cooks even faster than rice or potatoes. You can serve it plain, embellish it with peas and onion as it is here, or experiment with just about any fresh herb or chopped vegetable.

 1   onion, diced
 1   crushed garlic clove
 1   tablespoon olive oil
 1   cup frozen peas
 1   tablespoon minced fresh dill
     Salt and pepper to taste
1½   cups vegetable or chicken stock
 1   cup couscous

Sauté the onion and garlic in the oil in a saucepan over medium heat until translucent, about 5 minutes. Stir in the peas, dill, salt, pepper, and stock and bring to a boil. Add the couscous, cover, and return to a boil. Remove from the heat and let the mixture sit for 5 minutes, or until the liquid is absorbed. This can sit, covered, for about 10 more minutes or may be served immediately. Fluff with a fork before serving. Serves 4.

White Long-
Grain Rice

White
Short-Grain
Rice

Brown
Rice

Wild Rice

How To Cook Rice

Cooked just right, plain rice makes a wonderful, healthy side dish. Enhance the flavor by using broth or sprinkling it with herbs and spices. Directions are for 3 to 4 cups cooked rice.
Long-Grain: Boil 2 cups water, add 1 cup rice, stir, cover, and simmer for 15 to 20 minutes.
Short-Grain: Boil 1½ cups water, add 1 cup rice, stir, cover, and simmer for 15 to 20 minutes.
Brown Rice: Boil 2½ cups water, add 1 cup rice, stir, cover, and simmer for 30 minutes.
Wild Rice: Boil 4 cups water, add 1 cup rice, stir, cover, and simmer for 35 to 40 minutes.

FunFact
Fifty percent of all the world's rice is eaten within 8 miles of where it is grown.

Mexican Rice

A meal wouldn't be Mexican without a side of rice and beans, whether inside or alongside a tortilla. This seasoned rice is flavored with everything Mexican — cumin, jalapeño, garlic, and more. To save time preparing it, use a food processor to chop the onion, garlic, and pepper.

1	tablespoon vegetable oil
1½	cups white rice
1	16-ounce can Italian plum tomatoes, peeled and chopped, with their juice
2	onions, chopped
2	crushed garlic cloves
1	jalapeño pepper, seeded, veined, and chopped
½	teaspoon cumin
2	cups chicken stock, tomato juice, or water
1	cup frozen corn kernels (optional)
1	cup frozen peas (optional)
½	cup chopped fresh or frozen carrots (optional)
	Fresh parsley or cilantro (optional)

Heat the oil in a large saucepan and add the rice. Stir for about 3 minutes. Add the tomatoes, onion, garlic, pepper, cumin, and the stock, tomato juice, or water, as well as a combination or all of the corn, peas, and carrots.

Bring to a boil and simmer, covered, until the liquid is absorbed and the rice is tender, about 15 minutes. Garnish with chopped fresh parsley or cilantro. Serves 6 to 8.

Seasoned Rice Mix

Seasoned Rice Mixes

FamilyFun contributor Susan Purdy says these quick rice mixes make wonderful gifts from the kitchen. Store in widemouthed jars or take-out cartons.

Herb Rice:

1	cup uncooked long-grain white rice
2	beef or vegetable bouillon cubes
1	teaspoon green onion flakes
½	teaspoon each: rosemary, marjoram or oregano, and thyme leaves
½	teaspoon salt or celery salt

Curried Rice:

1	cup uncooked long-grain white rice
2	chicken or vegetable bouillon cubes
½ to 1	teaspoon curry powder
1	teaspoon dried minced onion
½	teaspoon ground cumin
½	teaspoon parsley flakes
½	teaspoon salt or celery salt

In a large mixing bowl, stir all the ingredients for either rice and pour into a sealable container.

Seasoned Rice:

In a large saucepan combine either the Herb or Curried Rice mixture with 2 cups cold water. Bring to a boil. Reduce the heat to low, stir once, and cover. Simmer for 14 to 20 minutes, or until the liquid is absorbed. Serves 4.

Kids Dig Rice

At nursery school, the favorite activity of *FamilyFun* reader Janet Buckley's four-year-old son is playing at the rice table, so she decided to create one for home use. After sealing the cracks of a large cardboard box with colorful hockey tape and decorating it with stickers, they filled the box with ten pounds of uncooked, inexpensive rice and added small pasta (orzo and tubettini), which they had painted with watercolors. With spoons, cups, and scoops, Sean pours and measures the rice, hides things in it, and builds hills and valleys.

Potatoes

Red Potatoes with Garlic and Rosemary

The garlic in this side dish is cooked in its skin, so that it comes out sweet and creamy. To eat, just hold a clove by its "tail" and pull out the insides.

- 2 pounds of small, new red potatoes, scrubbed and halved
- 10 cloves of garlic, left in their skins, excess paper removed
- Sea salt to taste
- Black pepper to taste
- 1 tablespoon chopped fresh rosemary or 1 teaspoon dried

Preheat the oven to 350°. Lightly oil a large roasting pan or baking dish and arrange the potatoes and garlic in one layer. Sprinkle with the salt, pepper, and rosemary. Cover tightly with foil and bake for 1 hour, or until the potatoes are soft when poked with a fork. Serves about 6.

Classic Mashed Potatoes

Hand-mashed and flavored to perfection, homemade mashed potatoes are my favorite comfort food. They may seem like a lot of work, but a little peeling and mashing are certainly worth the effort. Serve them as they are or embellish them with toppings.

- 4 to 5 large potatoes, peeled
- ½ to 1 cup milk
- 2 tablespoons butter
- Salt and pepper to taste
- Pinch of nutmeg (optional)

Cover the potatoes with cold water and bring to a boil. Cook for 20 minutes, or until tender. (Be careful to watch the pot; potatoes have a tendency to boil over.)

While the spuds are cooking, slowly heat the milk and butter. When the potatoes are done, drain them and add half the hot milk mixture. Mash the potatoes with a handheld potato masher or an electric mixer. Keep adding the hot milk until you reach the proper consistency (which, of course, varies from family to family). Season with salt, pepper, and nutmeg, if desired. Serves 4 to 6.

Spuds with Jewels:

In a frying pan, heat 1 teaspoon of vegetable oil and briefly sauté 1 diced red pepper (add hot peppers such as green jalapeño for fire). Stir in ½ teaspoon basil. Immediately pour on top of mashed potatoes.

Green Potatoes:

Use an electric mixer to blend 1 to 2 cups chopped cooked spinach into mashed potatoes until they turn green.

Red Coats:

Use purple, red, or new potatoes with their skins on.

The Cheddar Broccoli:

Mix grated Cheddar cheese with 1 cup chopped, steamed broccoli florets and fold into the mashed spuds.

Prague Potatoes:

Panfry 4 strips of bacon until crisp. Remove from the pan and add 1 diced onion, cooking until translucent. Crumble the bacon into the onion. Top mashed potatoes with bacon, onion, and drippings, using about 1½ teaspoons or less of fat per serving.

Golden Broil:

Spread prepared mashed potatoes in an oven-to-table baking dish. Drizzle ½ cup heavy cream over the top and sprinkle with Parmesan cheese. Broil until the top turns golden.

Breakfast for Dinner:

Serve mashed potatoes in a large bowl topped with 3 to 4 chopped hard-boiled eggs and chopped fresh parsley and chives.

Tatties 'n' Neeps:

For the Scots' way of using up leftover mashed potatoes, mix equal amounts of mashed potatoes and mashed turnips.

Colcannon:

Mix mashed potatoes with 1½ cups shredded, cooked, and drained cabbage or kale.

Bangers and Mash:

Try this English recipe: serve plain mashed potatoes with broiled or pan-seared sausages ("bangers") on the side.

Fenced-in Spuds:

Surround a mound of mashed potatoes with a "fence" of steamed green beans and carrot sticks.

Toppings for Mashed Spuds:

- ☛ Chopped black olives and scallions
- ☛ Sautéed mushrooms
- ☛ Crosscut leeks cooked in butter until soft
- ☛ Herbed bread crumbs
- ☛ Toasted sesame seeds
- ☛ Salsa
- ☛ Cheddar or Parmesan cheese
- ☛ Crumbled cooked bacon
- ☛ Sautéed onion with red or green peppers
- ☛ Chopped basil and fresh tomatoes
- ☛ Cumin and/or chili powder

Red Coats

The Cheddar Broccoli

Prague Potatoes

Green Potatoes

Spuds with Jewels

Baked Potatoes a la Mode

Teach your kids how to fix baked potatoes with toppings — grated cheese, stir-fried broccoli, olives, and more — and they'll grow to love the humble potato.

4 to 6 medium-size
baking potatoes

1 red bell
pepper

1 medium-size
bunch of broccoli

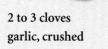
2 to 3 cloves
garlic, crushed

sliced olives

¼ pound mushrooms, sliced

salt

1 tablespoon
vegetable oil

1 Preheat the oven to 400°. Let the chef scrub the potatoes (younger kids will get into "washing" them with a scrub brush). Prick them with a fork, then wrap tightly in foil and bake for about 40 minutes.

2 Heat a wok or frying pan, add the oil, then add the broccoli and stir-fry over high heat for about 5 minutes, sprinkling with salt and crushed garlic as you go. Remove from the heat and spoon into a bowl.

Cooking Tip: Give the chef a long-handled spoon, tell him to hold tightly, and watch him closely while he stir-fries.

3 Cut a red bell pepper into 1-inch chunks and cook in a little water until tender. Place in a blender with a few shakes of salt and a small clove of garlic. Let your child puree the pepper until smooth and strain it into a small bowl so the skins are left behind in the strainer.

4 Melt about 2 teaspoons of butter in the wok or frying pan. Add the mushrooms and salt lightly. Sauté over medium heat for about 10 minutes, then spoon into a bowl.

Cooking Tip: To wash mushrooms, wipe them with a damp paper towel rather than submerging them in water. If they are very dirty, quickly rinse them under the faucet.

182

1 ripe tomato, diced

1 cup grated Cheddar cheese

2 minced scallions or chives

butter

¼ cup pesto (homemade or a good commercial brand)

milk

sour cream or cottage cheese

5 Help the chef assemble the toppings in bowls — the broccoli, pepper puree, mushrooms, olives, tomato, scallions, pesto, grated cheese, and sour cream or cottage cheese.

Cooking Tip: Older kids can help cut the tomatoes and scallions with a sharp knife. Smaller kids can use a plastic or serrated dinner knife. Please supervise, whatever your child's age.

6 Slit the potato and use a fork to mash the insides with a little butter and/or milk to make them creamy (so the toppings will blend in more easily).

Cooking Tip: Smaller children may need some help getting started, but they will thoroughly enjoy the mashing.

7 Add spoons to the bowls of toppings and let the children help themselves. Encourage them to decorate their potatoes as simply or lavishly as they wish. Serves 6.

Cooking Tip: Let your child invite a friend for dinner — he may be more adventurous about trying a new topping if he sees a friend try it first.

Side Dishes & Salads

Potato Salad Vinaigrette

Unlike most potato salads, which are coated with mayonnaise (an unwelcome picnic condiment), this version has a light oil and vinegar dressing. Be sure to pour the dressing over the potatoes while they are still warm, so it can be thoroughly absorbed. Potato salad always seems to taste better after the flavors have mingled, so you may want to mix up this one a day in advance.

- 1½ pounds small, new red potatoes, washed and quartered
- ¼ cup vegetable oil
- ¼ cup red wine vinegar
  Salt and pepper to taste
- ½ pound bacon, cooked until crisp, drained, and crumbled
- 3 eggs, hard-boiled and chopped
- 1 onion, grated
- 1 bunch scallions, chopped
- 2 tablespoons sweet pickle relish

Bring a pot of salted water to a boil and add the potatoes. Cook until just tender, about 15 minutes. Be careful not to overcook — potatoes can become mushy.

Drain the water and transfer the potatoes to a large bowl. Using a fork and knife, roughly cut the potatoes into bite-size pieces. In a small bowl, whisk the oil and vinegar and add the salt and pepper. Pour the mixture over the potatoes and toss.

Let the potato salad sit for 30 minutes, then add the bacon, eggs, onion, scallions, and relish, tossing gently until the ingredients are well combined. Refrigerate covered. Serves about 6.

Flavored French Fries

In France, they're called *pomme frites*. But the term "french fry" has nothing to do with France. It refers to a method, called frenching, or cutting the potatoes into narrow strips. Bake your next bag of frozen fries with a little flavor:

- ☛ **Cheese Fries: Melt grated cheese over fries.**
- ☛ **Herb Fries: Sprinkle herbs over fries before baking.**
- ☛ **Italian Fries: Melt Mozzarella cheese over baked fries and dip in spaghetti sauce.**
- ☛ **Thanksgiving Fries: Serve your fries with gravy.**

Oven-Baked French Fries

These fries are healthier than their fast-food counterparts. For a lower-fat version, use olive-oil-flavored cooking spray instead of the peanut oil.

- 1 medium-size potato per person, such as all-purpose, Yukon Gold, or red
- 2 teaspoons peanut oil
  Salt to taste

Preheat your oven to 425°. Peel the potato and slice it into squared fries, about ¼ inch thick. Dry off any excess starch with paper towels.

In a baking dish, toss the potatoes with the oil to coat. Bake for 15 to 20 minutes, turning at least once. Salt the fries and serve while hot. Serves 1 person per potato.

Tater Boats

The basic baked spud seems more adventurous when it's tricked out with a ship's rigging. To save time, bake a few potatoes ahead or use frozen skins, then let kids stuff and decorate them with carrot stick masts and red or yellow pepper sails.

1   medium baked potato
⅛   cup grated Cheddar cheese
2   to 3 tablespoons milk
½   tablespoon butter or margarine
    Salt and pepper to taste
    Extra grated Cheddar cheese, carrot sticks, red or yellow pepper, and peas or corn

Cut the baked potato in half lengthwise. Leaving a ¼-inch layer of potato along the skins, scoop the insides into a bowl. Mash in the cheese, milk, butter, salt, and pepper, then spoon the mixture back into the potato skins.

Warm the potatoes for 2 minutes on high in the microwave. Decorate the halves with the extra cheese, then add carrot stick masts, pepper sails, and a deck of peas or corn. Makes 2 boats.

Baked Sweet Potatoes with Orange Sauce

Spice up the sweetest of potatoes with orange juice and the flavors of fall — ginger, nutmeg, allspice, and walnuts. You can find sweet potatoes in most grocery stores year-round, but the best arrive in September and October.

3   sweet potatoes (about ½ pound each), scrubbed and pierced with a fork
¾   cup fresh orange juice
3   tablespoons brown sugar
½   teaspoon grated ginger
⅛   teaspoon nutmeg
¼   teaspoon allspice
2   tablespoons chopped walnuts (optional)

Preheat the oven to 400°. Place the potatoes on foil to catch the drippings and bake for 30 minutes, or until tender on the outside. Meanwhile, mix the juice, brown sugar, and spices in a bowl and set aside. Remove the sweet potatoes and cool slightly. Reduce the oven temperature to 375°. When the potatoes are cool enough to handle, peel and cut into 1-inch chunks. Place them in a casserole dish and top with the sauce. Bake for 25 to 30 minutes, spooning the liquid over the potatoes two to three times. Garnish with the nuts. Serves 4 to 6.

Tater Boats

How To Make Potato Prints

While you're cooking potatoes, set up a potato print craft for your child. Cut a potato in half, then have your child draw simple designs on the flat surfaces of the two halves with a ballpoint pen. When each image is ready, an adult can cut down about ½ inch around the shapes with an X-Acto knife, then remove the excess.

Pour acrylic paint into a pie plate. Dry the potatoes with a paper towel, then let your child press them into the paint, making sure that the shapes are well coated. Try a few test prints on scrap paper (pressing down with firm, even pressure will make the clearest print). Now your child can stamp away, decorating paper, cards, gift wrap, or fabric.

CHAPTER 9

Can I Have Dessert?

VER SINCE she was a kid, *FamilyFun* contributor Barbara Albright has always liked having dessert first — especially if it's a cookie, brownie, or piece of cake. But it wasn't until this former editor-in-chief of *Chocolatier* watched her daughter, Samantha, take her first taste of chocolate that she witnessed the truly magical effect of sweets.

From the earliest age, sweets make us happy. We are born with a natural love for sugar — it's the first flavor a baby responds to (yes, it's in a mother's milk). Growing up, it's the sweet stuff that we remember — a chocolate birthday cake, a trip to the candy store, or waiting for the ice-cream truck.

It's for this reason that Barbara doesn't mind having sweets around the house, from the giant chocolate chip cookies she developed for this chapter to the brownies she made for her latest cookbook. She believes that if you serve it in moderation, your kids won't crave it. She's also intent on developing their palates: "I want my kids to be discerning and to know what a really good cookie is supposed to taste like."

To help your family bake the kind of quality desserts Barbara is talking about, try the recipes that follow, keeping these guidelines in mind as you bake.

Don't forbid sweets. Children who aren't allowed to eat candy and other sweets are more likely to overeat goodies when adults aren't around. Also, if you make a big deal about desserts and consider them

Monster Pops: *Page 189*

Wild Oatmeal Cookies: *Page 192*

Blueberry Lattice Pie: *Page 204*

Keep flour, sugar, and butter on hand for dessert making. Instead of picking up packaged sweets at the store, buy flour, sugar, baking powder, chocolate chips, and other baking essentials. Making cookies or brownies from scratch is more rewarding than opening a store-bought version, and your home-baked goodies will taste much better.

Encourage your kids to bake. Baking a sweet can actually hook kids on cooking — it all starts when they lick the batter or frost the cake. First try the Wild Oatmeal Cookies cooking class on page 192, then test any other recipe in this chapter.

When baking desserts, measure flour carefully. Unlike cooking, baking is a science, and for best results, you want to measure precisely. Spoon flour into a dry measuring cup and level it off with a dinner knife. You also should level off your teaspoons of baking soda and powder. (Another tip: Be sure to use fresh baking powder.)

Keep your ingredients at room temperature. For best results, take your eggs out of the refrigerator a few hours before you plan to use them for a recipe.

Invest in an oven thermometer. Although your oven dial may say 375°, you should double-check the temperature by keeping a thermometer in your oven. This will help you get evenly baked cookies or cakes.

a "special treat," your kids may crave them when they're older.

Balance sweets with a nutritional diet. It's okay to eat desserts as long as they are figured into the overall diet for the day. If your child starts the day with a sugar cereal and has a cupcake after school, consider skipping dessert or offering fresh fruit.

Serve small portions. Generally, one cookie or a small piece of pie or cake is enough to feed a child for dessert. If you set an example of moderate eating, your kids are apt to follow your lead.

Cookies & Bars

Giant Chocolate Chip Cookies

When Ruth Wakefield added chopped chocolate to her basic butter cookie recipe at the Toll House Inn, chocolate chip became the most popular cookie in America. Here, we've updated Ruth's 1930s recipe to a '90s extravaganza. The goodies that go in them are up to you (chocolate chips, crushed toffee bars, butterscotch chips, or M&M's). The size they take is your decision, too — you can make them as small as a dime or as big as your hands.

2¼	cups all-purpose flour
¾	teaspoon baking powder
½	teaspoon salt
1	cup unsalted butter, softened
¾	cup sugar
½	cup packed light brown sugar
2	eggs
2	teaspoons vanilla extract
2	cups semisweet chocolate chips

In a large bowl, mix the flour, baking powder, and salt. In a separate bowl, cream the butter and sugars, then add the eggs, one at a time, mixing well after each addition. Stir in the vanilla extract, then gradually stir in the flour mixture until combined. Add the chips and stir again. For chewy cookies, refrigerate the dough for 2 hours or overnight.

Preheat the oven to 300°. Using a ⅓-cup measuring cup, drop the dough onto a baking sheet, leaving 3 inches between mounds.

Bake for 30 to 35 minutes, or until light brown. Cool for 5 minutes, then transfer to a wire rack and cool completely. Makes 15 giant cookies.

Monster M&M's:
Substitute M&M's for the 2 cups of chocolate chips.

Monster Chip & Nut:
Stir in 1 cup chopped walnuts, pecans, or other nuts with the chips.

Monster Pops:
Before baking the cookies, insert a Popsicle stick into the dough.

Monster Stir-ins:
Try other chips, such as peanut butter, butterscotch, or white chocolate.

Mini Cookies:
Use mini chips or M&M's. Measure out rounded teaspoons of dough, leaving 1½ inches between cookies. Bake for 17 to 20 minutes. Makes 85.

Can I Have Dessert?

Cookie Decorating

You don't need a lot of expensive equipment to create edible works of art — most of the stuff is already in your kitchen.

- Cookie cutters
- Aspic cutters (tiny cookie cutters)
- Garlic press for squeezing dough to make hair, manes, and swirls (don't pile it on too thick or it won't cook all the way through)
- Kitchen utensils and clean toys to make patterns in the dough
- Tubes of decorator's icing and/or assorted colors of All-Purpose Buttercream (see page 198) in pastry bags for frosting the cookies
- Colored sprinkles, M&M's, jelly beans, gumdrops, red hots, licorice, chocolate chips, or raisins for decorating the cookies

Sugar Cookies

This foolproof recipe will unleash the cookie monster in anyone. Creative cooks can cut the dough with any size cookie cutter, color it red, white, and blue, flavor it with chocolate, almond, and lemon, or use the baked cookies as an empty canvas for a frosting design.

1	cup butter, softened
¾	cup sugar
1	large egg
1	teaspoon vanilla extract
2¾	cups all-purpose flour
1	teaspoon baking soda
1	teaspoon cream of tartar

In a large bowl, cream the butter and sugar until fluffy. Add the egg and beat well, then mix in the vanilla extract. In a separate bowl, combine the flour, baking soda, and cream of tartar. Add the flour mixture to the butter mixture, one third at a time, until thoroughly combined.

Divide the dough into two equal portions and flatten each into a disk. Cover each disk in plastic wrap and refrigerate for 2 to 3 hours, or until the dough is firm enough to work with. If it becomes too firm, soften at room temperature for about 5 minutes.

Preheat the oven to 350°. On a lightly floured board, roll out the dough until it is about ¼ inch thick. Cut out cookies with cutters or by hand.

Using a metal spatula, carefully transfer the cookies to a baking sheet, leaving about 2 inches between them. Bake for 8 to 10 minutes, or until lightly browned around the edges.

Remove the cookie sheet from the oven, place it on a wire rack, and cool for 2 to 3 minutes. Using a metal spatula, transfer the cookies to the rack and cool completely. Repeat this procedure with the remaining chilled dough. Form any extra dough scraps into a disk, chill if necessary before rerolling, then continue until all the dough has been used. Baked cookies can be stored in an airtight container in the freezer for up to 1 month before frosting and decorating and for up to 3 days at room temperature. Makes about 3 dozen cookies, depending on their size.

Colored Sugar Cookies:

To make colored sugar cookies, mix and knead liquid or paste food coloring, drop by drop, into the basic sugar cookie dough until it reaches the desired hue.

Chocolate Cookie Dough:

After the last third of flour has been incorporated in the dough, mix in 2 ounces of melted and slightly cooled unsweetened chocolate.

Almond Cookie Dough:

Stir 1 teaspoon of almond extract into the dough right after the last third of flour has been incorporated.

Lemon Cookie Dough:

After the last third of flour has been added to the dough, stir in 2 teaspoons of grated lemon peel.

Appliquéd Stars

Appliquéd Stars:

For this multicolored cookie, you'll need three different dough colors and two or three similarly shaped cutters in differing sizes. Cut a large star (or another shape) out of one color of cookie dough and place it on a baking sheet. Using a smaller star cutter, cut out the center of the first star and remove it. Use the smaller cutter to cut out a star from a contrasting color and insert it into the center of the big star. Repeat with a third color of dough and the smallest cutter, if desired. Gently pinch the seams between the doughs so they won't separate during baking. Bake for 10 to 12 minutes.

Pinwheel Cookies:

Roll out chocolate and sugar doughs separately between sheets of plastic wrap into 12- by 8-inch rectangles. Remove the top sheet of wrap from one dough rectangle. Remove both sheets from the second rectangle and place that dough on top of the first. Starting with one of the 12-inch sides, roll up the doughs, jelly roll fashion. (Do not roll the plastic wrap up in between the dough, but wrap it around the outside of the roll.) Refrigerate or freeze for

1 hour, or until firm. Remove the plastic wrap, cut the roll into ¼-inch-thick slices, and place them on baking sheets. Bake for 10 minutes, or until the cookies are just lightly browned.

Cookie Necklaces:

Use letter-shaped cutters or cardboard templates to create names and words from the dough. Punch a hole in the top of each letter with a drinking straw. After baking the cookies for 10 minutes, cool and decorate. String them together on a piece of thin licorice.

Alphabet Cookies:

These edible letters can be used as spelling aids, word game pieces, or treats. Roll the dough into three cylinders (about 1 inch in diameter), cover, and refrigerate for 1 hour. Slice the logs into ¼-inch-thick rounds. Bake for about 10 minutes. When cool, use icing to inscribe a letter on each one. The most commonly used letters in the English language are *A, E, I, S,* and *T,* so make extras of these. The least commonly used are *Q, X,* and *Z,* so one of each should suffice.

Easier Cookie Baking

☞ Cut from the edge of the dough to the center, removing the cookies as you go.

☞ Position the oven rack in the center of the oven. If you use two racks, switch the positions of the baking sheets halfway through baking.

☞ Bake similar-size cookies together on one baking sheet so they are done at the same time.

☞ Don't run your hot baking sheets under cold water — the abrupt temperature change can cause them to warp.

Alphabet Cookies

Wild Oatmeal Cookies

When Mollie's mother added chocolate chips to her oatmeal cookie dough, a family tradition was born. Now Mollie and her kids have added their own favorite stir-ins (dried cranberries, apricots, chocolate chips, and more).

3 sticks softened butter or margarine

2 large eggs

1½ teaspoons vanilla extract

2 cups all-purpose flour

½ cup sugar

1 cup packed light brown sugar

1 Place the butter or margarine in a large mixing bowl. It's a good idea to do this ahead of time so the butter will soften. When your baker is ready to start making the batter, pre-heat the oven to 375°.

2 Beat the butter with an electric mixer until fluffy (about 1 minute). Add the sugars, then beat for another minute. Add the eggs and beat for 2 more minutes.

Cooking Tip: Explain to children under age ten that the electric mixer is for adults only. Turn off the mixer between additions so your child can put in the ingredients.

3 Add the vanilla extract and stir with a spoon. Mix in the flour, baking soda, and salt until "you don't see any more white," advises Mollie's daughter, Eve.

Cooking Tip: Even the youngest child will enjoy measuring the sugars, flour, and oatmeal (do this over a plate to catch any spills) and dumping them in at the appropriate time.

4 Stir in the rolled oats until they are well combined. At this point, you can divide the batter into separate bowls, one for each cookie flavor.

Cooking Tip: After the flour and oatmeal are put in, the batter will be stiff, and a parent may need to take over the stirring.

4½ cups rolled oats

up to ⅓ cup dried apricots, chopped (optional)

½ teaspoon salt

1 teaspoon baking soda

up to ½ teaspoon cinnamon (optional)

up to 2 cups semisweet chocolate chips (optional)

Kids' Reviews

"You tuck the flour into the batter."
— Lev, age 5

"When you put the cookies in the oven, they get wider."
— Jenni, age 7

"I know all about how to crack eggs and how to make cookies out of dough, right?"
— Eve, age 4

up to ½ cup raisins (optional)

up to ⅓ cup finely chopped walnuts (optional)

up to ⅓ cup dried cranberries or cherries (optional)

5 Add the optional goodies. Use some or all, in any combination. The amounts are flexible, so add as much or as little as the chef decides, within reason, of course. Try making oatmeal-raisin-chocolate chip cookies in one bowl and apricot oaties in another. Stir as well as possible; the goodies may not be evenly distributed, but that's okay.

6 Drop by rounded teaspoonfuls onto an ungreased cookie sheet. Bake for 10 to 12 minutes, or until the cookies are browned on the bottom.

Cooking Tip: Putting trays into or taking them out of the oven is a job for parents or kids over age ten.

7 Cool the cookies on a wire rack or a plate for at least 10 minutes before eating. The cookies will keep well in an airtight container. Makes about 5 dozen 2½-inch cookies.

Cooking Tip: Younger kids can remove the cookies from the tray with a spatula, but supervise them closely. Warn them about the hot tray and be sure to hold it steady.

Can I Have Dessert?

¼ teaspoon salt
2 cups chopped walnuts or pecans
   (optional)

Preheat the oven to 350°. Lightly butter a 13- by 9-inch baking pan (or line the pan with foil so that it extends 2 inches beyond each end of the pan, then lightly butter the foil).

In a large microwave-safe bowl, heat the butter and chocolates on high for 1 to 3 minutes, or until the chocolates are melted, stirring halfway through cooking. Let stand at room temperature for 10 minutes.

In a large bowl, using an electric mixer, beat the eggs and sugars for 3 minutes, or until light in color. Beat in the chocolate mixture and vanilla extract until blended. Mix in the flour and salt until just combined. Using a wooden spoon, stir in the nuts, if desired.

Scrape the batter into the prepared baking pan. Bake for 28 to 33 minutes, or until a knife inserted 2 inches from the center comes out almost clean (do not overbake). Set the pan on a wire rack to cool. Store the completely cooled brownies in an airtight container at room temperature. These brownies also freeze well. Makes about 20 squares.

Chocolate-Lover's Brownies

Chocolate-Lover's Brownies

When nothing but chocolate will do, these richly flavored, fudgy brownies will satisfy your craving. One square is downright decadent when topped with a scoop of ice cream and a confectioners' sugar heart.

1 cup unsalted butter
8 ounces semisweet chocolate
4 ounces unsweetened chocolate
4 large eggs
¾ cup firmly packed brown sugar
¾ cup sugar
2 teaspoons vanilla extract
1 cup all-purpose flour

Tiger-Striped Brownies

The three best-selling candies in the United States — Snickers, Reese's Peanut Butter Cups, and Peanut M&M's — all feature the dynamic duo of chocolate and peanuts. The same combo makes these chewy brownies so popular.

1	ounce semisweet chocolate
1	ounce unsweetened chocolate
1	tablespoon unsalted butter
⅓	cup creamy peanut butter
2	tablespoons vegetable oil
½	cup firmly packed brown sugar
½	cup sugar
2	large eggs, at room temperature
1½	teaspoons vanilla extract
¾	cup all-purpose flour
¼	teaspoon salt

Preheat the oven to 325° and butter an 8-inch square baking pan. In a microwave-safe bowl, melt the chocolates and butter on high for 1 to 2 minutes, stirring halfway through cooking. Set aside to cool slightly.

In a medium-size bowl, beat the peanut butter and oil. Add the sugars and continue beating until the mixture is light and fluffy. Add the eggs, one at a time, beating well after each addition. Mix in the vanilla extract, then the flour and salt until just combined.

Stir ⅓ cup of the peanut butter batter into the chocolate mixture. Scrape the remaining batter into the baking pan. Spoon the chocolate mixture over the batter. Using a table knife, make a zigzag through the layers to create a marbled effect. Bake for 30 to 35 minutes, or until a toothpick inserted in the center comes out almost clean.

Cool in the pan, then cut into bars. Store in an airtight container at room temperature. Makes 16 bars.

Can I Have Dessert?

Oat Date Bars

FamilyFun contributor Barbara Albright invites her kids to help prepare this not-too-sweet oaty mixture, press it into the baking pan, and cut it into chewy bars. The results are just right as lunch-box fare or as a quick energy boost on an autumn hike.

1	8-ounce package chopped dates
½	cup water
1	tablespoon fresh lemon juice
1½	cups rolled oats
1	cup all-purpose flour
⅓	cup chopped walnuts
⅛	teaspoon salt
½	cup butter, softened
¼	cup packed brown sugar

Preheat the oven to 350° and lightly butter an 8-inch square baking pan. In a small saucepan over medium heat, cook the dates with the water for 7 minutes, or until softened. Remove the pan from the heat and cool. Stir in the lemon juice. In a large bowl, mix the oats, flour, walnuts, and salt.

In a separate bowl, cream the butter and sugar. Gradually stir in the oat mixture, reserving 1 cup. Press the batter into the pan and spread the dates over the top. Sprinkle the surface with the reserved oat mixture and lightly press it with your fingertips. Bake for 20 to 25 minutes, or until lightly browned. Cool, then cut into bars. Makes 16 squares.

Tiger-Striped Brownies

Cakes

Chocolate Celebration Cake

Cubcakes

Chocolate Celebration Cake

When frosted with Chocolate Ganache (see page 198), this cake is a celebration of the richest chocolate flavor around.

5	ounces unsweetened chocolate, coarsely chopped
2	cups all-purpose flour
2½	teaspoons baking powder
¼	teaspoon salt
¾	cup unsalted butter, softened
1½	cups sugar
2	teaspoons vanilla extract
3	large eggs, at room temperature
1¼	cups milk

Preheat the oven to 350°. Lightly butter two 9-inch round cake pans. Line the bottoms of the pans with circles of baking parchment or waxed paper. Dust the sides of the pans with flour and tap out the excess. In a microwave-safe bowl, melt the chocolate on high for 1 to 2 minutes, or until melted, stirring halfway through cooking. Set the chocolate aside to cool to room temperature for 10 minutes.

In a large bowl, stir the flour, baking powder, and salt. In another large bowl, using a handheld electric mixer, beat the butter and sugar until combined. Beat in the melted chocolate and vanilla extract. One at a time, add the eggs, beating well after each addition. Add the flour mixture and milk in thirds, beating until just combined. Scrape the batter into the prepared pans and spread evenly. Bake for 25 to 30 minutes, or until a toothpick inserted in the center of each layer comes out clean. Transfer the pans to a wire rack. Cool 10 minutes. Carefully invert the cake layers onto the rack and cool completely.

Place one layer on a serving plate. Spread frosting over the cake and top with the second cake layer. Frost the outside of the cake, then the top. Store in the refrigerator. Serves 12.

Cubcakes:

To make pawprint cupcakes, bake the Chocolate Celebration Cake in two 12-cup muffin tins for 20 minutes. Frost the cupcakes with All-Purpose Buttercream (see page 198) or store-bought icing (for a furry paw, mix the frosting with grated coconut first). Top each cupcake with a small mint patty. Then place three Junior Mints or chocolate chips around the patty for claw marks. Beware — cubcakes walk away fast. Makes 24.

Devilish Devil's Food Cake

Sinfully rich, delicious chocolate gives this cake its name.

- ½ cup butter
- 1 cup sugar
- 2 eggs, at room temperature
- 2 ounces unsweetened chocolate, melted and cooled
- 1 teaspoon vanilla extract
- 1 cup milk
- 1¾ cups all-purpose flour
- 1½ teaspoons baking soda
- ½ teaspoon salt

Preheat the oven to 350°. Grease two 8-inch cake pans or one 13- by 9- by 2-inch pan. Cream the butter and sugar in a large mixing bowl, then beat in the eggs, one at a time. Add the cooled, melted chocolate and vanilla extract and mix well, then stir in the milk.

In a separate bowl, combine the flour, baking soda, and salt. Gradually add the flour mixture to the butter mixture and stir until just combined. Pour the batter into the pre-pared pans and bake the rounds for 25 to 30 minutes, or the baking pan for 40 to 45 minutes. Cool in the pans for 10 minutes, then turn onto a wire rack and cool completely. Serves 10.

Caterpillar Cake:

Bake the Devilish Devil's Food Cake in two 12-cup muffin tins lined with paper liners for 20 minutes. Mix up a batch of All-Purpose Buttercream (see page 198) or about 2 cups of store-bought white frosting and tint it with green or orange food coloring. Frost the cupcakes and arrange them in a curving, crawling pattern on top of a large cutting board or a piece of cardboard covered with foil. For a fuzzy look, tint the coconut with food coloring and sprinkle it over the cupcakes. Snip shoestring licorice into short lengths to form the antennae and legs. For eyes, try licorice candies or jelly beans.

Caterpillar Cake

THE CHOCOLATE FAMILY

Unsweetened Chocolate:
After cocoa beans are processed and roasted, they are ground to form this smooth, pure form of chocolate.

Bittersweet, Semisweet, and Sweet Chocolate:
Depending on the manufacturer, these dark chocolates have varying amounts of sugar and flavorings, such as vanilla, added.

Milk Chocolate:
This favorite is made of chocolate, milk solids, sugar, and flavorings, such as vanilla. It is sensitive to heat, so be careful when melting it.

White Chocolate:
True white chocolate contains cocoa butter and is ivory colored. It also contains milk solids, sugar, and flavorings, such as vanilla. The more common white confectionery coatings use vegetable fat in place of cocoa butter.

Chocolate Chips:
The addition of stabilizers helps chips hold their shape when baked. Because they contain milk solids, milk chocolate chips may burn when they touch the pan.

Cocoa Powder:
This easy-to-use form of chocolate is made from plain chocolate that has nearly all of the cocoa butter pressed out of it.

Frosting

The Frosting on the Cake

Follow these steps to smooth frosting:
☛ Let the cake cool thoroughly.
☛ For a flat-top cake, slice off the bumpy top and invert.
☛ Brush off crumbs before frosting.
☛ For a clean platter, place waxed paper under the edges of the cake before frosting, then remove.
☛ Frost with a thin layer of icing to seal in remaining crumbs before applying the final coat.
☛ For a smooth finish, keep a glass of hot water nearby to dip your spreader in.

All-Purpose Buttercream

This basic icing recipe can be spread on cakes and cookies or applied as decorative piping with a pastry bag. If you plan to use it for piping, make it a little stiffer by adding less milk.

> 3½ cups sifted confectioners' sugar
> 1 cup unsalted butter, softened
> 1 teaspoon vanilla extract
> 2 to 4 tablespoons milk

In the bowl of an electric mixer, beat the sugar, butter, and vanilla extract on low speed. Add in the milk bit by bit until the mixture has reached a spreadable consistency. Makes about 3 cups.

Chocolate Icing

FamilyFun contributor Becky Okrent recommends using the back of a spoon to spread this simple, shiny icing.

> 12 ounces semisweet chocolate chips
> 2 cups sour cream
> 4 tablespoons confectioners' sugar

In a heatproof dish, microwave the chips on high for 1 minute, or until melted, stirring halfway through cooking time. When the chips are melted, stir in the sour cream a few tablespoons at a time, until smooth and shiny, then stir in the sugar. Refrigerate for ½ hour, or until thick enough to spread. Makes 3 cups.

Cream Cheese Icing

This tangy icing complements carrot cake, banana cake, and pound cake.

> 8 ounces cream cheese, at room temperature
> 4 tablespoons unsalted butter, at room temperature
> 2 cups confectioners' sugar, sifted
> 1 teaspoon lemon juice

In a processor, mixer, or by hand, beat all of the ingredients together until smooth. Makes 1¾ cups.

Chocolate Ganache

Ganache frosting, flavored here with raspberry, is a mixture of chocolate and heavy cream. With more than a pound of bittersweet chocolate, it's for chocolate aficionados only.

> 18 ounces bittersweet chocolate, finely chopped
> 1½ cups heavy cream
> ⅓ cup seedless raspberry jam
> ¼ cup unsalted butter, cut into ½-inch cubes
> Pinch of salt
> 1½ teaspoons vanilla extract

Place the chocolate in a large bowl. In a saucepan, bring the cream, raspberry jam, butter, and salt just to a boil. Pour over the chocolate and let it stand for 1 minute. Whisk until smooth, then mix in the vanilla extract.

Cover with plastic wrap and let the frosting thicken overnight at room temperature, or refrigerate it for no longer than 1½ hours. Makes about 2 cups.

Better-Than-Basic Yellow Cake

Although it certainly is easier to reach for a cake mix, all the ingredients for this moist yellow cake are in your pantry. Try it — it's worth the effort.

4	eggs, separated
2¾	cups all-purpose flour
1½	teaspoons baking powder
½	teaspoon salt
1	cup butter, softened
2	cups sugar
2	teaspoons vanilla extract
1	cup milk

Lightly grease and dust with flour two 9-inch round cake pans, or one 13- by 9- by 2-inch pan. Preheat the oven to 350°. Using an electric mixer, beat the egg whites until stiff, but not too dry, and set aside. Sift the flour along with the baking powder and salt.

In a large bowl, cream the butter, gradually pouring in the sugar, beating until the mixture is fluffy. Beat in the egg yolks, one at a time. Add the vanilla extract and continue to beat.

Using a spatula or wooden spoon, add the flour mixture to the butter mixture in three additions, alternating with the milk. Fold the egg whites gently and thoroughly into the batter.

Pour the batter into the baking pan(s), spreading it out with a spatula. Bake the rounds for 35 to 40 minutes and the rectangle for 40 to 50 minutes, or until a toothpick inserted in the middle comes out clean. Cool in the pan for 5 minutes before inverting onto a wire rack to cool completely. Serves 10.

Hopscotch Cake:

Follow the Better-Than-Basic directions for a 13- by 9- by 2-inch cake. Once cooled, cut the cake into eight equal rectangular pieces. Arrange the pieces on a board or serving tray in the classic hopscotch pattern (see diagram at right). Use about 2 cups of frosting to ice the cake. Decorate each rectangle with snipped licorice strings, shredded coconut, colored crystal sugars, or rainbow sprinkles. Make numbers with candies, raisins, peanuts, or pieces of fruit leather. Then let your kids take turns standing a short way from the cake and tossing a piece of candy or cereal onto it. The "tosser" gets to eat the slice of cake on which his marker lands.

Hopscotch Cake

How To Grease Cake Pans

☞ For an easy flip out of the pan, grease your cake pans (bottom and sides) with shortening — not butter — and then dust with flour.

Can I Have Dessert?

199

Carrot Cake

"Cake made of *carrots*?" your five-year-old may ask. Don't worry — the moist, sweet results will soothe his fears. He'll never know it's healthier (at least a little) than your standard white or chocolate cake. Frost with Cream Cheese Icing (see page 198).

2	cups grated carrot
	Juice of 1 lemon
½	teaspoon lemon zest
½	cup raisins
½	cup chopped walnuts
2	cups packed light brown sugar
3	eggs, lightly beaten
1	teaspoon vanilla extract
½	cup buttermilk
½	cup vegetable oil
¼	cup honey
2	cups all-purpose flour (or 1 cup each of white and whole wheat)
1	teaspoon cinnamon
1	teaspoon baking soda
½	teaspoon salt
½	teaspoon baking powder

Preheat the oven to 350°. Grease and lightly flour two 8-inch round cake pans. Sprinkle the carrots with the lemon juice and stir in the zest; add the raisins and walnuts and set aside.

In an electric mixer or food processor, cream the sugar, eggs, vanilla extract, buttermilk, oil, and honey. Sift together the remaining dry ingredients and gradually add them to the creamed mixture, stirring just until smooth. Stir the carrot mixture evenly into the batter and pour into prepared pans.

Bake for 35 minutes, or until the top feels firm to the touch. Wait for the rounds to cool before removing them from the pans. Serves 8 to 10.

Dino Carrot Cake:

The itinerary for a great dinosaur birthday party? Make this purple dinosaur cake, hold a cavekids costume contest, and play pin the horn on the triceratops. Before frosting the cooled carrot cake rounds with Cream Cheese Icing (see page 198), cut both into dinosaurs (see diagram at left). Use candy corn for the dinosaur's ridged back and sharp teeth, sliced marshmallows for spots, gumdrops for toes, and Life Savers for an eye. Makes a pair of dinosaurs or a two-layer dino cake.

Dino Carrot Cake

200

Cheesecake

As a child, my brother requested cheesecake every birthday, which I thought was strange until I, too, acquired a taste for the deliciously creamy cake. It is surprisingly simple to make; for easy cutting, make it a day ahead and slice it with a sharp, wet knife.

Crust:

⅔	cup all-purpose flour
2	tablespoons sugar
5	tablespoons unsalted butter, cold
½	teaspoon lemon or orange zest
2	egg yolks
½	teaspoon vanilla extract
1	tablespoon heavy cream

Filling:

3	8-ounce packages cream cheese, softened
1	cup sugar
2	tablespoons all-purpose flour
2	teaspoons lemon or orange zest
¼	teaspoon vanilla extract
3	eggs
1	egg yolk
3	tablespoons heavy cream

Preheat the oven to 350°. In a food processor or electric mixer, blend the flour, sugar, and butter until the mixture resembles a coarse meal. Add the zest, egg yolks, vanilla extract, and heavy cream and blend until the dough combines. Press the mixture into the bottom of an 8-inch springform pan. Bake for 20 minutes, or until lightly toasted.

For the filling, whip the cream cheese in the food processor or mixer until fluffy. Add the sugar, flour, zest, vanilla extract, eggs, egg yolk, and heavy cream. Blend thoroughly. Wrap the bottom and outsides of the pan tightly with tinfoil and pour the filling over the baked crust. Set the pan in a larger baking dish, fill with water to just below the top of the foil. Bake for

Cheesecake with Blueberry Sauce

10 minutes at 400°, then lower the heat to 250° and continue baking for 1 hour, or until the center is set. Cool completely before serving. Serves 8 to 10.

Blueberry Sauce:

When the cheesecake is cool, drizzle each slice with a spoonful of this sauce. Bring 1 cup blueberries, ¼ cup sugar, and 1 tablespoon orange juice just to a boil in a saucepan. Reduce the heat and simmer, covered, for 15 minutes, stirring occasionally. Mash the berries with a fork or puree them in a blender or food processor. Makes 1 cup.

Strawberry Swirl Cheesecake:

Pour the cheesecake into the baked crust. Puree 8 strawberries and dot the liquid over the top of the batter. Using a small rubber spatula, gently swirl the puree into the batter. Proceed with the baking directions.

FunFact
At the turn of the century, Jewish immigrants made cheesecake with a smooth, cream cheese filling, and the "New York" cheesecake was born.

THE PICK OF THE PATCH

Whether you venture to a U-pick strawberry farm or happen upon a tangle of woodland beauties, your family will always remember the sweet taste of a fresh-picked strawberry. For a list of the farms in your area, check the classified ads, your local shoppers' guide, or County Extension Service. Most strawberry farms welcome children, but call ahead to be sure. Ask if the berries are ripe and whether you should bring your own containers.

Giant Strawberry Shortcake

Our plate-size shortcake is meant to impress picnic guests — and to be shared. For individual portions, you can make six conventional-size shortcakes.

1¾	cups all-purpose flour
5	tablespoons sugar
½	teaspoon salt
1	tablespoon baking powder
4	tablespoons butter
¼	cup heavy cream
¼	cup milk
3	pints strawberries, stems removed and sliced
	Whipped cream for topping
	Chocolate chips (optional)

Preheat the oven to 350°. In the bowl of a food processor or an electric mixer, blend the flour, 3 tablespoons of the sugar, salt, baking powder, and butter until the mixture resembles a coarse meal. Add the cream and milk, and mix to form a soft dough.

Turn the dough out onto a lightly floured surface and roll to a ½-inch thickness. Form the dough into one circle 7 inches in diameter or cut out small shortcakes with a 2-inch round cookie cutter. Place the round on an ungreased cookie sheet and bake for 12 to 20 minutes (depending on size), or until the cake springs back. Remove the shortcake from the cookie sheet onto a wire rack.

Place the strawberries in a large bowl and toss with the remaining sugar. Let the berries sit, covered, for at least 2 hours, or until a juicy syrup forms in the bowl.

When you are ready to serve the dessert, slice the shortcake in half and place the bottom half on a plate. Spoon strawberries and some of the syrup over the cake, then top with whipped cream. Place the other half of the shortcake on top of the whipped cream, followed by another layer of whipped cream, additional berries, and chocolate chips. Serves 6.

Giant Strawberry Shortcake

Pies

My First Apple Pie

Every kid deserves the chance to make an apple pie — and a child can easily learn with a little help from a patient adult.

1	unbaked double pie crust (see page 205)
5	cups apple slices
½	cup sugar
1	tablespoon all-purpose flour
2	teaspoons apple pie spice (or ¼ teaspoon each nutmeg and allspice and ½ teaspoon cinnamon)
	Juice of half a lemon
2	tablespoons butter

Preheat the oven to 400°. Roll out half the pie crust dough and line an 8-inch pie plate. Trim the edges allowing a slight overhang. Place the apple slices in a large bowl. Add the sugar, flour, apple pie spice, and lemon juice and toss until well combined. Spoon the mixture into the unbaked pie crust and dot with the butter.

Roll out the remaining pie dough into a ⅛-inch thickness. Fold the top crust in half, set it over the fruit, and unfold. Crimp the edges with your fingers or press the tines of a fork around the edges to seal. Cut slits in the crust in a decorative pattern. Bake the pie for 40 minutes, or until bubbly and golden brown. Serves 6.

Apple Crumb Pie:

Skip the top crust and add this crowning touch. In a medium bowl, mix ⅔ cup all-purpose flour, ½ cup sugar, ½ teaspoon cinnamon, and ½ teaspoon salt. With a pastry cutter or your fingers, blend in 5 tablespoons butter

My First Apple Pie

until the texture resembles a coarse meal. Sprinkle over the apples and bake for 40 minutes. If the topping browns too quickly, lightly cover it with tinfoil.

Cranberry-Apple Pie:

In a saucepan, cook 1½ cups chopped cranberries with 1 cup sugar, ½ teaspoon lemon zest, 2 tablespoons tapioca, and ⅓ cup cranberry juice until slightly thickened. Mix with the apples and continue with the directions.

Raisin & Nut Apple Pie:

Mix the apples with ½ cup raisins and ½ cup chopped walnuts before baking.

Pie Shortcuts

Use a ready-made pie crust or frozen unbaked crusts instead of home-made.

Roll out and freeze your own pie crusts in your pie plates for 1 to 2 weeks.

Cut the apples a day ahead and mix them with lemon juice to prevent browning.

Strawberry-Rhubarb Pie

Strawberry-Rhubarb Pie

You can make the most of delectable strawberries and rhubarb by baking them in a pie. The bright red color, not to mention the taste, pleases any crowd.

1 unbaked double pie crust (see page 205)
4 cups sliced strawberries
2 cups ½-inch pieces rhubarb
¾ cup sugar
¼ cup all-purpose flour
1 teaspoon orange zest
1 tablespoon butter
1 egg, beaten

Preheat the oven to 400°. In a large bowl, mix the strawberries and rhubarb with the sugar, flour, and orange zest. Roll out half of the pie crust dough into a ⅛-inch thickness and line the bottom of 9-inch pie pan. Add the filling and dot with the butter.

Roll out the remaining pie dough and use a pastry wheel or knife to slice it into ¾-inch-wide strips. Weave the strips over the filling and crimp the edges. Brush the crust with the beaten egg. Bake for 45 minutes, or until the

Frozen Berries

In most recipes, dry-packed frozen berries can be substituted for fresh: Just lightly toss them in flour before adding to your batter. To freeze fresh strawberries and blueberries, wash them, then let them dry on paper towels. Spread the berries on a cookie sheet and place them in the freezer (this keeps them from sticking together). Once frozen, put them in plastic containers with tight lids or place them in sealable plastic bags. Blueberries will last as long as two years in the freezer — and they make an excellent cold, quick snack.

filling bubbles and the crust turns golden brown. If the crust browns too quickly, cover it with foil. Serves 6 to 8.

Blueberry Lattice Pie

Sweet, plump, and fresh off the bush, blueberries require no peeling, pitting, or slicing before they are added to pie. During the off-season, use frozen berries (see at left) instead.

1 unbaked double pie crust (see page 205)
5 cups blueberries, washed and stems removed
⅔ cup sugar
¼ cup all-purpose flour
1 tablespoon lemon juice
1 teaspoon lemon zest
   Pinch of salt
2 tablespoons butter
1 egg, beaten

In a large bowl, mix the blueberries with the sugar, flour, lemon juice, zest, and salt. Let the filling sit for at least a ½ hour.

Preheat the oven to 425°. Roll out half of the pie crust dough into a ⅛-inch thickness and line the bottom of a 9-inch pie pan. Snip the edges evenly, allowing a slight overhang. Fill the pie shell with the blueberry mixture and dot with the butter.

Roll out the remaining pie dough and use a pastry wheel or knife to slice it into ¾-inch-wide strips. Weave the strips over the filling and crimp the edges. Brush the crust with the beaten egg. Bake for 35 minutes, or until the filling bubbles and the crust turns golden brown. If the crust browns too quickly, cover it with foil. Serves 6 to 8.

Pie Crusts

Create a lattice crust with a pastry wheel or knife. Cut rolled dough into ½-inch-wide strips and weave over pie filling.

Processor Pie Crust

With good reflexes, you can use a food processor to make pie dough. The trick here is to press the pulse button for mere seconds.

- 3 cups all-purpose flour
- 2 tablespoons sugar
- ¼ teaspoon salt
- 1½ cups cold, unsweetened butter, cut into chunks
- 4 tablespoons ice water or fruit juice

Place the flour, sugar, and salt in the bowl of a food processor and process for 5 seconds. Scatter the butter pieces over the flour, then pulse until the mixture resembles a coarse meal. Sprinkle with the water and process until the dough starts to come together (but not until it forms a ball). Carefully take out the blade, and press the mixture together to pick up all the bits of dough. Divide the dough in half, flatten into disks, wrap in plastic wrap, and refrigerate for at least 30 minutes before rolling and baking. Makes enough for 2 single crusts, or 1 double crust.

Cream Cheese Crust

A batch of this no-fail pie crust goes a long way. Use any leftover dough for pie ornaments (see page 208).

- 4 cups all-purpose flour
- 1½ cups cold, unsalted butter, cut into bits
- 1 8-ounce package cream cheese, cut into bits

In a large bowl, mix all the ingredients with your fingers or a pastry cutter until it forms a ball. Divide the ball in half and flatten each half into a disk, wrap, and refrigerate for at least 30 minutes. When you're ready to bake, roll out the dough on a lightly floured surface or between sheets of waxed paper, working the dough from the center outward until you have a circle large enough to line your pie pan. Makes 2 single crusts, or 1 double crust.

Chocolate Cookie Crumb Crust

Finally, a job the kids will love to do — smash cookies with a rolling pin.

- 1½ cups crumbs from plain chocolate cookies (use a processor or rolling pin)
- 2 tablespoons confectioners' sugar
- 6 tablespoons unsalted butter, melted

Mix the cookie crumbs, sugar, and butter in a bowl until thoroughly combined. Distribute the mixture evenly around a pie pan. Press it against the pan, the bottom first and then the sides. Bake at 350° for 10 minutes and cool before filling. Makes 1 single crust.

Graham Cracker Crust:

Use graham cracker crumbs instead of the chocolate cookie crumbs.

Gingersnap Crust:

Substitute crushed gingersnaps for the chocolate cookie crumbs.

One quick way to decorate your crust edge is to press the tines of a fork around the edge.

Crimp your crust by pinching the thumb and index finger of your right hand against your left index finger.

Banana Cream Pie

Your family has no doubt figured out that the banana is great when topping cereal or smeared with peanut butter. Now see what they think when it's layered with creamy pudding in a pie. To save time, use instant vanilla pudding.

    1   baked Graham Cracker Crust
        (see page 205)
Filling:
    1   cup sugar
    ⅓   cup cornstarch
    3   cups milk
    2   eggs, beaten
    1   teaspoon vanilla extract
    3   tablespoons unsalted butter
    2   large ripe bananas
        Whipped cream
        Dried banana chips (optional)

Prepare the Graham Cracker Crust in a 10-inch pie pan. To make the filling, blend the sugar, cornstarch, milk, and eggs in a large saucepan. Stirring constantly over medium-high heat, bring the mixture to a boil for about 15 minutes. Continue stirring until the filling is thick and coats the back of a wooden spoon. Remove from the heat and stir in the vanilla extract and butter. Cover the pudding with plastic wrap so that a skin doesn't form and let the mixture cool for 30 minutes.

Restir and pour half of the pudding into the baked pie crust. Swirl the pie plate so the sides of the crusts are coated with the cream. Slice the bananas evenly over the cream. Pour the remaining pudding over the bananas, then refrigerate until ready to serve. Spread whipped cream over the pie and garnish with banana chips, if desired. Serves 8 to 10.

Banana Trivia

According to an old wives' tale, the inside of a banana peel makes a great shoeshine for patent leather shoes. (We haven't tested this, so you're on your own with this one!)

The earliest dessert recipe ever written was a banana recipe — a mushy mixture of bananas, almonds, and honey.

If your kids have a tough time falling asleep, give them a banana. Like a cup of warm milk, a banana is a sleep enhancer.

The average American eats 26 pounds of bananas a year, making it our most consumed fruit.

There are more than 200 varieties of bananas in the world.

The biggest banana split ever made was 4.55 miles long!

Bananas are botanically classified as a berry.

Chocolate Cream Pie with Oreo Crust

Each year, Americans consume more than 10.5 pounds of chocolate per person in the form of candy, ice cream, cakes, and brownies. You can get your fill with this pie, but be sure to cut small slices — the chocolate flavor is intense.

Crust:
- 1½ cups finely crushed Oreo cookies (crush 15 in a food processor or blender)
- 3 tablespoons butter, melted

Filling:
- 1 cup sugar
- ⅓ cup cornstarch
- ⅛ teaspoon salt
- 4 large egg yolks, lightly beaten
- 3½ cups milk
- 1½ teaspoons vanilla extract
- 6 ounces bittersweet chocolate, finely chopped
- 2 ounces unsweetened chocolate, finely chopped

To make the crust, generously butter a 9-inch glass pie plate. In a large bowl, stir the cookie crumbs and the melted butter. Using your fingertips, firmly and evenly press the mixture into the bottom and sides of the pie plate.

In a large saucepan, combine the sugar, cornstarch, and salt. Whisk in the egg yolks until combined. Gradually mix in the milk. Whisking constantly, cook over medium heat for about 10 minutes, or until the mixture thickens and comes to a boil. Remove the pan from the heat and mix in the vanilla extract and chocolates, whisking until smooth. Immediately pour the mixture through a medium-fine strainer

into the prepared pie crust. Cover the surface of the pie with a piece of plastic wrap to prevent a skin from forming. Cool at room temperature, then refrigerate for several hours or overnight.

Mud Pie

When your kids tire of making real mud pies, serve them slices of edible mud. *FamilyFun* contributor Cynthia Caldwell suggests using Haagen-Dazs ice cream.

- 1 baked Chocolate Cookie Crumb Crust (see page 205)
- 6 cups or 3 pints chocolate ice cream, softened
- 1 cup ready-made fudge topping
- 4 cups whipped cream
- ¾ cup crushed chocolate cookies or chocolate graham crackers

Fill your baked, cooled pie shell halfway with half of the chocolate ice cream and freeze for 30 minutes. Spread the fudge topping over the ice cream and freeze for another 15 minutes. Top with the remaining ice cream, the whipped cream, and cookie crumbs. Then freeze for at least 3 hours. Serves 8 to 10.

Pudding Parfaits

For individual pudding parfaits, spoon alternating layers of Chocolate Cream Pie filling (see at left) and crushed Oreo cookies into stemmed glasses. Top with whipped cream and crushed cookies.

Mud Pie

Pie Ornaments

For a decorative top crust, use cookie cutters or a knife to cut leftover dough into leaves, stars, bows, or other festive shapes. Glaze the uncooked top crust with eggwash (see page 118), add the shapes, then bake (if the crust browns too quickly, cover with tinfoil).

Real Pumpkin Pie

For years, I made my pumpkin pies from canned pureed pumpkin, and they always tasted fine. But one year, I grew more pumpkins than I needed for jack-o'-lanterns and was determined to turn one into pie. I enlisted the help of an eleven-year-old friend, and making pie became a rewarding afternoon project. Now we always make our pies from real pumpkins.

1   unbaked single pie crust (see page 205)
1   small pumpkin
3   eggs
½   cup sugar
¼   cup brown sugar
2   teaspoons cinnamon
1   teaspoon ginger
½   teaspoon cloves
½   teaspoon salt
1   12-ounce can of evaporated milk

Roll out the pie dough and line a 9- or 10-inch pie pan. Cut the pumpkin in half, remove the seeds, and place the halves face down on a greased cookie sheet. Bake at 350° for 40 minutes, or until tender. Cool, then scoop out the meat, and mash or puree it.

Beat the eggs and sugars. Blend in 2 cups of the puree and the rest of the ingredients. Pour into the pie crust. Bake at 450° for 10 minutes, then reduce to 350°. Bake for another

50 minutes, or until the pie sets. Cool, then slice. Serves 6 to 8.

Pecan Pie

When approaching any holiday dinner, *FamilyFun* contributor Becky Okrent has been known to mutter "Save room for pie!" She prefers to make this rich dessert in a 12-inch tart pan with a removable bottom to show it off.

1   unbaked single pie crust (see page 205)
4   eggs, lightly beaten
¾   cup packed dark brown sugar
½   cup dark corn syrup
½   cup maple syrup or 4 tablespoons molasses
6   tablespoons unsalted butter, melted
2   teaspoons vanilla extract
2½   cups coarsely chopped pecans
½   cup pecan halves

Roll out the dough and line a 12-inch tart pan or 10-inch pie pan. In a large mixing bowl, blend the eggs, brown sugar, corn syrup, maple syrup, butter, and vanilla extract. Stir in the chopped nuts, then pour the filling into the tart shell. Sprinkle with the pecan halves. Bake at 325° for 30 minutes, or until the center has set. Serves 10.

Pecan Pie

Candy

The World's Simplest Candy

Candymaking doesn't necessarily involve boiling sugar and using a candy thermometer. These clusters — made of melted chips and nuts or dried fruits — are a cinch.

- 1 cup semisweet or milk chocolate chips
- 1 cup peanuts, walnuts, raisins, or chopped dried fruit

Place the chips in a microwave-safe bowl and microwave on high for 1 to 2 minutes, or until melted, stirring halfway through cooking. Stir in the nuts or fruit (or a combination). Drop by the teaspoonful onto a waxed paper–lined baking sheet and refrigerate until firm. Makes about 15 candies.

Chocolate Lollipops

While you can't make chocolate from scratch (it's a complex blend of more than 500 flavor components), you can make your own candies and lollipops.

Candy molds, chocolate melts, and lollipop sticks for this recipe can be found at department or party stores that sell cake-decorating supplies, or by calling Wilton Enterprises at 800-772-7111 or Sweet Celebrations at 800-328-6722.

> Plastic lollipop molds
> Small bags of chocolate and colored candy melts
> Small, clean paintbrush
> Lollipop sticks

Place the chocolate and colored candy melts into small glass dishes, using a separate dish for each color, and microwave until soft (if you don't have a microwave, place the dishes in a pan of simmering water, making sure that no water gets into the melts). Use a paintbrush to paint the colors into the molds. To keep the colors from running, harden each one in the refrigerator before adding the next.

Set the lollipop sticks into the molds, then spoon more chocolate over them. Smooth the top with a knife and tap the mold to remove bubbles. Refrigerate until hardened. Make as many as you want.

The World's Simplest Candy

Chocolate Lollipops

Caramel Turtles

More S'mores

The first recipe for this messy campfire dessert appeared in the 1940 *Girl Scout Handbook*.

The Classic: Toast 1 marshmallow over hot coals until brown, then sandwich it between 4 squares of chocolate (a 1.5-ounce Hershey's Milk Chocolate bar works best) and 2 graham crackers.

Robinson Crusoes: Spread 1 tablespoon peanut butter on the graham crackers before sandwiching.

Chocolate Dream: Use chocolate graham crackers instead of plain.

Mighty Mints: Sandwich the marshmallow between 2 thin mint patties.

Sophisticates: Use chocolate biscuits or cookies instead of graham crackers.

Caramel Turtles

A sweet-tooth's dream, caramel turtles are easy and fun for a child to make. They do, however, require an adult to move the pans in and out of the oven when melting the caramel onto the nuts. For gifts, *FamilyFun* contributor Susan Purdy individually wraps the turtles in plastic wrap tied with ribbon or stores them in single layers between waxed paper in a decorative tin or box.

1⅓ cups pecan halves
18 squares caramel candies, individually wrapped
½ cup semisweet chocolate chips or chopped chocolate

Preheat the oven to 350°. Slice or break pecan halves lengthwise to make slivers for the head, tail, and four feet. For each turtle, arrange 6 nut pieces in a 6-point star on a foil-lined cookie sheet. Unwrap one caramel square and cut it in half. Set one half on top of the cluster of nut pieces. Without disturbing the arrangement, place the tray of turtles in the oven for about 4 to 5 minutes, watching carefully so the nuts don't burn. The caramels will melt onto the nuts, creating the turtle's shell.

Remove the tray from the oven and set 4 to 5 chocolate chips on top of each caramel. Return to the oven for a few seconds to melt the chocolate. You can spread out the melted chocolate with the back of a spoon if you wish. Remove the foil with the candies on it from the baking sheet and allow the turtles to cool completely. Makes 36 turtles.

Hand-Dipped Candies

One of the microwave oven's specialties is melting chocolate, and you can take advantage of it with this recipe.

1 3- to 4-ounce high-quality chocolate bar (not milk chocolate)
Dried apricots, pretzels, cherries, granola bars, or cookies

Place the chocolate in a microwave-safe bowl and microwave on high for 1 to 2 minutes, or until melted, stirring midway through cooking. Cool slightly and be sure it is not too hot for your kids to work with. Dip the dried apricots or any treat into the chocolate and place them on a cookie sheet covered with waxed paper. To avoid messy hands, dip with skewers or toothpicks. Refrigerate or freeze until hardened. Make as many as you want.

Marzipan Fruits

These confections were brought to Europe from the Near East during the Crusades and for centuries were the dessert of choice for all who could afford them. Marzipan is made from easy-to-shape almond paste that you model and paint with food coloring (no cooking is necessary).

1   cup almond paste
2   cups confectioners' sugar
1   large egg white (or 2 teaspoons Wilton Meringue powder plus 2 tablespoons water)
2   teaspoons almond extract
     Food coloring

Marzipan Fruits

Crumble the almond paste into a large bowl. Sift the confectioners' sugar into the same bowl and add the egg white and almond extract. Mix the dough until it forms a ball, sifting in more sugar if the dough is sticky.

Turn the dough out on a surface sprinkled with confectioners' sugar and knead until smooth and satiny. Break off small lumps of dough and mold them like clay, shaping them into balls to form a cluster of grapes, pears, oranges, lemons, strawberries, apples, and peaches. For finer details, use toothpicks. Set on waxed paper to dry.

After the marzipan has dried, mix a drop of food coloring with water (the less water you use, the more intense the color) and use a clean paintbrush to delicately paint the fruits.

To make the stem for a strawberry, dip the end of a toothpick into green food coloring, then poke it into the fruit. For a pear's stem, press a whole clove, stem end up, into the fruit. Cut tiny leaves from green construction paper and pierce them with toothpick stems to fasten to the fruits. Dry for 4 hours, or overnight, then store in an airtight container. Makes about 40.

Rock Candy

As this sugar water evaporates, it forms a sweet, hard crystal candy on a string.

1½   cups water
6   cups sugar
     Food coloring
3   6-inch lengths of string

Bring the water to a boil in a saucepan. Remove from the heat and add 3 cups of the sugar, stirring until it dissolves. Slowly add the remaining sugar, reheating the water if necessary. When all the sugar has dissolved, pour into three heatproof jars or glasses. Stir 3 drops of food coloring into each jar. Tie each length of string around the middle of a pencil. Lay atop the jars so the strings hang down into the liquid. Crystals will begin to form in 1 hour and continue to solidify for several days. If a layer forms on the surface of the water, break it. When the water evaporates, the candy is ready to eat. Makes 3.

Gumdrop Tetrahedron

Did you know the triangle is stronger than the square? Let your kids prove it with gumdrops and toothpicks. Form a triangle with 3 toothpicks for sides and 3 gumdrops, firmly speared, for corners. Add 2 more toothpicks and 1 more gumdrop to form adjoining triangles. Once they get the hang of it, challenge them to build a structure that's strong enough to hold a pile of books.

Can I Have Dessert?

At Home Sundae Bar

Sundae Makers

A sundae bar is a dessert that creates its own party. Its an all-or-nothing affair, so don't hold back. Lay out the messiest, most delightful elements and go at it whole hog, so to speak.

Sweet Sauces

☛ **Hot Fudge in a Flash:** Bring ⅔ cup heavy cream to a boil in a saucepan. Add 1 cup semisweet chocolate chips and let stand 1 minute. Whisk until the chips melt. Stir in ½ teaspoon vanilla extract. Makes 1 cup.

☛ **Gooey Caramel Sauce:** In a double boiler, melt 12 ounces of caramel candies in 1 cup evaporated milk; stir until smooth. Makes 2 cups.

☛ **Minty Fudge Sauce:** Heat ½ cup milk and ¼ cup butter in a double boiler until the butter melts. Stir in 12 ounces semisweet chocolate chips and ¼ teaspoon peppermint extract, whisking until smooth. Makes 2 cups.

Frozen Bases

Ice cream
Frozen yogurt
Sherbet

Diced fruit in your favorite juice
Fruit puree
Melted peanut butter
Blueberry sauce

Sundae Sauces

Hot fudge sauce (see recipe at left or store-bought)
Minty Fudge Sauce (see recipe at left)
Gooey Caramel Sauce (see recipe at left)
Coffee syrup
Chocolate syrup
Maple syrup
Melted candy bars, such as Mars Bars or Milky Way Bars
Melted jam or jelly

Add-ons & Smoosh-ins:

M&M's
Crumbled brownies
Chocolate chip cookie dough
Broken or mini cookies, graham crackers, vanilla wafers, or animal crackers
Chocolate, butter-scotch, mint, or peanut butter chips
Crushed candy bars

Crushed pretzels
Fresh berries, sliced banana, or pine-apple
Cereals
Wheat germ
Mini marshmallows

Garnishes

Whipped cream
Chocolate-dipped spoons and cones (see recipe at right)
Shredded coconut
Grated chocolate
Malted milk powder
Fresh mint leaves
Cherries
Chopped nuts
Chopped dried fruit

The Brownie Trooper:

Top a Chocolate-Lover's Brownie (see page 194) with chocolate chip ice cream, Minty Fudge Sauce, whipped cream, mixed nuts, and a cherry.

Avalanche:

Gather as many friends as possible. This event is a group effort — and the only way to take complete advantage of a sundae bar. Start with a huge shallow bowl, add one scoop of every ice cream offered, smother with at least three sauces, and cover with as many add-ons as you can fit. Plop on some whipped cream, top with a cherry, then pass out the spoons and dig in.

S'more Sundae:

Cover rocky road ice cream with Hot Fudge in a Flash, mini marshmallows, whipped cream, and Teddy Grahams or graham cracker crumbs.

The Friday, Saturday, Sundae:

In a parfait glass, layer orange, lemon, and raspberry sherbet. Top with Blueberry Sauce (see page 201), shredded coconut, and a paper umbrella.

Mount St. Helens:

A variation on the dusty miller, this sundae tops vanilla ice cream with hot fudge sauce, malted milk powder, whipped cream, and, if you can take the heat, red hots.

Leaning Tower of Oreos:

This sundae honors its Italian namesake — and lends itself to a messy contest. Using chocolate fudge swirl ice cream as cement, stack as many Oreos as you can. Drizzle Minty Fudge Sauce over the top and finish with whipped cream and a homemade Italian flag.

Go Nuts:

Top peanut butter cup ice cream with hot fudge sauce, broken-up peanut butter cups, peanut brittle, and a garnish of whipped cream, grated chocolate, and a cherry.

Chocolate Extras

For a taste of chocolate in every bite (literally), try these simple treats. To make 12 spoons, 12 cones, plus 12 ice-cream cups, melt 12 ounces semisweet chocolate chips in a double boiler, stirring until smooth.

Chocolate Spoons: Dip the head of each spoon into the melted chocolate; quickly remove it, flip it over, and place it cup side down on waxed paper until the chocolate hardens.

Chocolate Cones: Dip the top of each sugar cone into the chocolate to a depth of about 1 inch; quickly remove it and place it on waxed paper until it hardens.

Edible Ice-Cream Cups: Using a spoon or brush, completely coat the insides of 12 foil muffin liners with the melted chocolate. Cover with plastic wrap and refrigerate for 1 hour, or until firm. Carefully peel off the foil. Use leftover chocolate to touch up any missed spots.

Go Nuts

Leaning Tower of Oreos

Avalanche

More Sweet Treats

Apple Crumb

When topped with vanilla ice cream, this autumn dessert is anything but crummy. Substitute 5 cups of any fruit in season — pears, peaches, or berries — for the apples.

- 5 large apples
- 1 cup rolled oats
- ⅔ cup brown sugar
- ½ cup all-purpose flour
- 6 tablespoons butter
- 1 teaspoon cinnamon
- ¼ teaspoon salt
- ¼ teaspoon allspice
- 2 tablespoons apple or orange juice

Preheat the oven to 375°. Lightly butter an 8-inch square baking pan or a casserole of equivalent size, then dust it with flour. Peel, core, and slice the apples and arrange them in the pan. In the bowl of an electric mixer, blend the oats, brown sugar, flour, butter, cinnamon, salt, and allspice on low speed until it forms a coarse meal. Crumble the mixture evenly over the apple slices and sprinkle with the juice. Bake for 35 minutes, or until the topping turns golden brown. Serves 6.

Apple Crumb

Strawberry Mousse

Light and airy, this fruit-based treat can be whipped up in minutes and kept on hand for a summer snack. When garnished with strawberries, whipped cream, and mint leaves, it also makes an elegant dinner-party dessert. If fresh strawberries aren't available, dry-packed frozen berries work well, too.

¼	cup cold water
1	package unflavored gelatin
¼	cup boiling water
2¼	cups strawberries
1	teaspoon lemon zest
⅓	cup sugar
1½	cups heavy cream
4	to 6 mint leaves (optional)

Pour the cold water into a small bowl and sprinkle with the gelatin. Let stand for 2 minutes. Pour the boiling water over the gelatin mixture and whisk until the gelatin is dissolved. Set aside 6 perfect strawberries for the garnish. Wash and remove the stems from the rest of the strawberries. Place the gelatin mixture, strawberries, lemon zest, and sugar into a blender or the bowl of a food processor and puree until smooth. Whip the cream with an electric mixer until it forms soft peaks; set aside a few dollops for garnish. Pour the strawberry mixture over the whipped cream and gently fold the ingredients together. Spoon the mixture into parfait or stemmed glasses, cover, and refrigerate for at least 3 hours. Just before serving, garnish each glass with the reserved whipped cream, strawberries, and the mint leaves. Serves 4 to 6.

Strawberry Mousse in a Chocolate Cup:

Spoon prepared strawberry mousse into Edible Ice-Cream Cups (see page 213) and garnish as directed.

Strawberry Mousse

Blueberry Fool

Don't let the name fool you — this old English pudding is easy and delicious. It's best served either icy cold or semi-frozen.

1	tablespoon butter
2	cups blueberries, washed and stems removed
⅓	cup sugar
1½	cups heavy cream

Melt the butter in a small saucepan over medium heat. Stir in the blueberries and sugar and cook, covered, for 15 minutes. Stir occasionally. Remove from the heat, then mash with a fork or puree in a blender or food processor. Allow the sauce to cool thoroughly.

Whip the cream until soft peaks form, then gently fold in the blueberry sauce. Refrigerate the fool until ready to serve. Scoop it into frosted bowls or stemmed glasses and garnish with additional berries and a dollop of whipped cream. Serves 4.

Blueberry Fool

CHAPTER 10

Home for the Holidays

O_{F ALL} the recipes we run in *FamilyFun* magazine, our holiday ones are treasured the most. Last year, swarms of readers counted down the days before Christmas with a cookie Advent calender; a year before, the Jell-O eyeballs for Halloween were *the* hit with trick-or-treaters; and this year, the Village People place markers showed up on Thanksgiving tables across America. Why are these holiday recipes and ideas so popular?

For most of the year, families' lives are too overscheduled for indulgence. But during the holidays, we take the time to celebrate, to make special meals, and to bake something incredibly, delightfully sweet. We do it because we have vacation time (hopefully) but, more importantly, because our par-

ents did it for us when we were kids.

Just like eating chocolate on Valentine's Day, jelly beans on Easter, and turkey on Thanksgiving, the recipes in this chapter have become rituals with *FamilyFun* readers. We hope your family, too, will try them once, then look forward to them again next year.

Involve your kids in the holiday preparation. Invite your kids to help you cut the holiday cookie dough with cookie cutters or stuff the turkey on Thanksgiving. They will feel a great sense of pride, having contributed to the holiday meal.

Plan ahead. To relieve some of the holiday pressure, prepare cookie dough and pie crusts when you have spare time, then wrap in sealable plastic bags or freezer paper and

Lucky Red Shake: Page 219

or make the Village People place markers, page 231, for your Thanksgiving spread.

dressed up with themed napkins and centerpieces. Sprinkle confetti on a New Year's Day buffet table, set up a red, white, and blue flower arrangement for the Fourth of July on your picnic table,

Look in your grandparents' recipe box. In this chapter, you will find new recipes to add to your holiday repertoire, but be sure to serve your children the traditional foods from your ethnic or religious heritage as well. These foods teach kids about their family history and are a special way to connect one generation to the next.

Celebrate once a month. *FamilyFun* contributor Cynthia Caldwell says it's important to serve a fancy dinner every month or so to celebrate a holiday or birthday (a special event, such as a good report card or winning soccer season, is reason enough, too). Pull out the cloth napkins, china, silverware, and candles, dress up a little, and carve the turkey or roast at the table. Your kids will enjoy the meals and become more comfortable with polite table manners.

Plan Ahead for the Holidays

Make holiday punches (page 219)

Prepare Sugar Cookie dough (page 190) and freeze for up to a week

Roll out pie crusts (page 205), line pie plates with them, and freeze in pie plates for 1 to 2 weeks

freeze. During the holiday rush, just defrost and proceed with the recipes.

Be prepared. Stock up on food coloring (red and green for Christmas, orange and black for Halloween, and so on) to add to cookies, frosting, and drinks. Also, pick up cookie cutters and, if you feel like splurging, baking pans (a heart shape for Valentine's Day, a bunny for Easter, a turkey for Thanksgiving).

Make the dinner table special. Any holiday dinner can be appropriately

New Year's

Lucky Red Shake

New Year's Eve has all the fixings for a true kid's celebration — the chance to toss confetti, sport silly hats, and stay up late. Toast to the new year with frosted mugs of this ruby-red drink, a lucky color according to Chinese legend.

- 1 cup strawberry soda
- 2 strawberries, stemmed and sliced
- 1 scoop strawberry ice cream

Pour the soda into a mug; add the ice cream and the strawberries. Serves 1.

Chocolate Resolution

Raise a glass of foamy chocolate, a parting gift to parents who swear they will diet in the new year. Garnish the shake with a homemade sparkler: Cut fringe out of a piece of tinfoil, twist one end, and stuff it into the tip of a bendy straw.

- 2 scoops chocolate ice cream
- 3 tablespoons chocolate syrup
- ½ cup milk

Mix all the ingredients in a blender until smooth. Serves 1.

Cloud Nine

When your family makes toasts with this heavenly shake, you'll have sweet dreams for the new year. Splash it up with a frozen grape kabob.

- 2 scoops vanilla frozen yogurt
- 1 banana
- ½ cup white grape juice

Mix the ingredients in a blender until smooth. Serves 1.

Celebration Sticks

FamilyFun reader Sarah Rosemarino, age eight, of North Canton, Ohio, dipped pretzels into a bowl of leftover melted chocolate, and her festive treat was born.

- 1 cup chocolate chips
- 12 8-inch pretzel rods
  Colored sprinkles

Melt the chocolate in the top of a double boiler. Dunk the pretzels halfway into the chocolate, then roll in a bowl of sprinkles. Dry on waxed paper. Makes 12.

Ring in the New Year

Whether you want to celebrate the new year with a family party or a sleep-over bash for your kids, here are some ideas to start the year right:

☛ **Clockface Cake:** Frost a round cake with white icing and use decorating gel to draw clock hands striking midnight.

☛ **Resolution Letters:** Write letters to yourselves, seal them in envelopes, and promise not to open them until the next New Year's Eve.

☛ **Fresh New Year:** Open all your doors and windows (for just a minute if it's cold out) and let the new year breeze into your home.

☛ **Good Luck:** Serve Hoppin' John or black-eyed peas, a traditional New Year's good luck charm in the South.

Valentine's Day

CAKE-DECORATING TIPS

Fancy frosting designs are easy to create using a pastry bag and decorating tips. You can buy starter kits at grocery, kitchen supply, and party stores. The most versatile tips are the writing, star, and leaf ones. Before decorating your cake, kids should practice on waxed paper. Use the writing tip's plain line for letters, stems, squiggles, dots, and outlines. Make stars with the star tip by holding the tip straight down near the cake and squeezing until the star forms. For a neat finish, stop the pressure before pulling away. The leaf tip makes a ribbon with a ridge down the center. Squeeze out the icing to form the bottom edge, then relax the pressure and pull the tip away to make a rippling leaf.

Saint Valentine's Sweetheart Cake

Legend has it that ever since Saint Valentine drew a picture of a heart and wrote inside it "From your Valentine" back in 270 A.D., hearts have been a symbol of love. If this saint was still around, his message would be even sweeter written on a heart-shaped cake. In his honor, hand some cake-decorating supplies over to your kids and help them write sweet messages in icing. Here's to love, cakes, and all that good stuff.

> 1 unbaked cake (see recipes on pages 196 to 199) or cake mix
>
> 3 cups All-Purpose Buttercream (see page 198)

Pour the cake batter into a heart-shaped cake pan (available at kitchen supply stores), or into an 8-inch round pan plus an 8-inch-square pan. Bake according to directions; cool completely. If you used the second cake pan option, cut the round cake in half. On a serving platter, set each semicircle against adjoining sides of the square to form the top of the heart. Frost with the icing, reserving a portion for decorating. Divide the leftover icing into bowls and tint each one a color, then decorate the cake. Serves 10 to 12.

Saint Valentine's Sweetheart Cakes

220

Chocolate Valentines

Which do kids love more: Giving surprises or getting them? I'm not sure, but I do know they'll have fun making these sweet pops — whether they gobble them up or give them away.

1   3- to 4-ounce high-quality dark or white chocolate bar
Lollipop or Popsicle sticks
Shredded coconut, chopped nuts, or sprinkles (optional)

Place the chocolate in a sturdy sealable plastic bag. Microwave 1 minute on high until just barely melted, or melt the bag of chocolate in simmering water (with white chocolate, use only the water method).

Cover a cookie sheet with waxed paper and lay down a lollipop or Popsicle stick. Snip a small hole in a corner of the plastic bag. With the slightly cooled chocolate, draw a heart shape around the top part of the stick and then fill it in. If your kids have trouble making the heart shape, just have them form a circle. Make more lollipops until the chocolate is used up. You can decorate the still-warm lollipops with shredded coconut, nuts, or sprinkles. Place the cookie sheet in the refrigerator or freezer to harden. Wrap the cooled pops in plastic and tie a red bow around the sticks. Makes 3 to 4.

Edible Valentine's Day Cards:

Children can paint messages on these chocolate "cards" with a colorful icing. As described above, melt white chocolate (so the messages will show up more clearly). On a cookie sheet covered with waxed paper, squeeze the chocolate into a 3- by 5-inch rectangle or a large heart. Smooth the surface with a knife dipped in warm water and refrigerate or freeze until hardened. Meanwhile, whisk 1 egg white and 1½ cups sifted confectioners' sugar to make the "paint." Divide into bowls and add food coloring to each bowl to make red, purple, green, blue, or any other colors. When the chocolate has hardened, flip it over and use a small clean paintbrush to write messages or draw simple pictures on the chocolate card.

Heart Cookie Pops

Heart Cookie Pops

Once frosted and decorated, these big conversation heart cookies on sticks say "I love you" with more gusto than those tiny candy conversation hearts. If your time is tight, use store-bought cookie dough instead of homemade.

Sugar Cookie dough (see recipe on page 190)
Popsicle sticks, soaked in water

When the cookie dough has thoroughly chilled, preheat the oven to 350°. On a lightly floured board, roll out the dough until it is about ⅛ inch thick. With a cookie cutter, cut out heart shapes. Place one heart on a greased cookie sheet. Lay a Popsicle stick in the center of the heart and place another heart directly on top of the first. Pinch the sides together so that the two pieces become one. Bake for 10 to 12 minutes, or until the edges are slightly browned. When the cookies are cool, let the kids decorate them with icing, cinnamon hearts, sprinkles, or messages. Makes about 24 cookie pops, depending on their size.

Love Potion #1

Recipes for romance are a part of nearly every culture. This easy-to-concoct brew is light on romantic witchcraft and heavy on red color and tart taste. Blend on high ½ cup each of slightly thawed frozen strawberries and raspberries, and 1 cup white grape juice (or apple juice). Blend until the color is uniform. To make the potion thicker, add more fruit; to thin it out, add more juice. Garnish with cherries and sip, sigh, and swoon... Serves 2.

Easter

Braided Easter Bread

1½ teaspoons salt
6 soft-boiled, dyed eggs (nontoxic dyes only, see at left)
Egg wash (see page 118)

In a large mixing bowl, dissolve the yeast in the water. Meanwhile, melt the butter in a saucepan, turn off the heat, and add the milk. Pour the mixture into the bowl with the yeast. Add the sugar and eggs and stir well. Mix in 1 cup of the flour and then the salt. Continue mixing in the flour, 1 cup at a time, until a soft dough has formed. Turn the dough onto a floured surface, adding flour if the dough is too sticky to handle. Knead until it becomes elastic. Place in a lightly oiled bowl, cover, and set in a warm, draft-free area until doubled in size (about 1 hour).

Punch down the dough. Divide it into three equal parts and roll each piece into a 25-inch-long strand. Lay the strands side by side and loosely braid them (to avoid tearing the dough, braid from the middle out to each end). Place the braid in a wreath shape on a greased cookie sheet; tuck the ends under. Sink the eggs into the dough, between braided strands. Cover and let rise until double in size, about 30 minutes. Brush the egg wash over the dough. Bake in a preheated 350° oven for 25 minutes, or until golden brown. Serves 6 to 8.

Bunny Cake

Every Easter when I was a kid, my sister and I made this rabbit-face cake and decorated it with licorice whiskers and coconut fur.

1 unbaked cake (see recipes on pages 196 to 199) or cake mix
3 cups All-Purpose Buttercream (see page 198) or white frosting
Pink crystal sugars
1 cup shredded coconut

Homemade Egg Dye

To mix up a batch of nontoxic dye for dipping white eggs, place ½ cup hot tap water, 2 teaspoons vinegar, and 6 drops food coloring into a small bowl and stir well. Your kids can mix together a few different food colors to produce purple, turquoise, or other hues.

Braided Easter Bread

Wake your family on Easter morning to a basket from the Easter Bunny and a delicious breakfast bread from you. If the braided loaf is a hit this year, turn it into an annual tradition.

2 tablespoons active dry yeast
½ cup warm water
½ cup butter
¾ cup milk
½ cup sugar
2 eggs, lightly beaten
5 to 6 cups all-purpose flour

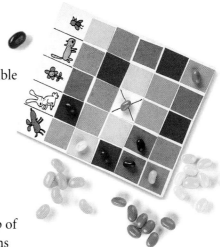

Bunny Cake

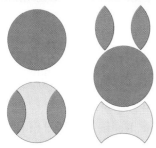

Jelly beans, gumdrops, and black
licorice
Decorating gel

Bake the cake in two 8-inch round cake pans. Cool thoroughly. Lay one round on a platter or cookie sheet covered with tinfoil. Cut the other round into three pieces (see diagram), positioning the two petal shapes above the face for the bunny's ears, and placing the remaining cake below the face for the bunny's bow tie.

Frost with the icing, then sprinkle a line of pink crystal sugars down the center of each ear. Cover the face and ears with the shredded coconut. Place 2 jelly beans for the eyes, a black gumdrop for a nose, a red gumdrop for a tongue, and black licorice for the lips and eyebrows. To decorate the bow tie,

squirt on the decorating gel to resemble polka dots. Serves 10 to 12.

Edible Easter Baskets

This Easter, don't put all your jelly beans in one basket. Put them on top of cupcakes and make edible decorations for the dinner table.

>   12   cupcakes
>   1½   cups All-Purpose Buttercream (see
>   page 198) or white frosting
>   12   pipe cleaners
>   1   cup shredded coconut
>   Green food coloring
>   Jelly beans

Frost the cupcakes with the icing. Bend a pipe cleaner into an arch and push the ends into the sides of each cupcake. Make green coconut grass by adding a few drops of the food coloring to the coconut. Then, rest jelly bean eggs on top of the grass. Tie a ribbon bow on the pipe cleaner handle at a jaunty angle. Put one cupcake basket by each place setting or give them as gifts. Serves 12.

Edible Easter Baskets

Jelly Bean Bingo

Playing bingo has never been this sweet. Across the top row of each bingo card, affix the same sequence of stickers, then randomly color the remaining squares with jelly bean–colored markers. To play, the caller draws 1 sticker and 1 jelly bean and announces them. If a frog sticker and a pink jelly bean are chosen, a player with a pink square in the frog column can cover it with a pink jelly bean. The first to complete a line horizontally, vertically, or diagonally wins all his jelly beans.

Mother's & Father's Day

A Hat for Mother

Mom deserves royal treatment on Mother's Day, so here's a cake her littlest fans can make with help from Dad or a big sibling.

1	18-ounce package yellow cake mix
4	eggs
¾	cup vegetable oil
¾	cup apricot nectar
3	teaspoons almond extract
1	recipe Lemon Icing (see below)
	Gumdrops

A Hat for Mother

Preheat the oven to 325° and grease and lightly flour two pans: a rimmed, 12-inch round pizza or cake pan and a 1½-quart metal or ovenproof baking bowl. Combine all the ingredients except the icing, then beat in an electric mixer at medium speed for 4 minutes. Divide the batter between the pan and bowl; bake the pan for 20 to 25 minutes and the bowl for 45 to 50 (both are ready when a toothpick inserted in the center comes out clean). Let the cakes rest for 5 minutes before removing from the pans. Cool completely.

Center the bowl-shaped cake over the flat one. Ice the cake and finish with a hat ribbon and gumdrop "flowers" (see at left). Serves 10 to 12.

Lemon Icing

This buttercream frosting is flavored with lemon, but raspberry, mint, and vanilla are just as delicious.

½	cup unsalted butter
4	cups confectioners' sugar
2	teaspoons lemon extract, or zest and juice of 1 lemon
	Pinch of salt
4 to 6	tablespoons heavy cream

Cream the butter, then gradually beat in 1 cup of the sugar. Mix in the lemon extract and salt. Add the remaining sugar and just enough cream to create a spreadable icing. Makes 3 cups.

A Shirt for Dad

FamilyFun contributor Phyllis Fiorotta says you don't have to be a baker or tailor to create this shirt cake for Father's Day.

Cardboard shirt box, at least 9 by 13 inches
1   unbaked cake (see recipes on pages 196 to 199) or cake mix
3   cups All-Purpose Buttercream (see page 198) or white frosting
Food coloring

Line the shirt box with tissue paper. Prepare the cake batter according to directions. Bake in a 9- by 13-inch cake pan, remove from the pan, cool, and place on waxed paper. Cover with a larger piece of waxed paper and flip the cake over and into the box (the cake bottom should face up).

Reserving a small portion for the tie, tint the frosting a pastel color with a couple drops of food coloring. Frost the cake with the pastel icing. Tint the reserved icing a bright color and spread it into a tie shape on the cake. Cut a collar and two cuffs out of white paper. The collar is a strip, rolled into a ring and taped, with a small V cut out of the center. The cuffs are rectangles with candy cuff links. Just before serving, trim away the waxed paper and add the collar and cuffs. Serves 10 to 12.

A Shirt for Dad

Queen for a Day

On Mother's Day, make Mom feel like a queen by laying down the red carpet and giving her the royal treatment.
A Royal Brunch: Insist that Her Highness sleep late. Meanwhile, the king and his court jesters can *quietly* create a festive brunch including Pineapple Boats (see page 175), Royal Ham 'n' Eggs (see page 20), and Monkey Bread (see page 123).
The Palace Dining Room: Prepare a throne by padding a table chair with a pillow. Decorate the table with fresh flowers, cloth napkins, and full table settings (two sizes of forks and spoons). Add colorful construction paper place mats.

King for a Day

On Father's Day, there's nothing grander for Dad than being treated like a king.
A Royal Barbecue: Let Dad lounge the afternoon away in his favorite outdoor chair while Mom and the kids prepare a regal feast of shish kabob (see page 138), Cheese Wedge Biscuits (see page 112), and Roasted Corn on the Cob (see page 168).
Graffiti Tablecloth: To humor the king, his court jesters can cover the picnic table with a white paper tablecloth personalized with messages to Dad.
Gold Coins: Offer Dad the riches of his kingdom with homemade coins. Cut circles from yellow construction paper and draw a self-portrait on each coin. Then add a value: A chore that the king can redeem whenever he cashes the coin in.

Fourth of July

Fourth of July Picnic

Fourth of July Picnic
★ ★ ★ ★

On July 4th, feasts have always been the order of the day. This year, feed a crowd of friends with a potluck. Divide the guest list into groups, assigning salads to one, desserts to another, and beverages to the third. Each family can bring its own chicken to grill.

Barbecued Chicken

Potato Salad Vinaigrette (page 184)

Roasted Corn on the Cob (page 168)

Giant Strawberry Shortcake (page 202)

Barbecued Chicken

In summer, the language of barbecue is spoken everywhere. There's something about cooking and eating outdoors that seems to make food taste even better. Here's an easy-to-spread sauce to keep grillside for those who want a little tang with their chicken.

- 1 yellow onion, minced
- 2 crushed garlic cloves
- 2 tablespoons butter
- 2 tablespoons water
- ¼ cup brown sugar
- 1 cup catsup
- 2 tablespoons white vinegar
- 1 tablespoon Dijon mustard
- 2 tablespoons Worcestershire sauce
- 1 teaspoon grated orange rind
- ¼ cup orange juice
- 10 chicken pieces (breasts, thighs, or legs)

Sauté the onion and garlic in the butter until translucent. Add the water and brown sugar and simmer for 1 minute. Add the catsup, vinegar, mustard, Worcestershire sauce, and orange rind, stirring constantly. Pour in the orange juice and stir until blended. Simmer over very low heat for 15 to 20 minutes, stirring occasionally.

Brush the sauce on the chicken pieces several times while grilling. Makes 2 cups of sauce, enough to coat 4 chicken breasts and 6 legs or thighs.

Fruit Salad

None of the watermelon goes to waste with this decorative salad. The rind becomes a basket full of melon stars and sweet grapes.

- 1 medium-size watermelon
- 1 cantaloupe
- 1 honeydew melon
- 2 pounds seedless grapes

To make the basket, rinse the outer rind of the watermelon. Lay it on its side and slice off the end, about one quarter of the melon. Scoop out the flesh of the entire watermelon and reserve it. Using the tip of a vegetable peeler or lemon zester, inscribe large stars on the rind's outer surface.

Next, cut the cantaloupe in half, scoop out the seeds, and use a melon baller to remove the flesh from one of the halves. Use the second half to make melon stars: Cut the half into 1-inch slices and, using a star-shaped cookie cutter, cut out the melon. Repeat this process with the honeydew melon.

Remove the seeds from the scooped out watermelon and cut stars out of it. Wash the grapes and remove their stems. Fill the watermelon basket with the fruit. Create festive fruit kabobs with any leftovers. Serves 10 to 12.

Red, White & Blueberry Freeze Pops

Sweet, cool, and relatively healthy, these fruity, frozen pops are great pick-me-ups after a Fourth of July parade.

- 10 5-ounce plastic or paper cups
- 1 quart raspberry juice
- 10 Popsicle sticks
- 2 cups cold water
- 1 pint frozen vanilla yogurt
- ¾ cup fresh or frozen blueberries

Assemble the cups on a cookie tray. Pour 1 inch of the raspberry juice into each cup, then place the tray in the freezer. When the juice is partially frozen, set a Popsicle stick in the center of each cup and let the juice freeze solid. Next, blend 1 cup of the water and 4 large scoops of the frozen yogurt until smooth. Pour 1 inch of the yogurt mix on top of the frozen juice layer in each cup and freeze again. Once the yogurt layer sets, blend the second cup of water, the blueberries, and a large scoop of the frozen yogurt. Spoon the blueberry mix into the cups and freeze overnight. To serve, slide the pop out of the cup. Makes 10 pops.

Old-Fashioned Lemonade

After helping cut the lemons, you may want to turn this recipe over to the kids, who tend to be the lemon squeezing experts.

- 5 to 6 large lemons
- 1 cup sugar
- 2 quarts cold water

Slice the lemons in half and squeeze each of them into a large measuring cup (this should yield about 1½ cups of juice). Remove any seeds.

In a large pitcher or Mason jar, combine the juice and the sugar. Stir in the cold water and serve over ice. (For a nice touch, place mint leaves in the ice cube trays before freezing.) Makes about 10 cups.

Popcorn Relay

Fancy footwork is the ticket to success in this Fourth of July game. Everyone has a unique shuffle, waddle, or twist, making this relay as much fun to watch as it is to run. Beforehand, prepare a pair of plastic or paper cups for each runner. Poke a hole in the center of each cup bottom. Push one end of a thick rubber band through the hole and into the cup. Then, slip a paper clip on the end of the band inside the cup and gently pull the other end until the clip rests on the bottom of the cup. The rubber band, worn around the ball of the foot, holds the cup in place atop a player's shoe. Just prior to the race, a member from each team is issued a big bag of popcorn and charged with filling teammates' cups. Two large, shallow boxes are set five yards beyond the starting line, opposite the teams. When the whistle blows, the first person in each team's line sprints to their box and empties his cups into it, trying to lose as little popcorn as possible along the way (it's harder than it sounds). He then runs back and tags the next sprinter in line. The relay continues for 2 minutes or until one of the bags is emptied. Then, the popcorn in each box is measured and the team with the most wins.

Frozen Witches

with the fruit. Carve a small face in each orange (triangle shapes for eyes? circles on the sides for ears? a diamond for a nose? a mouth with a solitary tooth?). Fill the orange with the fruit salad and replace its top. As a finishing touch, garnish each top with mint leaves for stems. Make as many as you like.

Frozen Witches

Throw a fiendish party the neighborhood kids will never forget. They'll screech with delight over these bewitched desserts, but the real pleasure will be your family's — the little witches are a kick to decorate. For best results, assemble ahead of time and freeze.

> Tube of chocolate decorating gel
> 8 chocolate sugar cones
> 8 thin, round chocolate wafers
> 1 pint pistachio ice cream
>   Black shoestring licorice
>   Chocolate chips
>   Candy corn

To avoid witch meltdowns, make these desserts in batches of four. For each witch hat, squeeze a ring of the decorating gel around the edge of a cone and attach the cone to a chocolate wafer "rim," then set it aside. Using an ice-cream scoop, drop "heads" of the ice cream onto a cookie sheet lined with waxed paper. Arrange cut licorice pieces into hair and a mouth. Add chocolate chip eyes and a candy corn nose. Top each ice-cream head with a cone hat (flatten the ice cream slightly so the hat doesn't fall off). Freeze for at least 2 hours, or until the hats are set in place. Makes 8.

Jack-O'-Lantern Fruit Salad

This Halloween, carve jack-o'-lanterns out of oranges instead of pumpkins. Fill them with fruit salad, and serve as snack, appetizer, or dessert.

> Assorted fruit, such as melon, strawberries, apples, and kiwis
> Oranges (1 per person)
> Mint leaves

Chop the assorted fruits and mix them in a large bowl (you will need about ½ cup per orange). To carve a pumpkin cup, slice off the top of an orange (as you would a jack-o'-lantern). Using a knife to loosen the edges, scoop out the inside of the orange with a spoon. Toss the juice in

Haunted Graham Cracker House

If you can't turn your house into a diabolical mansion for Halloween, then use graham crackers to create an equally scary one with a rickety porch, a Keep Out sign, and a graveyard. Increase the recipe and you can make a complete ghost town.

The Paste:

- 2 egg whites
- 3 cups confectioners' sugar
- 1 teaspoon black cake-decorating paste (available at party and kitchen supply stores)

The Structure:

- 1 empty cereal or cracker box
  Graham crackers
  Black and orange candies, such as black shoestring and twisted licorice, candy corn, orange candy sticks, Tic Tacs, M&M's, and Necco wafers
  Marshmallows
  Crushed chocolate cookies

In the bowl of an electric mixer, blend the egg whites with the confectioners' sugar and the black paste until smooth. Cover the bowl with a damp cloth to keep the paste from hardening and set it aside.

Arrange the empty cereal or cracker box upright on a piece of foil-covered cardboard (you can tape it down to secure it). Use the paste to glue the graham crackers onto the sides of the box. Tape the top flaps of the box together to form a pitched roof, then cover them with graham crackers.

Next, fill in the cracks by squeezing the paste through a pastry bag with a plain tip (you also can use a plastic bag with a small hole cut from the corner). Draw crooked windows and board them up with graham cracker scraps.

Home for the Holidays

Cover the roof with candy corn and M&M's. You can add a porch by gluing a graham cracker horizontally to the side of the house; support it with licorice or candy sticks. For a backyard graveyard, flatten the marshmallows, snip off the sides with scissors, then use paste to stand them up in the courtyard. As a finishing touch, add a crooked walkway of Necco wafers and ice a Keep Out sign on a graham cracker. Finally, sprinkle crushed chocolate cookies to make the yard.

Haunted Graham Cracker House

Thanksgiving

Turkey Potpies

Looking for a fun way to polish off Thanksgiving leftovers? Set them up buffet style, starting with the turkey tray. Add bowls of peas, green beans, carrots, corn, and the gravy bowl. Hand out individual-size, pastry-lined pie tins and let your kids customize their potpies. Adventurous diners might want to try adding cranberry sauce, mashed potatoes, stuffing, or herbs. Add the top crusts, crimp the edges, poke vent holes in the tops, and bake at 425° for 20 to 30 minutes, or until lightly browned.

Roasted Turkey

Roasted Turkey

Preparing a holiday turkey can give any cook jitters. With a few of *FamilyFun*'s pointers on your side, though, it needn't be such a daunting task.

1 12- to 15-pound turkey (neck, giblets, and excess fat removed)
Salt and pepper
6 to 8 cups Country Herb Stuffing (see page 231)
Double thickness of cheesecloth
⅓ to ½ cup melted butter

Preheat the oven to 325°. Rinse the turkey inside and out with cold water and pat dry. Lightly salt and pepper the cavities. Loosely fill the neck and body cavities with the stuffing. Using a thin

metal skewer or needle and thread, skewer or sew the openings shut. Tie the legs together with kitchen twine and fold the wings back and under the body of the turkey.

Place the turkey breast side up on a roasting rack in a roasting pan. Next, soak the cheesecloth in water and squeeze it dry. Saturate it in the melted butter and drape it over the turkey. Pour 1 cup of water in the bottom of the pan and bake the turkey for about 15 to 20 minutes per pound. The cheesecloth will help keep the meat moist, but you also should baste the bird once every hour or so.

Forty-five minutes before the turkey is done, remove the cheesecloth and let the turkey brown. If the legs and breast are browning too quickly, cover them with foil. The turkey is cooked when an instant-read meat thermometer inserted into the thickest part of the thigh registers between 180° and 185°. Remove the turkey to a serving platter. Cover it loosely with foil and let it rest for 20 to 30 minutes before carving. Serves 8 to 10 with enough for leftovers.

Country Herb Stuffing

Most families want more stuffing than can fit into the bird, so this recipe makes enough extras to bake in a side dish. For safety reasons, cook the bird immediately after stuffing it.

- 2 tablespoons butter
- 1 onion, diced
- 4 celery ribs, diced
- 2 tart apples, peeled, cored, and finely diced
- 1 loaf Italian bread, cubed and dried in a 350° oven
- ½ loaf whole wheat or oatmeal bread, cubed and dried in a 350° oven
- 2 to 3 tablespoons poultry seasoning
  Salt to taste
- 3 to 5 cups turkey or chicken stock

In a medium skillet, melt the butter and sauté the onions and celery until soft. Add the apples and sauté for about 5 minutes. Lightly toss the bread cubes with the apple-onion mixture, seasonings, and salt. Bring the stock to a simmer and pour it over the seasoned bread cubes. Stuffing moistness is a personal preference, so adjust to your family's taste and then refrigerate until ready to stuff the bird. Makes about 10 cups.

Pumpkin Ice-Cream Pie

Pumpkin Ice-Cream Pie

FamilyFun contributor Drew Kristofik, of Westport, Connecticut, says her family eats this from Halloween through Thanksgiving, pausing occasionally for the odd fruit, vegetable, and protein meal. Her kids like to decorate the pie with a pumpkin seed face.

- 1 quart vanilla ice cream or frozen yogurt (allow to get soupy before adding to the mix)
- 1 cup plain canned pumpkin
- ¼ cup sugar
- ¼ teaspoon cinnamon
- ¼ teaspoon ginger
- 1 Graham Cracker Crust (see page 205)

You can add the ingredients in any order you like and it still comes out great. Throw everything (except the crust, of course) into a large bowl and stir. When the filling is mixed, which in Drew's house means everyone has had several turns with the spoon, pour it into the prepared crust and set it in a level place in the freezer to harden overnight. Serves 8 to 10.

Village People

Spice up the Thanksgiving table with these handcrafted place markers. Make Native American and Pilgrim figures with toilet paper tubes and construction paper. Draw facial features, make hair, and add headbands and feathers for Native Americans as well as collars and hats for the Pilgrims.

salt, pepper, flour or matzo meal, and baking powder.

In a large skillet, heat about 1 inch of the oil. When the oil is bubbling, gently drop about 2 tablespoons of the potato batter into the pan (it should hold a round shape). Gently flatten each latke with the back of a spoon. Fry over medium heat for 3 to 4 minutes on each side, or until golden brown and crisp (use two spatulas when flipping latkes so the oil doesn't splatter). Drain cooked latkes on paper towels and set them aside in a warm oven. Add more oil to the pan as needed for frying the rest of the pancakes. Serve hot with applesauce, sour cream, jam, or sugar. Makes about 18 latkes.

A Week of Guests

In Santa Fe, New Mexico, Miriam Sagan's family celebrates Hanukkah with the traditional rituals — lighting menorah candles, frying latkes, and giving gifts. They also follow an old European custom of inviting friends to their house every night of the eight-day holiday. They host a mix of people, including non-Jewish families. Word gets around, so when one of their guests can't make it, someone else is sure to call and say, "Hey, we heard you need people on night number six, and we're volunteering!"

Luscious Latkes

Hanukkah isn't Hanukkah without a steaming plate of latkes. These potato pancakes are fried in oil to commemorate the two-thousand-year-old Hanukkah story of the jar of oil that miraculously burned for eight days in a Jerusalem temple.

4	large potatoes, peeled
1	onion
2	large eggs
1½	teaspoons salt
¼	teaspoon white pepper
2	tablespoons all-purpose flour or matzo meal
¾	teaspoon baking powder
	About 1 cup peanut or vegetable oil

Coarsely grate the potatoes and onion in a food processor or with the large holes of a grater. Place in a colander, then press to squeeze out as much liquid as possible. In a large bowl, combine the potato mixture with the eggs,

Homemade Applesauce

Sweet, tart, homemade applesauce is a perfect complement for a plateful of piping hot latkes. Because the apple skins are left on during cooking, this sauce comes out a rosy pink.

12	medium apples
1	cup water
½	cup sugar
1	tablespoon lemon juice
½	teaspoon cinnamon

Wash, quarter, and core the apples. Place them in a large cooking pot and add the water. Over medium heat, cook the apples until they are nearly soft. Add the sugar, lemon juice, and cinnamon. Cook for a few minutes longer, then press the apples through a medium sieve and let cool. Serve warm or cold. Makes about 4 cups.

Hanukkah Doughnuts

These holeless, jelly-filled doughnuts, also known as sufganiyot, are a popular Hanukkah food in Israel. Like latkes, they are deep-fried in oil to celebrate the Hanukkah miracle. This recipe is adapted from Faye Levy's *International Jewish Cookbook* (Warner Books).

- ¾   cup lukewarm water
- 2   packages active dry yeast
- ¼   cup sugar
- 4   cups all-purpose flour
- 2   large eggs
- 2   large egg yolks
- 7   tablespoons butter, at room temperature
- 1   teaspoon vanilla extract
- 2   teaspoons salt
- ¼   cup apricot or strawberry jam
      Vegetable oil (at least 5 cups)
      Confectioners' sugar

Pour ½ cup of the water into a small bowl. Add the yeast and 1 teaspoon of the sugar. Let stand for 10 minutes.

Spoon the flour into a large mixing bowl. Make a well in the center and add the remaining sugar and water, plus the eggs, yolks, butter, vanilla extract, and salt. Mix until the ingredients are blended. Add the dissolved yeast and mix again until a dough forms.

Knead on a lightly floured surface for about 10 minutes to form a smooth ball (if the dough is sticky, add extra flour). Place in a lightly oiled bowl, turn to coat, and cover with a damp cloth. Let the dough rise in a warm place for 1 to 1½ hours, or until doubled in size.

On a lightly floured surface, roll out half the dough to a ¼-inch thickness. Using a 2½- to 3-inch cutter, cut the dough into 28 rounds. Put ½ to 1 teaspoon of the jam in the center of half

the rounds. Lightly brush the rim of each round with water, then set a plain round on top. With floured fingers, firmly press the edges together to seal. Transfer this "sandwich" to a floured tray. If it has stretched out to an oval, plump it gently back into a round shape. Continue with the remaining dough. Cover with a slightly damp cloth and let them rise for 30 minutes.

In a large skillet or deep fryer, heat the oil to 350° (measure the temperature with a candy thermometer). Carefully slide in 4 doughnuts or enough to fill the pan without crowding. Fry the doughnuts for 3 minutes on each side, or until golden brown. Drain on paper towels. Repeat with the remaining half of the dough.

Cool (the jam is very hot), garnish with the confectioners' sugar, then serve. Makes about 28 doughnuts.

OH DREIDEL, DREIDEL, DREIDEL

The dreidel game is a form of an old German gambling game. The stakes are low with players betting their fortune in chocolates with a spin of the top. If *Nun* comes up after a spin, that player gets nothing from the communal pot. *Gimel* means the player takes the whole pot. If *Heh* turns up, the player takes half of what's in the pot. *Shin* means the player must add to the pot. The game is over when one player has won all the "chips."

Quick and Easy Banana Bread

*This holiday season, teach your kids how to bake banana bread —
a homey and inexpensive gift that says thank-you to a special teacher,
baby-sitter, or friend.*

1 tablespoon plus
½ cup softened
butter

1 to 2
tablespoons
sesame seeds
(optional)

¾ cup
packed brown sugar

1 teaspoon
vanilla extract

2½ cups all-purpose
flour

2 eggs

1 Preheat oven to 350° (325° for glass pans). Melt the tablespoon of butter and pour it into a medium or large loaf pan. Let the chef use a pastry brush to coat the pan and sprinkle in sesame seeds, if desired.

2 Place the softened ½ cup butter in a large mixing bowl. Beat with an electric mixer or by hand until it's whipped. Crumble in the brown sugar (a good job for a child) and mix until creamy.

Cooking Tip: A quick way to soften butter is to unwrap it, place it in a small glass bowl, and microwave at 5-second increments for 20 seconds.

3 Break the eggs into a small bowl and lightly beat with a fork. Add the eggs to the butter mixture and beat well for about 1 minute, adding the vanilla extract along the way. Set aside.

Cooking Tip: Remind your kids to whack each egg hard. (Don't worry if you have to pick out a little bit of shell!)

4 Measure the flour into a separate bowl. Add the baking soda, baking powder, and salt and mix well. Add a third of this dry mixture to the wet one and stir slowly. When the flour is mostly mixed in, add half the banana.

Cooking Tip: Even the youngest child can peel a banana, slice it with a dinner knife, if supervised, and mash it.

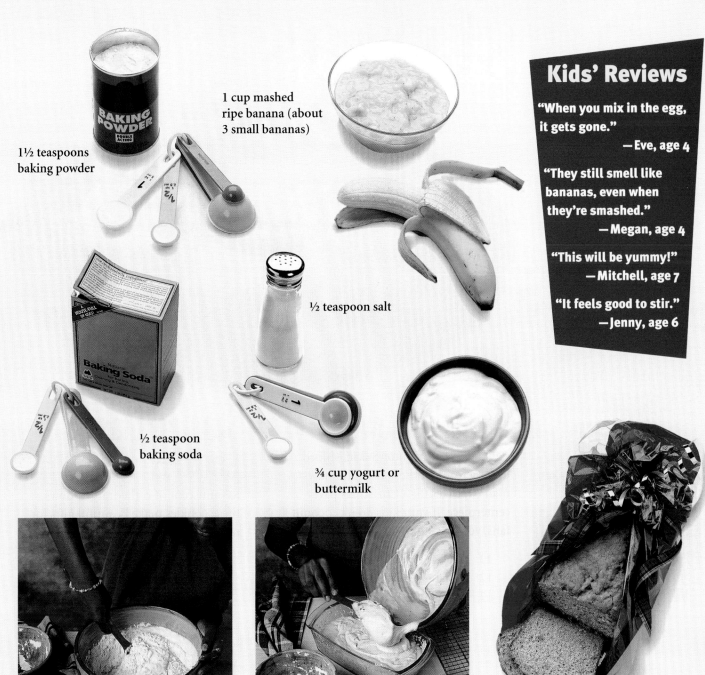

1½ teaspoons
baking powder

1 cup mashed
ripe banana (about
3 small bananas)

½ teaspoon salt

½ teaspoon
baking soda

¾ cup yogurt or
buttermilk

5 Add another third of the flour and the rest of the banana. Continue to stir and add the remaining flour and the yogurt or buttermilk. Mix from the bottom until combined.

Cooking Tip: Make the batter in a large bowl so the kids can enjoy stirring without worrying about spills.

6 Pour into the prepared pan and gently spread to fill evenly. Place in the preheated oven and bake undisturbed for 60 to 70 minutes, or until a knife inserted into the middle comes out clean.

Cooking Tip: Kids think spreading the batter is especially fun (but packing brown sugar with their fingers and mashing bananas are close rivals).

7 Allow to cool in the pan for at least 10 minutes, then remove by tapping the pan sharply and inverting it onto a rack. Cool completely before wrapping or slicing.

Cooking Tip: Kids can wrap the loaf in colored cellophane or cut a few slices and present them on a paper plate wrapped in plastic. Adorn with ribbons and a handwritten card.

Tasty Tags

FamilyFun contributor Heidi King came up with a sweet way to label her holiday gifts — she bakes tags out of cookie dough and inscribes them with icing. To make one, cut rectangles or another shape out of Sugar Cookie dough (see page 190). Poke a small hole (it will close up a bit when baked) for attaching the "tag." Bake the cookies according to the directions and let them cool. Using tinted All-Purpose Buttercream (see page 198), thinly spread each tag with one color, then, with a pastry tip, add names and designs in a contrasting color. When the icing is dry, thread a thin ribbon through the hole. Seal each cookie in plastic wrap, then attach the tag to the gift.

Frosted Snowmen

FamilyFun contributor Susan Milord made a troop of these friendly snowman cupcakes for a Christmas party centerpiece. If your kids aren't coconut fans, you can eliminate the extra layer.

- 12 regular-size cupcakes (with liners)
- 12 miniature cupcakes (no liners)
- 2 to 3 cups All-Purpose Buttercream (see page 198) or white frosting
  Shredded coconut
  Candy corn or orange gumdrops
  Chocolate chips
  Strips of ribbon or fabric

To assemble the snowmen, frost the tops of the regular-size cupcakes with the icing and set aside. Frost the tops and sides of the miniature cupcakes, then roll them in the coconut. Center the miniature cupcakes on top of the larger ones and sprinkle with coconut.

To decorate the faces, use the candy corns or slivers of the gumdrops for noses, and chocolate chips for eyes and mouths. Tie the decorative strips of ribbon or fabric around the smaller cupcakes like scarves. Makes 12.

Stained-Glass Cookies

Reminiscent of cathedral windows, these cookies make beautiful gifts for neighbors, grandparents, and friends.

Sugar Cookie dough (see recipe on page 190)
Colored hard candies

While the cookie dough is chilling, sort the hard candies by color. Place each batch in a heavy-duty plastic bag and seal. Crush the candies into small chunks with a mallet or rolling pin and set aside. Cover a baking sheet with foil. Roll out the dough and cut out tree-shaped cookies, then use small cutters, such as aspic cutters, to cut out stars or other shapes within each tree. Place the cookies on the baking sheet and fill the cutout holes with the crushed candy so it is even with the cookies' surface. Do not overfill. Bake the cookies at 350° for 10 to 12 minutes. When they are cool, carefully remove them from the foil. Makes about 3 dozen cookies, depending on their size.

Christmas Stockings

These merry cookies make sweet stocking presents or late-night treats for Santa.

> Sugar Cookie dough (see recipe on page 190)
> All-Purpose Buttercream (see page 198)
> Colored sprinkles
> Candies

Roll out the dough to about a ¼-inch thickness. Cut out a sock shape using a cookie cutter or a pattern made of cardboard. If you want to hang the stockings, use the end of a drinking straw to cut a hole through the cuff of the sock, but not too close to the edge. Bake the cookies at 350° for 10 to 12 minutes. When completely cooled, decorate the stockings with frosting, sprinkles, and candies. For the recipient's name, pipe out frosting. Makes about 3 dozen, depending on their size.

Cookie Advent Calendar

After we ran the directions for making this cookie Advent calendar in *FamilyFun* magazine, a host of our readers counted down the days before Christmas one cookie at a time.

To make the calendar, take a piece of colorful felt, about 30 inches by 15 inches, and turn one of the shorter edges over 2 inches (to form the top casing). Rough-stitch it to the back of the calendar, leaving room in the fold to run a ¼ -inch-thick dowel for hanging.

To number the days, use store-bought cookies or bake a batch of your favorites, such as Sugar Cookies (see page 190) or Gingerbread Cookies (see page 238) — you'll need 25 cookies plus a few extra for hungry helpers. If you bake your own, let them cool thoroughly.

Using a tube of colored frosting, number the cookies from 1 to 25. When the frosting dries, wrap each cookie in plastic wrap, twisting the plastic at the top part of the cookie. Arrange them on the calendar, evenly spaced, for placement. Make a small mark with a pen, centered ½ inch above each cookie. Then, set the cookies aside.

Next, secure ribbons to the calendar face. Thread a large-eyed darning needle with a piece of ribbon (or colorful yarn), about 10 inches long and ⅛ inch wide. Make a small stitch at one mark on the calendar. Pull the ribbon through the felt so that both ends of the ribbon are on the face of the calendar. Set the cookies back in place and tie the ribbon in a bow around the twisted plastic wrap at the top of each cookie. To hang your Advent calendar, slide the dowel into the casing. Tie the ends of a 2-foot-long piece of ribbon to the dowel tips, then hang it within reach of your little elves.

Gingerbread Cookies

three or four equal portions and flatten each into a disk. Cover in plastic wrap and refrigerate for 2 hours, or until firm enough to roll.

Preheat the oven to 350°. Roll and cut out the dough, then transfer the cookies to greased baking sheets. Bake for 10 minutes, or until brown around the edges. Remove the baking sheet to a wire rack; cool for 5 minutes. Transfer the cookies to racks and cool thoroughly. Cookies can be stored in an airtight container in the freezer for 1 month and up to 3 days at room temperature before they are decorated with frosting. Makes about 4 dozen cookies.

Popcorn Snowmen

These marshmallow treats disappear faster than a parking spot on the day before Christmas.

>   15   cups popped popcorn
>   ½   cup butter or margarine
>   2   10-ounce packages marshmallows
>   Thin pretzel sticks, raisins, candy
>   corn, mini jawbreakers, red
>   hots, gumdrops, and fruit
>   leather
>   Royal Icing (see page 239)

Pour the popcorn into a large bowl; set aside. Melt the butter in a nonstick saucepan over medium-low heat. Add the marshmallows, stirring constantly until melted. Pour over the popcorn and stir to coat. When cool enough to touch, rub margarine on your hands and form popcorn balls.

Stack three popcorn balls for a snowman. Using Royal Icing for glue, add pretzel stick arms, raisin eyes, and a candy corn nose. Arrange mini jawbreakers into a broad grin. For buttons, use gumdrops or red hots. For scarves, cut rectangles out of fruit leather and fringe the ends. Makes about 5 snowmen.

Ice-Cream Cone Ornament

Assembling this ornament, always a hit with ice-cream fans, is simple enough for pint-size attention spans. Glue a ribbon loop into a sugar cone for hanging the ornament. Run glue along the top edge and stuff a ball of fiberfill into the cone. Add ribbon and glitter "sprinkles" and a red pom-pom "cherry." Hang for all to see.

Gingerbread Cookies

With this standard holiday recipe, you can whip up sturdy gingerbread canvases to ice and decorate. The baked cookies are light and delicious.

>   4½   cups all-purpose flour
>   1   tablespoon cinnamon
>   1½   teaspoons ginger
>   ½   teaspoon ground cloves
>   ½   teaspoon nutmeg
>   1   teaspoon baking soda
>   ½   teaspoon salt
>   ¾   cup molasses
>   ½   cup firmly packed brown sugar
>   ½   cup butter, softened
>   2   large eggs, at room temperature

In a large bowl, combine the flour, cinnamon, ginger, cloves, nutmeg, baking soda, and salt. In another large bowl, beat the molasses, brown sugar, butter, and eggs. One third at a time, beat in the flour mixture until thoroughly mixed. Divide the dough into

Graham Cracker Village

What to do with your restless brood on a snowbound day? Let them raise the roof, of course, by building a confectionary village.

The Royal Icing:

- 2   egg whites
- 3   cups confectioners' sugar
- ¼   teaspoon cream of tartar

The Structure:

- Pint-size milk cartons (thoroughly washed out and dried)
- Graham crackers
- Nonpareils, Necco wafers, slivered almonds, or peanut halves
- Assorted candy, such as caramels, marshmallows, red hots, gumdrops, candy fruit slices, fruit leather, licorice, gum slices, hard candies, Life Savers, mini jawbreakers, lollipops, or rock candy sticks
- Sugar or shredded coconut

To make the icing for gluing the houses together, beat the egg whites with the sugar and cream of tartar in an electric mixer until creamy and smooth. Spoon half into a pastry bag fitted with a writing tip or a sealable plastic bag with a hole cut in one corner. Reserve the rest of the icing in the bowl, covered with a damp cloth to prevent it from hardening.

Arrange the milk cartons upright on a piece of foil-covered cardboard (you can tape them down to secure them). Use the icing to glue graham crackers to the sides of each carton. Frost two roof crackers to the top of each carton, then apply shingles of nonpareils, Necco wafers, slivered almonds, or peanut halves. Pipe icing along the roof ridge and cap with another row of candy. Use caramels or a marshmallow covered with red hots for a chimney.

For windowpanes, apply gumdrops, candy fruit slices, or fruit leather and trim with piped icing. Make doors out of decorated graham crackers. To create a wreath, attach a shoestring licorice bow to a green Life Saver. "String" colorful holiday lights by decorating roof edges with rows of mini jawbreakers.

For landscaping, plant spearmint gumdrop shrubs. Lay cobblestone walkways of nonpareils or Necco wafers. You can even build a snowman — use toothpicks to skewer marshmallows. For lampposts, top peppermint sticks with yellow gumdrops. Fix them along the village street with frosting. Use whip licorice and mini jawbreakers to string holiday lights between the lampposts. Once all the details are set, let it snow with a generous sprinkling of sugar or shredded coconut.

Kwanzaa Cookies

From December 26th to January 1st, your family can celebrate the African American holiday Kwanzaa by baking Kwanzaa flag cookies. Roll Sugar Cookie dough (page 190) to ⅛ inch thickness and cut it into rectangles. Sandwich a Popsicle stick flagpole between 2 rectangles. Bake as directed, then cool. Decorate with colored frosting to match the picture above.

Graham Cracker Village

Index

**Asparagus with Sesame-
Orange Dipping Sauce:**
Page 165

A Shirt for Dad: *Page 225*

C

Peanut Butter Granola Bars: *Page 38*

**Cheddar Broccoli
Mashed Potatoes:**
Page 181

I

Couscous with Peas: *Page 178*

J

K

L

Mud Pie: *Page 207*

S

Egg Heads: *Page 19*

Oven-Baked Cherry Tomatoes:
Page 170

Cold Zucchini Soup: *Page 102*

W

Y

Z

Art & Photography Credits

Special thanks to the following *FamilyFun* magazine photographers and stylists for their excellent work.

Michael McAndrews: *86; 88; 89 (top right); 94 (top right); 96.*

Steven Mark Needham: *32; 33 (bottom left); 48 (top left); 50 (top left); 51 (bottom right); 188; 201; 204; 215.*

Kevin Roberts: *194 (top left).*

Joanne Schmaltz: *49 (top right); 119 (bottom right); 199; 223 (top left).*

Shaffer/Smith Photography: *28–29; 35 (bottom left); 41; 46; 50 (bottom left); 53 (top, middle & bottom right); 58–59; 61 (bottom right); 74–75; 93 (top right); 94 (bottom right); 100–101; 109 (top right); 119 (middle right); 150–151; 153 (bottom right); 163; 182–183; 192–193; 206 (bottom left); 234–235.*

Steve Smith: *217; 238 (bottom left).*

Stayner/Stayner: *30 (top left); 42; 43 (top right); 44 (top left); 51 (top right); 63 (top & middle right); 64 (top right); 85 (top center); 139 (bottom right); 143; 146; 161 (top right); 203; 214.*

Edwina Stevenson: *218.*

Chip Yates: *45 (top left); 69 (middle right).*

STYLISTS:

Bonnie Anderson/Team, Laurie Baer, Cynthia W. Caldwell, Debrah E. Donahue, Myrosha Dziuk, Erica Ell/Team, Elizabeth Fassberg, Karen Gillingham, Petra Henttonen, Kimberly Huson, Jacqueline Lemieux, Karin Lidbeck, Susan McClellan, Randy Mon, Amy Malkin Pearl, Marie Piraino/Ennis, Roberta Rall, Sandi Ransone, George Simonds, Hilda Shum, William Smith, Norman Stewart, Janet Street, Karen Tack, and Diane Vezza.

ACCESSORIES:

Special thanks to Different Drummer, Pinch Pottery, and The Coffee Gallery of Northampton, Massachusetts, as well as Crate & Barrel and Williams and Sonoma, for providing props.

Dipped Strawberries: *Page 79*

Dino Carrot Cake *Page 200*

Also from FamilyFun magazine

★ **FamilyFun magazine:** a creative guide to all the great things families can do together. Call 800-289-4849 for a subscription.

★ **FamilyFun's Cookies for Christmas** by Deanna F. Cook and the experts at *FamilyFun* magazine: a batch of 50 recipes for creative holiday treats.

★ **FamilyFun's Crafts** by Deanna F. Cook and the experts at *FamilyFun* magazine: a step-by-step guide to more than 500 of the best crafts and activities to do with your kids.

★ **FamilyFun's Parties** by Deanna F. Cook and the experts at *FamilyFun* magazine: a collection of more than 100 complete party plans for birthdays, holidays, and every day.

★ **FamilyFun's Games on the Go** by Lisa Stiepock and the experts at *FamilyFun* magazine: a roundup of 250 great games and tips for families traveling by car, plane, or train.

★ **FamilyFun.com:** visit us at http://www.familyfun.com and search for articles, post messages, and e-mail editors.